Is there reall

HEAVEN KNOWS

A personal journey in search of evidence

SANDY COGHLAN

Pegasus Education Group

My sincere thanks to
Dr. Raymond Moody
for his generous permission
to use quotes from his books.

Published by Pegasus Education Group
PO Box 223, McCrae, Victoria, 3938, Australia

First published November 2016
Australian edition: March 2017

reprinted August 2019

ISBN: 978-0-9945355-4-2

Mum ...

for all your love and encouragement
for all you shared with me
for all you taught me
for all you gave me
and for your gift that became this book

Chapters

PREFACE

"I'm 82 years old, and I have to accept that soon…"

I clutched the phone to my ear and waited for her to continue.

"I mean… I know I won't be here much longer."

"Oh Betty, come on…"

"No, listen, please!" she interrupted, her voice still crackling with emotion. There was another long pause, and I waited while she composed herself. Heaven knows, I was trying to do the same.

"I've been thinking about it a lot lately and I admit that it frightens me. But…"

Again I waited in silence, fighting back tears.

I didn't need this. Not now. Whatever had I been thinking? I should never have made this call. I barely knew this woman. I had only met her once or twice, many years ago.

Perhaps I could just find my jolly voice and say: "Well, Betty, it's been nice talking to you. Stay in touch." Then I could hang up and not have to deal with it. I didn't need this now. Please God, if you do exist, not now.

But I didn't hang up. I waited. What she said next would change my life.

"I'm sorry." Her voice was stronger, calmer. "I want you to know that what you just told me has given me so much comfort. Thank you. Thank you so very, very much."

That was the moment. I knew what I had to do.

I had to write this book.

INTRODUCTION

In 1976, an innocuous little paperback called *Life After Life* created quite a stir when it hit bookshop shelves around the world. People everywhere were reading it, or intending to read it, or had recently finished reading it, or were recommending that everyone else read it. People who had already read it would stop strangers who were reading it while travelling on trains or eating lunch in cafes, and they would enter into animated conversations about it.

This phenomenon had also occurred a few years earlier, in 1969, with a book called *Chariots of the Gods* by Eric Von Daniken. I was twenty when 'Chariots' shot to the bestseller list, and because I didn't want to be the only person in the world who hadn't read it, I purchased a copy.

I tried to read it. But whenever I removed the paperback from my handbag in a public place, gushing strangers would rush up and make comments like "Isn't it wonderful? It never occurred to me that instead of apes, our ancestors might have been aliens!" Or they would ask me mind-boggling questions like "Now tell me, honestly, has it or has it not changed all your ideas about religion yet?"

I didn't have any ideas about religion. I didn't even think about it. Until the age of seven, I had lived with, and later near, my feisty Irish grandmother Nora, who dismissed religion as superstitious nonsense. And so, therefore, did I.

Neither had I ever considered the possibility that I'd descended from apes, so switching to aliens was hardly a giant leap. Besides, I felt a little intimidated by these profound interpretations of Von Daniken's findings. Unlike them, I hadn't "oohed and aahed" my way through the book, pausing occasionally to think "well, well, little green men must really be our ancestors, and doesn't *that* now throw a whole new light on our bible's teachings!"

Frankly, I thought I'd been reading a book about recent archaeological findings!

Seven years passed, and the Von Daniken scenario happened all over again. This time it wasn't about Martian ancestors. This time, it was a book about the possibility of life after death.

Dilemma. Should I purchase a copy so I could enter into deep and meaningful conversations with total strangers in public places? Or was I now far too mature and past the need for peer-group approval?

The title, *Life After Life,* suggested that another life awaited us after this one. To me, this smacked of reincarnation. I knew (didn't everyone?) that reincarnation was total nonsense. Coming back to life as a sacred cow in India did not excite me.

However, it had recently occurred to me that I was going to die. I wasn't terminally ill. I didn't have a psychic premonition or even a visit from an angel. I simply came to the sudden and shocking realization that I was mortal. However and whenever it happened, one day I would cease to exist.

Now, it may seem strange that the inevitability of death could have escaped my attention for twenty-seven years, but it had. As the only child of a mother who was also an only child, and of a father who had deserted us two decades earlier, I wasn't blessed with an array of elderly aunts and uncles or ageing second cousins who might have been inclined to demonstrate their mortality for me, so it hadn't occurred to me that death was something we all had to face.

This sudden realization threw me for a loop, and I began to seriously question the purpose of life.

Why did we *do* anything? Why did we learn, love, communicate, laugh or cry? What did any of it matter? Why did we accumulate possessions, change jobs, make friends, cook meals, save money, make plans, read books and clean out cupboards? Everything suddenly seemed so pointless.

I tried to discuss it with friends and workmates, but they left me in no doubt they'd rather be anywhere else, talking to anyone else, about anything else. Some accused me of being morbid. Others pointed out it was a subject polite people didn't discuss. A few shuddered and uttered phrases like "ooooh, I don't want to talk about it! I don't even want to think about it!"

In 1977, death was still a taboo subject, except for those few who quoted biblical references and insisted that the afterlife was reserved for those who had been saved by embracing the true religion.

When I encountered this reaction, I was the one who politely excused myself.

I purchased a copy of *Life After Life,* took it home and carefully placed it beside my bed.

A week later, four newborn pups were dumped in the gutter outside my house late at night. Their cries woke me and I tiptoed through the rain to rescue them.

Two sleepless weeks of warming milk and holding baby bottles in four hungry mouths every hour left neither time nor energy to philosophise. When I found a surrogate mother for them, I forgot I'd been depressed, and why.

Life After Life remained beside my bed, unopened, for months. I eventually grew tired of seeing it there, so I wrapped it up and sent it to Nora, my paternal grandmother. Her husband—my grandfather—had died five years earlier.

'Pop' had been a quiet, unassuming man who spent most of his time reading the newspaper or pottering around his home-made caravan. I had not seen him since childhood, so his passing had not shocked me or left a gaping hole in my life, but it did give my grandmother the dubious distinction of being only person in my life who knew someone who had died. It may provide some comfort, I told myself, not even sure if she was still grieving for him!

A no-nonsense Belfast woman, Nora ruled with an iron fist and took every opportunity to make her opinions known to all. I posted the book to her without reading so much as a paragraph, later cringing when I considered it may have contained religious references.

I received no response from her.

If you knew my grandmother, you'd probably agree that under the circumstances, this was the most preferable reaction.

It would take eleven years before I was brave enough — perhaps even desperate enough — to buy another copy of *Life After Life.*

Sandy Coghlan, 2016

CHAPTER 1

AND SO IT BEGINS

It wasn't a booming voice from above. It wasn't even a voice, really. It was more a thought in sentence form.

I can't know how other peoples' minds work, but I rarely think in complete sentences. And while thoughts can be random, I'm usually at least vaguely aware of why I thought them, and the sequence of events or the reminders that put them there.

This, however, was a fully formed sentence that simply popped into my head for no apparent reason. It was a strange sentence, even strange wording, for me to think.

It was a wintry evening in 1987 when I bustled into the house after a day at the office and collapsed into a chair at the kitchen table. Muffin, one of the pups I had rescued eleven years earlier, bounded in and launched herself at me, covering my face with sloppy kisses. A Rottweiler German Shepherd cross, she had grown into a gentle and affectionate giant.

"What's for dinner?" I asked my mother as I tried to wrestle Muffin to the ground.

"I'm making you an omelette." Mum said quietly.

I looked up and noticed there was only one pan on the stove.

"What are *you* having?"

"Oh, nothing. I don't feel great."

"And so it begins" the voice said.

I tried to hide the sense of foreboding I suddenly felt.

"What's wrong?"

"Oh, I'm just a bit off," she shrugged. "I might have an early night."

Mum was a constant source of worry. She was wafer thin due to the muscle-weakening condition she'd developed two decades earlier. Baffled at the time, the doctors had conducted every test they could think of, including a spinal tap and muscle biopsy. They eventually shrugged and chose to label it Muscular Dystrophy, admitting there was no treatment. They warned she could expect to be wheelchair-bound within five years.

Although she used a walking stick and became thinner and frailer as the years went by, my mother was still on her feet twenty years after that dire warning. But I knew her condition was deteriorating, and I was aware that being "a bit off" could simply mean a headache, or it could mean something far more serious.

Later that evening, her abdomen was so bloated she resembled one of those starving Ethiopian children on World Health documentaries.

"My god!" I gasped when she pulled back the bedclothes. "I'm calling an ambulance!"

"No, no! I don't want to go to hospital. Just see if you can get a locum to come and have a look."

By the time the doctor arrived, Mum was nauseous and her pulse was racing.

"I think we'd better get you to a hospital!" he announced.

***

It was almost 3 am when the taxi dropped us back at our front gate. I struggled to get Mum out of the cab and into the house.

I helped her into bed and smiled encouragement. "It's all over. You'll be fine now." I told her, not totally believing it myself but anxious to put her mind at rest. Mum had never been strong when it came to illness or pain. It frightened her, as did the prospect of dying.

For over four hours, exhausted and worried, I had paced back and forth along the cold, soul-less hospital corridor, sat beside Mum in the noisy emergency room, and shivered in the car park during cigarette breaks. My mind hadn't functioned; it just went through the motions.

Now, snuggled up in my own bed, I pondered the possibilities.

"She could have died!" I kept repeating the doctor's words after he had diagnosed a bowel blockage. I shuddered at the thought.

My mother could have died.

She wasn't only my mother, she was also my best friend. I had lived a normal teenager's life and back-packed around Europe in my early twenties, but my mother's ever-diminishing muscle strength meant I was needed more and more as the years passed.

I bought a house in my early thirties and we moved in together so I could help with the activities she found difficult. It was an ideal arrangement. She cooked and cleaned, I worked and paid bills. We shared everything — our joys and our sorrows, our likes and dislikes, our opinions and interests. My mother's own mother, Nan, was 96 and we visited her at the nursing home weekly. The three of us were all we had.

I thumped my pillow into submission and tried to sleep, but those words kept coming back. "And so it begins." What did it mean? Where had it come from? Was I making too much of it? Was it just a random thought, or was it some mysterious cosmic message sent to prepare me?

A cosmic message? Where did I get such preposterous ideas? I dismissed 'the voice' as nonsense. Content that my mother was now comfortably asleep in her own bed and certain I would see the world from a saner perspective in the morning, I rolled over and finally drifted off to sleep.

And so began my year from hell. My mother didn't get up for a year.

***

Throughout the next twelve months, thoughts of death and the meaning of life kept returning. Mum slept throughout most of every day. During the few hours she was conscious, she ate little and complained of nausea, indigestion, dizziness, exhaustion and heart palpitations.

Doctors came, and doctors went. They examined her, ordered tests and prescribed medications. None could find a cause. It was as though she had simply given up on life.

For a few months, I phoned her from work every hour and threw a panic if the phone rang more than three or four times. Eventually, I left work altogether. I needed to be there to encourage her to eat, help her to the bathroom, and, I thought with trepidation, hold her hand when her time came.

I regularly tiptoed to her door and stood listening to ensure she was still breathing. If she was awake, I tried to jolly her into having a cup of tea or something to eat. She made an effort, but her eyes told the story I didn't want to hear.

"And so it begins" continued to haunt me. Although she was only sixty-four, I had no doubt my mother's dying process had begun.

Death was something that happened to faceless people on a page in the newspaper. I carefully avoided that page. I refused to imagine my mother no longer existing.

I spent many lonely evenings huddled on the back doorstep, gazing at the heavens and silently berating God, even though I doubted such a being existed. I angrily asked that non-existent God if there was any point to life, why we lived and died. No answer came, because there was no-one home up there to hear me.

Then, a television interview with the 1950's English heart-throb, singer and actor Tommy Steele, gave me permission to consider that perhaps, just perhaps, there was hope that we lived on after death.

***

In his usual effervescent way, Tommy talked about the time when, as a child, he had contracted spinal meningitis and was not expected to live. He was put into an isolation ward at the hospital and left to sleep in a screened-off bed.

During the night, Tommy became aware of the laughter of a child beyond his screen. He was semi-conscious, but managed to open his eyes when a brightly coloured ball plopped on his bed, just out of reach.

Assuming the ball belonged to another boy sharing his room, Tommy struggled to reach it and throw it back over the screen. Almost instantly, the ball was returned. Once again, feeling disgruntled but not wanting to deprive a sick child of his ball, Tommy summoned what little energy he had left to throw it back.

He was now utterly exhausted, but again the ball landed on his bed, and again he struggled to reach it and return it as the child beyond the screen giggled with delight.

During this painful game, which lasted throughout the night, Tommy began to notice some feeling returning to his legs. When the doctors examined him the following morning they found to their amazement that he appeared to be recovering.

Tommy insisted that the little boy in his room had given him the strength to fight. The doctors had no idea what he was talking about and removed the screen. No-one else shared his room.

When Tommy told his parents about the incident and described the ball in detail, his mother gasped. She reminded Tommy that when he was much younger, he'd given his three year old brother, Rodney, an identical ball for Christmas. It was to be the last present Rodney ever received, as he died shortly afterwards.

Tommy related his experience to the interviewer with enthusiasm and wide-eyed wonder. He had nothing to gain, and could only expect ridicule from those who dismissed it as nonsense.

Tommy Steele's experience was featured in the Logansport Press, Indiana, and in the Gastonia Gazette, North Carolina, in 1966. Unfortunately, I have been unable to obtain a copy of either. It was also included briefly in 'The Psychic Handbook' (1995) by Craig Hamilton Parker.

***

I spent that evening on the back doorstep, pondering Tommy Steele's story.

How was that possible?

Perhaps he had hallucinated due to medication.

Maybe the night-nurse had been bored and decided to play ball with the dying kid.

Could a sick child from another room have sneaked past the nursing station to throw balls over a screen because he couldn't sleep?

None of those explanations made sense, but considering them distanced me from being one of those gullible people who visited psychics, read astrology charts and believed in spirit guides.

The universe works in mysterious ways.

CHAPTER 2

MY FLYING MATRON

As my mother slept throughout most of every day, the loneliness of four walls began to close in. I made an effort to get out of the house for at least an hour each day.

During one of my 'escapes', I met a friend at a local café and listened with little interest as she told me about her brother-in-law. According to Murielle, Bill was a world-renowned medium, and he was due to visit Melbourne next month.

"Really, he's amazing!" Murielle insisted. "I met my husband, his brother, because my parents always went to Bill for readings when I was growing up in England. These days he's in such demand he travels the world. He only comes to Melbourne once a year to visit us. Really, you *must* see him while he's here."

I sighed into my coffee cup. "But Murielle, I'm not really into..."

"If I don't put your name down by tomorrow you'll miss your chance!" Murielle interrupted. "His appointment book fills up really fast when people know he's coming. He does his readings at my place so he's only 5 minutes down the road. Then she added solemnly, "He's getting on in years so who knows if he'll be back."

I hadn't seen a medium, psychic or clairvoyant since I'd lived in London in 1969. At 21, I'd been desperate to get answers to all the important questions in life, like who would I marry and when would I win the lottery. When I didn't get answers to those crucial questions, I relegated psychics to the same category as snake oil salesmen.

"Ok," I sighed, not wanting to offend her. "Pencil me in and I'll think about it."

Perhaps it was just a coincidence that the following day, another friend called by unexpectedly to tell me about a reading she'd just had with a woman she described as "the most amazing psychic I've ever been to!"

"She was incredible," Janice rattled on, "she told me things no-one else knew. Her name is Rhonda, do you know her?" she asked. "she lives..."

"Why would I know her?" I snapped, slightly annoyed.

I was beginning to think I must be one of the few people in the world who didn't get weekly psychic updates.

Janice shrugged. "Well, she just lives in the next street, you probably bump into her in the supermarket. Here," she said, taking out her notebook. "I'll leave her details for you anyway."

I smiled politely and thanked her, intending to discard it the moment she left. Then I remembered the interview with Tommy Steele and wondered if there might be something in it for me after all.

***

"Could a psychic tell me how I could help Mum get better?" I asked deep space that evening while hugging my knees on the back doorstep.

As expected, deep space ignored me.

***

"Hello! You're right on time." Rhonda said as she opened her door. "Please, come in."

Janice's psychic lived in a modest weatherboard house surrounded by a neat garden. Inside, the house was tidy and well lit, and two small children were playing in the lounge.

I was relieved. I almost expected to be greeted by a gypsy holding a crystal ball.

All the same, I wondered what I was doing here.

Janice was right, however. Rhonda was amazing.

She knew my mother wasn't well. She knew my interstate cousin was divorced and preparing to marry a man who drove a forklift, even though I didn't know at that time. I phoned my cousin that evening and to my astonishment, discovered it was true!

Even more amazing was what followed a few days after my appointment with her.

Due to Murielle's constant reminders, and perhaps also to Rhonda's accuracy which helped convince me that all psychics might not be frauds, I conceded defeat and agreed to have a reading by her brother-in-law, Bill.

When I compared the taped recordings later, I was amazed by their uncanny similarities.

Rhonda: A new spirit guide is moving in. She's, um, it's like she was some sort of sister.

Bill:... a new guide entering, an individual who was a nursing sister, a matron in fact, in a hospital

Rhonda:... in very olden days

Bill:... and I'm going back in time to the days when the starched uniforms were worn

Rhonda:... when they used to wear, you know, the starched one. She's got this big bib top on, and like a cape

Bill:.... a white bib, bombazine cloth material

Rhonda:... and this cape, it's flying out behind her

Bill: She walked quickly and her cape would billow out behind her.

Rhonda: There's very much a time coming that you'll be tossing and turning, she's saying that she's very much around you at that time.

Bill: She is exercising an influence over you to keep you as cool, calm and collected as possible, and her influence on you has been such that she's certainly calmed you down.

Rhonda:... because the things you know about healing, you will be asked more of and more of in the future

Bill: Pay close attention to her in the future because she says only by doing that can you begin to realise the potential which you have to give other people the help, the remedies which they need.

I played the tapes over and over again. What was I to make of them?

Could this have been a standard reading, one everyone receives? Highly unlikely. Sooner or later people would compare notes.

Was it a conspiracy? Did Rhonda and Bill know each other? No, I was confidant Rhonda had never heard of Bill because when I told her later about the similarities, she asked for his contact number.

Still refusing to be convinced, I phoned Murielle, and she assured me she knew no-one called Rhonda and had never made an appointment for anyone by that name.

Was it possible Bill and Rhonda had read each other's minds, or had both read mine? And if so, was mind reading any less amazing than spirit guides?

On reflection, I realised that couldn't apply to Rhonda, because I'd had no idea the new man in my cousin's life drove a forklift, or even that they were planning to marry.

Besides, how could either of them read my mind about a matron with a flying cape?

Whichever way I turned it around, the simplest solution was that I really did have a guide in spirit who had been a nursing sister and had worn a starched bib and cape.

To my sceptical mind, the implications of this were mind-boggling.

If either of them had mentioned a winged angel or a cute cherub, I could easily have dismissed it. But a nursing matron was presumably someone who had once been alive, unless winged angels also had occupations!

If we were being guided by people who had lived and died, then the prospect of an afterlife became far more credible.

I recalled the visit I had made to the Spiritualist Association in London eighteen years earlier. I had been shown into a small room and introduced to a plump, jolly lady called Beryl. As I entered the room, Beryl raised one eyebrow and in a strong cockney accent announced "D'ya know you've got a 'merican Indian with you?"

I groaned inwardly while smiling outwardly. Who hadn't laid claim to an American Indian spirit guide in the 1960's? They had been the flavour of the month. But having booked and paid well in advance for the privilege of a reading by the resident medium, I decided to go along with it.

"Blimey and he's a big strong 'un!" Beryl remarked, her eyes focusing on a point above my head and slowly travelling upwards.

"He's standing very tall and straight." She lifted her chin and thrust her shoulders back as though trying to stand to attention while seated. "And so full of energy, he is! He's telling me... he's saying he saved your mother! Did you know that?" she asked.

Then, not waiting for my response, waved her hand and added "but you were just a babe, you wouldn't remember! 'She nearly drowned,' he's saying. He's thumping his chest and saying 'I saved her, it was me. I did it!' Ask your Mum, she'll tell you, yes indeed she will, m'dear!"

I don't recall what other profound statements Beryl imparted during my twenty-minute reading. I had instantly dismissed everything as fantasy and "just a bit of fun".

Now, nearly two decades later, I had to wonder.

"Mum," I whispered as I entered her darkened bedroom. These days, I could never be sure if she was awake, asleep, or even still alive, so I tiptoed around the house daily and approached her nervously.

"Hmmmm?" she opened her eyes and peered at me in the half-light, trying to focus.

"Um, I know this is probably a silly question, but did you ever nearly drown when I was a baby?"

I was sure I knew what the answer would be. I had never seen my mother venture beyond the shallows.

She pushed herself up on one elbow with difficulty and looked at me quizzically. "How did you know?"

I told her that a medium I consulted in London had mentioned it to me.

To my amazement, my mother confirmed that over thirty years earlier she had been swimming at a local beach when she'd suddenly developed cramp.

"I was going under for the third time!" she said.

"What happened?" I asked.

She shrugged. "It just disappeared and I swam ashore. I'll never forget it. I was a goner."

I wasn't sure if I should tell her who might have saved her. I still wasn't sure I believed it myself, so I chose to keep quiet.

All the same, I was stunned, and promptly retreated to my thinking doorstep.

***

How could she have known that? Had it simply been a lucky guess, or was it just an uncanny coincidence?

I recalled how easily I had joked about being "looked after" a few years ago when, faced with the prospect of a forty-

minute drive across town in heavy traffic on a wet and windy morning, my car had refused to start.

The local mechanic responded quickly to my phone call and towed it back to his garage. He phoned a short time later. "It started without a hiccup as soon as we got here!" he announced.

"Wonderful! Can I come and pick it up now? I'm already late for work!"

"Well ..." he said a little hesitantly, "when did you get new tyres?"

It was a strange question, and I wondered if he was going to berate me for not buying tyres through his garage.

"Um, a few days ago," I replied, preparing to launch into an explanation about the hefty discount a neighbour had arranged for their purchase.

"Then you're a very lucky girl to still be alive! Whoever put them on didn't tighten three of the wheel nuts! One wheel was already wobbling when we got here."

"Gosh, someone up there must like me!" I laughed, more from relief that my car had chosen that moment to be uncooperative.

"Someone sure must!" he agreed. "You can pick it up in an hour."

An American Indian?

A flying matron?

Or was it just another happy coincidence?

CHAPTER 3

THE AFTERLIFE CAFÉ

I had no doubt my mother was dying, so I decided it was time to find out if the best-selling book that professed to contain "actual case histories that reveal there is life after death" could offer any real comfort. It had been published more than a decade earlier so I doubted I'd find a copy on the shelves of the local bookshop, but it was worth a try.

"Excuse me, would you happen to have a copy of 'Life After Life', by Dr. Raymond Moody?" I asked the young man behind the counter.

"Certainly!" he smiled and pointed to a shelf on the far side of the shop. "You'll find it in the "new age" section."

Uh oh. The New Age section hardly inspired my confidence. No doubt it would be surrounded by books about reincarnation, aura cleansing, ufo's and channelled messages from Atlanteans!

"Oh, I thought the author was a doctor." I said dismissively.

"Raymond Moody? He *is* a doctor. Now. When he wrote 'Life After Life' he was still a struggling medical student.

Why was I here? Why was I buying a book I had dismissed as nonsense a decade earlier even though I hadn't bothered to read it? What could I possibly expect to get from this 'innocuous little paperback', written by a medical student?

Would it convince me that it was ok my mother was dying because she'd survive death and be just fine, and that there was absolutely nothing to worry about?

Was I totally mad?

"Here it is!" he waved the book under my nose and jolted me back to the present.

"Hmmm. Have you read it?" I asked, flicking disinterestedly through the pages. "Do you really think it's true?" I had no doubt he'd insist it was. After all, he'd want to make a sale.

"Well... I read it. Who hasn't? Do I believe it? Um.... not really," he mumbled through his smirk, his eyes darting to the other end of the store where his boss was busy with another customer. "Even the author himself isn't convinced."

He took the book from me and flipped to the last few pages, then handed it back, pointing to a specific paragraph.

"In writing this book I have been acutely conscious that my purpose and perspectives might very easily be misunderstood. In particular, I would like to say to scientifically minded readers that I am fully aware that what I have done here does not constitute a scientific study. And to my fellow philosophers I would insist that I am not under the delusion that I have 'proven' there is life after death."

I sighed. On one hand, I was impressed by the author's honesty. On the other hand, I really, *really* wanted someone or something to convince me that we do survive death.

"Do you have anything else on the subject?" I asked. "Anything at all?"

"Nope," he shrugged. "That's it. Not really a lot of call for that type of thing. Although..." he rubbed his chin thoughtfully, "there might be something in the religious section."

"Don't bother!"

I put the book back on the counter, then on a sudden impulse changed my mind and purchased it. I was doubtful it would provide the answers I sought, but I didn't know where else to look.

I wondered why I was even seeking answers when I was sure there were none. I had chosen to dismiss stories of cape-flying nursing guides as coincidental fantasies, but the prospect of losing my mother to oblivion spurred me on.

I knew there were people who believed we survived death, but I suspected most of them only accepted it because their church or parents or bible told them it was so, or because the alternative terrified them so much they preferred to hang on to any slim thread of hope.

I bought coffee in a paper cup, then crossed the road and glanced around the park for somewhere to sit. It was a warm day and most of the seats were taken, but I found space on the end of a bench seat and retrieved the little paperback from my bag.

The cover announced that it was an 'astounding bestseller' and that it 'may change mankind's view of life, death and spiritual survival.'

"Good luck!" I thought cynically.

I flicked it open to a foreword by someone called Elisabeth Kubler-Ross, MD. I was tempted to skip that section and start with Moody's own words when a sentence by Dr. Kubler-Ross caught my eye:

"It is enlightening to read Dr. Moody's book at the time when I am ready to put my own research findings on paper."

I was mildly intrigued to learn that another doctor, perhaps this time a real one, had also done research in this area, then questioned how any scientifically minded person could actually conduct research on the afterlife.

"Interesting book, isn't it?" A gnarled hand gently touched my forearm and I turned to look into a pair of piercing blue eyes on a smiling face surrounded by a shock of white hair.

I didn't want to be rude to a nice old lady, so I nodded politely, then read the first sentence again.

"You must read his new one, too," she said as she leaned closer, her bony shoulder pressing against mine.

I closed the book and placed it on my lap. "He's written another book?" I asked, feigning interest.

"It's his third, it only came out this year. It's called 'The Light Beyond'. The TS Bookshop will have it, they'll have George Ritchie's book too."

"I... um... George Ritchie? Is he another doctor?" I asked, wondering why the man in my local bookshop hadn't mentioned it and what and where the TS Bookshop was.

"Yes, of course!" she smiled. "He was the first one Dr. Moody heard about. He had his NDE during the war and Dr. Moody attended a lecture he gave. That's what got him started. Look."

I wondered what an "NDE" was, but before I could ask, she reached over and took the book from my lap.

"See here, the dedication in the front?" She handed the book back and I read the page she indicated.

To George Ritchie, MD and, through him,

to the One whom he suggested

The One? I knew what the capital 'O' on One suggested. I cringed when I considered what my grandmother must have thought when she received her copy. A Belfast protestant who married an Irish catholic shortly after the first world war, Nora had seen first-hand how religion divided families and turned friends into enemies.

"Interesting." I smiled weakly and fixed my eyes on the first page again.

This lady was not about to be easily dismissed.

"You see dear, when George Ritchie died of pneumonia at an army camp, he went to a café in a town he'd never been to before, in Mississippi, and..."

"Wait!" I interrupted, wanting to kick myself for showing interest. "He went to a *café*? That's where you go when you die?"

She laughed. "Well, not exactly. He just flew out of his body and that's where he landed."

This was definitely becoming too bizarre. "He flew? Out of his body?"

"Yes dear!" She leaned forward and assumed one of those "*are you trying to tell me you don't know?*" expressions.

During the next 20 minutes I listened intently as she told me that while some people had survived close calls with death throughout history, advanced resuscitation techniques had become common practice in recent years and as a result, many more people were being revived after they'd been declared dead. According to her, quite a few had amazing stories to tell.

My new acquaintance explained that Life After Life's author Raymond Moody had initially come across the concept of the afterlife through ancient dialogues by philosopher Plato. Then he attended a lecture by Dr. Ritchie.

Ritchie, she explained, had been a 20-year old private in the U.S. army during world war 2 and had been singled out to attend Medical College in Virginia. A few days before he was due to report to the college, he caught a cold which rapidly developed into pneumonia, and he was hospitalised at the military base.

Although he had a dangerously high temperature and was coughing blood, he desperately wanted to take advantage of this opportunity. In the early hours of the morning, he jumped out of bed and began to make his way to the train station.

15

Incredibly, Ritchie found himself walking through an orderly, then through closed doors, then flying through the air. Confused and disoriented, he flew over a small town and decided to stop and get his bearings. He landed outside a white café with a red roof and a blue neon sign and attempted to ask directions from a man walking by.

The man took no notice and, as with the orderly, walked right through him!

Ritchie returned from the 'afterlife café' and made his way into the hospital ward, but by then his body had been covered by a sheet and he had to search through the wards looking for himself.

Was this fantasy, I wondered.

According to this lady, Ritchie visited this town for the first time many years later, and he was able to drive directly to the café. It looked exactly as he remembered it. His book, 'Return From Tomorrow', published in 1978, describes his experience in detail.

I scribbled the details on the paper bag, along with the name of the bookshop she mentioned, but it was more out of politeness than genuine interest. The idea of someone flying through the night sky, landing outside a café and searching hospital wards for his body seemed too bizarre to consider.

Our conversation was starting to make me a little uncomfortable. I wondered if I'd stumbled onto some strange cult that worshipped death and sent missionaries into parks to convert people.

Then I reminded myself that I was seeking answers to the most important questions in life, questions I had pondered nightly for months: what was the point of being born if we just became food for worms? Was all we achieved in life merely for the sake of our children, who would also cease to exist one day, as would their children?

I was now nudging 40 and it was highly unlikely I would ever have children of my own, so what was the point of everything I'd worked for? When my mother died and no longer needed my care, would there be any purpose to my life, any reason for me to go on existing? Complete self indulgence seemed the only option. "Live for today, for tomorrow we die!"

The sudden realization I'd been away from home for almost an hour brought me back to the present with a jolt. I turned to thank the lady for her interesting conversation and bid her goodbye, but she was nowhere to be seen. One moment she had been sitting beside me, chatting as though we were old friends. The next, she appeared to have evaporated into thin air.

16

I glanced around the park, but there was no sign of her.

"Hmmm, I must have been lost in my own little world longer than I thought!" I considered. "How rude of me. Strange, she didn't even say goodbye."

As I walked across the road, a well dressed young man approached and handed me a pamphlet. I took it and began to read it as I walked.

> We have all sinned. We have all disobeyed God and done wrong before Him. The wages of sin is death. God will ask us to give account of what we have done. After this, the judgement. If we reject God's salvation, a terrible sentence awaits us. Anyone not found written in the Book of Life will be *cast into the lake of fire.*

If this was the afterlife, I decided, then I'd rather become worm food!

CHAPTER 4

WHERE IT ALL BEGAN

I read 'Life After Life' from cover to cover in one intense afternoon. I read about people floating out of their bodies and viewing themselves from a corner of the ceiling. I read about people whizzing through tunnels, seeing bright lights and having conversations with beings of light.

I had to concede that these accounts were eerily similar, but I staunchly clung to my scepticism. Perhaps the questions had been framed in a way that led each person to provide specific answers, such as "and tell me, did you fly rapidly through a long tunnel, like others have said?"

Names were rarely used. Were these real people? Perhaps the accounts were similar because they had all been written by one person!

In 1988, all I knew, or thought I knew, about Raymond Moody was that he had been a struggling medical student who had written a sensational book.

In 1988, all I really knew about everything to do with this topic could have been written on a pinhead. I also didn't know that I was taking the first steps of a very long and exciting journey.

Raymond Moody had sought answers to all the big questions long before he became a medical student and author. His own journey began as an undergraduate student of philosophy at the University of Virginia in 1965. During this time, one of his psychiatry professors, John Marshall, had alerted the class that a colleague, psychiatrist and professor Dr. George Ritchie, was giving a talk to a group of students at the medical school that evening.

Ritchie, Moody's professor explained, had been pronounced dead for around nine minutes and had an "interesting experience".

Curious by nature, young Raymond went along to hear what he had to say. While he found Ritchie's talk fascinating, he was unsure how to process it. He simply "filed it away" as an hallucination and thought no more about it.

In a lecture many years later, Dr. Moody confessed: "I grew up assuming that death was just an elimination of consciousness. I believed that when you died, it was like the lights go out and you go into an impenetrable blackness and it was like turning off your consciousness, which was very threatening to me because I really do enjoy thinking, I'm a thinking and information junkie to a severe degree."

About four years after attending Ritchie's talk, Moody was teaching Philosophy at an East Carolina university when a student approached him and asked if they could talk about life after death in class one day.

"Why would you want to talk about that?" he asked, convinced that such a concept was nothing more than a myth.

The student explained that he'd had a bad accident about a year earlier and his doctor told him he had died. "I had an experience that totally changed my life," he added, "and I haven't had anybody to talk about it with."

Dr. Moody invited his student to tell him more, then listened with growing excitement. The description he heard was almost identical to the experience Ritchie had described four years earlier.

Moody's mind was spinning. Was it merely an amazing coincidence that he had met the only two people in the world who'd had such an experience?

On the other hand, he wondered, was it possible this had happened to others?

Dr. Moody had to know more! He made it known around the university that he was open to hearing about other heavenly experiences and was astounded when around one hundred and fifty people — students, parents of students, teachers and friends of teachers — came forward to tell him their stories.

Most confessed they had never told another soul.

He chose fifty of these for in-depth interviews, and was stunned to hear even more commonalities in the experiences they related.

People told him they had viewed their bodies from above and travelled rapidly through a tunnel. Many described seeing a blinding light and some stated they had been greeted by deceased loved ones.

Prior to publication of 'Life After Life', books or studies on such experiences were rare. There were obscure references in a few old philosophy books, but Dr. Moody recognised that these were hardly the choice of reading matter for the average person so felt it was highly unlikely those he interviewed were fabricating their experiences based on such accounts.

Besides, such references had not included tunnels.

A meticulous researcher, he began categorizing the various stages of these 'near death experiences', or as he termed it, the 'NDE'.

I had arbitrarily dismissed this author's credentials when the bookseller told me he was "just a medical student". I was humbled.

Now I knew that prior to becoming "just a medical student", Dr. Moody had been a Professor of Philosophy at a major university before attending medical school to gain qualifications as a psychiatrist. This second degree had provided him with an opportunity to interview more people who claimed to have taken a glimpse of 'the other side' which eventually served as the catalyst for him to write 'Life After Life'.

Two doctoral degrees before the age of thirty hardly suggested someone who had written a sensational book in the hope of making a quick buck.

But of course, I knew none of this in 1988 when I opened the covers of his book for the first time.

***

The first problem Dr. Moody encountered in his initial interviews was ineffability — the difficulty experiencers had in finding words to explain what had occurred to them. Time and again, those he interviewed insisted that "there are no words to express what I'm trying to say" or "they just don't make adjectives to explain what I experienced."

Subjects attempted to describe what it felt like to be out of their body. I was vaguely familiar with the phrase 'obe' (an acronym for 'out-of-body experience'). Books with titles like 'Easy Astral Travelling' and 'How to Leave Your Body' had been popular throughout the 60's.

Then again, so had experimentation with psychedelic drugs, so I had cynically assumed the two activities were closely connected.

During my backpacking journeys through Europe in that decade I had met too many zonked out travellers to give much credence to stories of out-of-body experiences.

Now, Dr. Moody's research seemed to be suggesting that death might actually be the ultimate high.

One woman described how she had watched her body bobbing up and down in the water as she drowned and reported an "airy feeling that's almost indescribable" adding that she felt almost like a feather.

Another was in hospital when she died. She floated to the ceiling and watched as the doctor tried to revive her. She described feeling: "almost as though I were a piece of paper that someone had blown up to the ceiling."

This comment put me in mind of a book I had once read about author Ernest Hemingway, who had been hit by 28 pieces of shrapnel while working as an ambulance driver in Italy during the first world war.

In a letter to a friend, and reproduced in the biography 'My Brother Ernest Hemingway' by Leicester Hemingway (1962), Ernest wrote:

"I died then... I felt my soul or something coming right out of my body, [the way] you'd pull a handkerchief out of the pocket by its corner. It flew around and then came back and went in again and I wasn't dead any more."

I recall closing the book on that page and trying to imagine what it might feel like to fly around your body.

"Dying is a very simple thing," Hemingway added. "I've looked at death and really I know."

He remained deeply affected by this experience. In his novel, 'A Farwell to Arms' (1929), one of his characters (Frederic Henry) undergoes the same confrontation with death:

> "I tried to breathe but my breath would not come and I felt myself rush bodily out of myself and out and out and out and all the time bodily in the wind. I went out swiftly, all of myself, and I knew I was dead and that it had all been a mistake to think you just died. Then I floated, and instead of going on I felt myself slide back. I breathed and I was back."

Another woman in Moody's book reported floating out of her body and thinking: "My God, I'm dead! I can't believe it!"

I wondered how French philosopher Descartes might have handled such a statement. In the seventeenth century, he wrote: "I think, therefore I am," reasoning that if one questioned their existence, that very thought proved they did, indeed, exist.

21

Did that philosophy still apply in death?

"I wasn't sorry that I was dead," this woman continued, "but I just couldn't figure out where I was supposed to go... and so I decided I was just going to wait until all the excitement died down and they carried my body away, and try to see if I could figure out where to go from here."

I found this prospect a little disturbing and made a hasty retreat to the back doorstep.

***

Propping my elbows on my knees, I pondered the implications of what I had read.

I tried to imagine being dead but still alive, being conscious yet invisible, desperately trying to make someone, anyone, see me or hear me.

Were we all destined to become ghostly forms, hovering around the scene of our deathbeds, haunting those left behind?

Was this heaven, or was it hell?

Perhaps it was true, ignorance was bliss. I had set out to find proof, or at least credible evidence, for the validity of an afterlife, but instead of providing comforting validation, this book was opening Pandora's box and showing me things I wasn't sure I wanted to see.

***

When I found the courage to return to the book, I read of another woman who had a cardiac arrest immediately before surgery.

Two surgeons tried unsuccessfully to resuscitate her, then one said: "Let's try one more time and then we'll give up."

They succeeded, and the woman later stunned the surgeon when she repeated his words back to him. That certainly got my attention!

"You never really believe, I don't think, fully, that you're going to die" one experiencer reflected, adding "it's always something that's going to happen to the other person."

Yes, I could relate to that. It had taken me almost the first three decades of my life to recognize my own mortality, and only then because I had faced the possibility of losing my mother. I had also never imagined *her* dying!

I read accounts of people who heard the pronouncement of their own death while trying to tell those around them they were "very much alive, thank you!"

One woman died as a result of a cardiac arrest while undergoing a liver scan. The radiologist immediately dialled her doctor's number and told him "Dr. James, I've killed your patient."

"I knew I wasn't dead," this woman later told Dr. Moody. "I tried to move or to let them know, but I couldn't."

***

If these accounts were true, then we could only leave our bodies if we were not our bodies. That begged the question: what were we?

I could look out through my physical eyes, but these experiences suggested those eyes were merely a camera lens, a tool we used to view the physical world.

So what, or who, was looking out through those eyes?

Neuroscience tells us that we interpret with our brains what we see through our eyes. But if the physical brain dies with the body, then how could these people have interpreted what they saw through eyes they didn't have, by a brain that was physically dead?

My own tired brain was spinning. This little paperback book was turning my world upside down.

It was no longer just about survival of death, now it was getting personal. If these people were telling the truth and we really did survive death, then what survived? It was just too easy to say "the soul survives". What was a soul, anyway?

What did we become after our physical shell disintegrated?

"If I am not my body," I pleaded with the universe, "then who or what am I?"

CHAPTER 5

SHOW ME THE EVIDENCE

"If we're not our bodies, then what are we?"

Pauline worked as a teller at my local bank and we began our friendship with brief chats over the counter. One day I took time out to call into a local café for a coffee and noticed Pauline sitting alone. She beckoned me to join her and we began meeting occasionally for lunch.

Our conversations rarely involved anything more challenging than recipes, our favourite movies or the latest antics of our dogs, but our lunch dates provided me with much needed time away from home and an opportunity to talk to another human being.

Aware that Pauline was a devout catholic, I always avoided controversial subjects. But on this day, there was only one question rattling around in my brain: if we're not our bodies, then what are we?

Foolishly, I allowed my thoughts to turn into spoken words.

Pauline was silent for a moment. Then, carefully placing her cutlery on her plate, she looked directly at me and smiled serenely.

"We're souls, of course! We're souls trapped in physical bodies because..."

"And what exactly is a soul?" I interrupted, becoming irritated at the ease with which she accepted this concept and fearing I was about to hear a sermon on how we were all sinners or fallen angels condemned to be eternally trapped in physical life.

When would I learn to keep my mouth shut?

"And how do you know this, Pauline? Have you ever seen a soul? What does this soul look like? Does it have eyes and ears and arms and legs? Does it think? And where is it? Tell me, where is your soul now, right now, while you're sitting here talking to me? Show me. Show me your soul, if there's such a thing!"

Pauline reached over the table to pat my hand. "Why are you so angry?" she whispered, her eyes darting either side of me to satisfy herself I wasn't attracting unwanted attention from other diners.

"I just wonder if you've ever questioned any of this? What if it's all a big lie and when we're dead, we're dead? What if you only believe it's true because your priest told you it was true, and your priest only believes it because he was told it was true, way, way back to the first person who ever said it, and everyone goes happily on their way being nice little people who hope to be good enough to go to heaven one day when really there's no soul and there's no heaven and..."

"Hey hey, slow down!" Pauline laughed. "What if, what if. What if you and I are just figments of each other's imagination?"

I reminded myself that this wasn't a conversation we should be having, so I made a valiant attempt at humour. "Well, we can't both be figments of each other's imagination," I laughed weakly, "because one of us needs to have the imagination to begin with! Besides, if that was true we wouldn't be anything, body or soul. We'd just be..."

I suddenly had a flashback. I was seven or eight years old and was stretched out on the back lawn enjoying the sunshine as I watched the clouds drift by. "Am I really alive?" I had wondered. "Or if there's a God, is He just having a dream and I'm in it?"

"We'd just be what?" Pauline's voice jolted me back.

"We'd just be... oh, I don't know." I shrugged, pretending to lose interest. "We'd be people we see in our dreams that just fade away when... um... when we wake up." I didn't want to encourage her by saying "when God wakes up!"

***

Our conversation unnerved me, so I went home and read 'Life After Life' again, slowly this time.

Account after account revealed that those who had died and returned to tell their tales did not feel the desperation I assumed they must as they approached the threshold of death. Instead, feelings of peace and quiet, even joy, were described by most.

Dr. Moody heard comments like "all I felt was warmth and the most extreme comfort I have ever experienced" and "I couldn't feel a thing in the world except peace, comfort, ease, just quietness".

These were people who had been suffering pain or discomfort moments earlier.

How was this possible? How could anyone approach death joyfully? People like Pauline may have unshakeable faith that Saint Peter would usher them through the pearly gates, but the rest of us could only hope there was something more, or nothing more, depending on our individual points of view.

Either way, it was still only blind hope.

I longed to believe. But I was not a faith-without-proof kind of person. I needed more.

I needed hard facts. Not anonymous anecdotes.

***

From my God-conversation doorstep, I threw out a challenge: "Show me the evidence!"

I could not face the rest of my life waiting for my own turn to become extinct, or worse, becoming a conscious, invisible handkerchief!

The fact that I was challenging a being I didn't believe in, and asking for hard evidence of something as nebulous and unprovable as an afterlife did not feel at all illogical to me at the time.

Perhaps I was teetering on the edge of insanity. Mum's illness, a mortgage to pay without a regular income, and the loneliness of enforced isolation were all beginning to take their toll.

***

'The Power of Positive Thinking' by the well-known motivational writer, Norman Vincent Peale, had been gathering dust on my bookshelf for years. A friend had given it to me shortly before moving to smaller premises and I had taken it to be polite.

I decided it was just what I needed. I snuggled further into my oversized lounge chair and prepared to learn all I could about the fundamentals of positive thinking.

Halfway through the book, I slammed it shut. There, in black and white, was yet another account of yet another near-death experience, this one having occurred to the author's friend, Mr. Clarke.

Was this some cosmic conspiracy?

26

The doctor had given up hope on Clarke, Peale explained. With failing heart, deathly low blood pressure and no reflexes, it was obvious he was dying. His family gathered at the bedside and waited for the inevitable.

Imagine their surprise next morning when Clarke opened his eyes. Within a few days, he also recovered his speech.

Clarke later reported to Peale: "At some time during my illness, something very peculiar happened to me. I cannot explain it. It seemed that I was a long distance away. I was in the most beautiful and attractive place I have ever seen. There were lights all about me, beautiful lights. I saw faces dimly revealed, kind faces they were, and I felt very peaceful and happy. In fact, I have never felt happier in my life."

"Then," he recalled, "the thought came to me: I must be dying. Then it occurred to me, perhaps I have died. Then I almost laughed out loud and asked myself: Why have I been afraid of death all my life? There is nothing to be afraid of in this."

Asked by Peale if he had wanted to return, Clarke replied: "It did not make the slightest difference. If anything, I think I would have preferred to stay in that beautiful place."

Peale did not doubt his friend's story, describing Clarke as a construction engineer with a scientific turn of mind, a quiet, restrained, factual, unemotional type of man.

Peale added that he had "spent too many years talking to people who have come to the edge of something and had a look across, who unanimously have reported beauty, light, and peace, to have any doubt in my own mind."

Had Clarke or Peale read 'Life After Life'? Was this simply a copycat account? I checked the publishing date and discovered that it pre-dated Moody's book by more than twenty years! No, it was certainly not a copycat account.

What a coincidence!

It would take many years, but I would eventually realise that when I asked questions on the back doorstep, then went to bed in disgust because no heavenly voice boomed a response, a 'coincidence' would invariably provide at least part of the answer within days.

I found myself becoming encouraged, even excited, by this brief account pre-dating 'Life After Life'. Was it possible there were others?

If any pre-Moody accounts had been recorded and still existed, I was determined to find them.

I needed to compare reports by people who had no opportunity to invent a scenario based on Dr. Moody's published research. I needed to know if other accounts prior to 1976, if any existed, also included tunnels, lights and boundaries. If so, this would lend far more credence to those in 'Life After Life'.

I had a mission! It was time to visit the bookshop that the lady in the park had recommended.

It still hadn't occurred to me that the words *"and so it begins"* had truly been prophetic.

CHAPTER 6

A KID IN A CANDY SHOP

As the train rocked me into a meditative state, my confidence began to wane.

What if my bookshelf contained the only two pre-Moody accounts (Hemingway and Clarke) that were ever recorded? 'Life After Life' had been a runaway success because Moody was the first person to systematically gather and record these accounts, but what if he had he also been the only one to do so?

Without supporting evidence, could I over-ride the tiresome little voice in my head that told me all accounts reported since 1976 were fabrications based on those in one best selling little book?

Could I hold firm to the belief that even if no-one had written them down, other people really had journeyed to heaven through tunnels, conversed with lights and had reunions with loved ones before Dr. Moody made such images popular?

Or, and I suspected this would be the outcome, would I finally have to dismiss Moody's book as fiction? If so, then I would also be forced to accept that death really did mean total annihilation and that there was no real purpose to life.

Norman Vincent Peale had indicated in 1952 that he had spoken to many who had such experiences. But, he had provided no details.

Elisabeth Kubler-Ross stated in the foreword to 'Life After Life' that she had been conducting research in this area for years. But, she had not yet made her findings public.

Ernest Hemingway had written about becoming a pocket handkerchief as he flew out of his body. But Hemingway was, first and foremost, a writer of fiction.

Millions of readers around the world had accepted Moody's accounts as credible, so why couldn't I?

Maybe the idea of God in His heaven was too steeped in religious concepts for me to consider. Perhaps it was simply that the prospect of a happy-ever-after was just too convenient, too comforting, too childish or too impractical to accept.

I was afraid of being gullible. I had come of age in the late 60's when everything weird and sensational had been enthusiastically embraced.

During my teens, I had been sufficiently curious to visit a few psychics for guidance. One or two had been vaguely interesting, but most were amateur 'cold readers' who made laughable predictions about tall dark handsome men and promised great career success.

In my late teens, I had read a book about 'Beatles style' meditation and made a half-hearted attempt to practice it, with little success.

In my early 20's, I had briefly studied astrology, dabbled in palmistry and read a book about creating your own reality.

I had embraced none of it.

Many I met while backpacking in Europe burnt incense, smoked pot, chanted mantras, smudged auras and sat on mountaintops at daybreak communing with Native American spirit guides.

I had found most aspects of new age thinking slightly ludicrous.

Perhaps I had been too young. I acknowledged that people were looking for answers, but at the time I hadn't even been sure what the questions were.

Now, I was the one looking for answers. But I was also acutely aware that if science eventually revealed a more mundane cause for near-death experiences, it would be a long and painful fall from the pinnacle of belief into the deep valley of disappointment.

The mission I chose to embark upon that day was fraught with danger.

***

As I approached the building, I noticed the front window displayed books on tarot cards, numerology and reincarnation.

I cringed. I peeked through the glass door but could see nothing more threatening than a dimly lit flight of stairs.

I took a deep breath, glanced around to ensure no-one would see me go in (after all, I was far too sensible for all this hocus-pocus) then ducked through the door. As I began to climb the stairs, each step creaked eerily under my feet. The sickly sweet aroma of incense wafted towards me. I imagined entering a small, dark room and being greeted by a woman in saffron robes, seated in the lotus position and probably chanting in tongues!

Was I ready for this?

On entering the huge, brightly lit room, I gasped in amazement. Floor-to-ceiling shelves spread out before me in every direction. Where to start? I wandered up and down aisles glancing at shelf labels: ufo's, astrology, channelling, Buddhism, spirit guides.

Every time I turned a corner, I encountered people — men, women, young, old — browsing bookshelves, flicking through books, choosing books, recommending books to each other, carrying armfuls of books. Others were gathered around the counter waiting to pay for books, asking for the location of specific books, leaving with bags full of books.

It was a whole new world I didn't even know existed.

I turned a corner and there it was. The afterlife. Five solidly packed shelves.

Months earlier, my local bookshop had offered Dr. Moody's book, or nothing. Now, I felt like a kid in a candy shop. I didn't know which colourful sweet to bite into first.

Alas, these sweets all proved sour.

Not one of these glossy paperbacks had been published before 1976. Most of them had been written by people who died and returned to tell their "amazing story of the world beyond". I had no interest in what I suspected would merely be copycat stories.

Others were by psychics who claimed to have channelled the information during their daily conversations with the spirit world.

No thanks.

Disappointed, I nervously approached the counter and explained my dilemma. Nervously, because I still believed that asking for books about death was just too weird.

I needn't have worried.

"I think we'll have just what you're looking for," the young man behind the counter smiled. He led me to a second-hand section occupying the entire back wall. The top shelves were so high I needed a stepladder to reach them. The stepladder was promptly provided.

"If you don't find what you need here," Brad said quietly, "just let me know. We've got at least twice this many in the storeroom out the back. We don't usually allow customers back there, but since you're looking for something specific..." He gave me a conspirational wink, then left me to it.

Oh joy. I spent the rest of the day browsing this goldmine. I agonised over each choice until I realised that, as used books, they were a fraction of the cost of new ones.

The stack on the floor beside me grew alarmingly and was threatening to topple when I chanced upon an old academic publication titled 'Deathbed Observations by Physicians and Nurses', written by Karlis Osis, Ph.D and published in 1961.

I grabbed it and clutched it protectively to my chest with both hands, looking furtively from side to side as though I expected other browsers to throw me to the floor and violently wrench it from me.

This was starting to get serious!

***

I left the T.S. Bookshop with two large carry bags I could barely lift and headed for the nearest coffee shop. Sipping a well earned cappuccino, I flicked through my selections.

One offered "eyewitness accounts of men and women who have experienced the hereafter". Another promised "the earliest known collection of first-person accounts confirming that this life is but one phase of our existence." Yet another claimed to be "the book that shatters every myth about mortality."

I opened one called 'The Waiting World' and read the introduction: "Once a man experiences a thing himself, there can be no more doubting. He knows! Whether it be Fiji, a new baby in the home, or the touch of God."

I could relate to this statement. I had recently considered that crossing the threshold of death might be similar to a tribesman from a remote indigenous tribe being taken to New York or Paris, then being returned to his village. Imagine his frustration when he tried to describe what he saw.

Would anyone believe him when he spoke of flying through the sky faster than a shooting star? Would they listen with interest when he described huts so tall they scraped the clouds? Would they ask questions about the moving boxes inside these huts that propelled people upwards towards the sky?

His fellow tribesmen would no doubt scoff at his silly stories, but he would always know that what he saw was not a dream. It had happened. That place existed.

The words "touch of God," however, suggested religious overtones and I noticed that the author, Archie Matson, was a Reverend. I was about to discard it for another. After all, I had an almost never-ending supply in the bags at my feet! But the next paragraph made me sit up and pay attention.

"Some thirty years ago," Matson wrote, "a greatly trusted friend told me of a personal experience... [and] I still remember the ecstatic thrill that went through me."

Matson explained that an 80-year-old family friend confided to him that 50 years earlier (and this takes us back to the late 19th century), she had left her body following surgery and found herself floating over the bed, looking down on her physical form.

"I have never dared tell it to a living soul," she confessed, "for fear people would think I had gone off the deep end."

Most of those Dr. Moody interviewed had also admitted keeping their experiences to themselves for fear of being labelled mentally unstable. Some confided in close friends and family but found that few believed them. One woman attempted to discuss it with her minister, only to have him dismiss her story as hallucination.

We can only imagine the relief these people must have felt when Dr. Moody not only made it known he was genuinely interested in hearing what they had to say, but also revealed that their experience was not unique.

Occasionally some experiencers were fortunate to find a sympathetic ear.

One girl's family had been doubtful about her story until they consulted her doctor. He admitted he had heard stories like hers before and explained to the concerned parents that when patients were in severe pain or had serious injuries, the soul temporarily left the body.

This was, indeed, a rare doctor.

The experience of Archie Matson's friend served as the catalyst for him to collect more accounts, and as Dr. Moody had discovered, a genuine desire to know attracted others with stories to tell.

Matson later wrote: "There have been scores... in recent years [of] personal experiences of ordinary people and their families. A sympathetic ear and the assurance that others have similar experiences are better than wine for loosening the tongue."

One account that came to Matson's attention occurred to Gene Albright from Arizona, who died in 1960. "Suddenly the darkness cleared," Albright reported. "My mind seemed sharper and clearer than it had ever been. Just as suddenly the pain was no more. With this I felt wonderfully and supremely free."

Yes, I was going to enjoy reading this one!

Dr. Moody's second book, 'Reflections on Life After Life', was one of the few post-Moody books I bought. Published eighteen months after his first, it promised "new vital research into near-death experiences"

I later learned that the main reason he wrote this follow-up book was that participants in the first book had made heaven sound so attractive that he feared it may have prompted a spate of suicides!

Dr. Ritchie's book, 'Return From Tomorrow', claimed to be "one of the most startling and hopeful descriptions of the realm beyond." Recalling the tale I had heard in the park about Ritchie flying out of his hospital bed and landing at a café in Mississippi, I wasn't hopeful.

'Journeys Out of the Body' by Robert Monroe, was included because I had revealed my confusion to Brad about reports of leaving the body at death. He had assured me this book would begin to make everything clear and offer a sound basis for my understanding.

According to the preface, it provided information on techniques for leaving the body, meeting with the dead, and visiting other planes. The author was described as "a solid citizen who's been 'out' a thousand times now and wants to pass his experiences on to others so they won't have to go through some of the confusion and terror he did while learning on his own."

I could feel the angel of scepticism snuggling into my shoulder.

CHAPTER 7

BEFORE IT ALL BEGAN

Once home, I stretched out on the couch and ran my eye over the tower of books stacked up beside me. I chose 'The Vestibule', simply because it was on the top of the pile. It had been published in 1972, and the author was Jess Weiss.

Weiss had been one among thousands of young American men drafted to serve his country in Europe and North Africa in 1941. He went into battle with the courage of one who has no thought or fear of death, not because he was incredibly brave but because he had never known death.

"I had never seen a corpse," he confessed. "I had never attended a funeral, and no family member or close friend of mine had died."

I was relieved to know I wasn't the only one!

By 1944, Weiss was a multi-decorated corporal squad leader. Throughout those years he had watched helplessly as friends and comrades died, some inches away. He had witnessed countless rotting corpses of adults, children and animals. Faced with such horrors, he doubted he would survive the war. Soon, he was no longer sure he wanted to survive.

The high velocity German mortar shell that found its way to Weiss' leg paralysed one side of his body, and he was sent home.

His physical disability was obvious, but the mental and emotional wounds were the hardest to bear. For more than a decade Jess woke in a cold sweat every night, screaming and struggling to escape. Any loud noise sent him running for cover.

He eventually married and had children, but the guilt of surviving when so many others had perished soon led to apathy and depression.

Weiss had two choices — give up and die, or find some meaning in living. He chose the latter. He found hope in a second-hand bookshop and became fascinated with books on metaphysics, spiritual life and mystical theology.

Through this reading he became familiar with the story of the biblical Lazarus who had died and returned to life four days later. He then came across a modern (for its time) article in Life magazine which told the story of David Snell's death and subsequent resuscitation.

Snell had gone into anaphylactic shock as a result of a penicillin shot. Fortunately, his wife had been able to summon help quickly, but for a few terrifying moments before the adrenalin took effect, he had no pulse and no discernible pressure or blood flow. He wrote that at the point of death he had gazed into something he believed to be life's supreme mystery.

"What was it?" he asked in his article. "I knew it so well when it was there, opening before me, something more beautiful, more gentle, more loving than the mind or imagination of a living creature could ever conceive. But it is gone."

From that moment, personal stories of death and resuscitation began to find their way to Jess Weiss. Like Dr. Moody three decades later, Weiss became fascinated by the similarities he heard in these stories.

He wrote: "[they] made me realize that mind and body exist separately, and that all I really am is consciousness."

Weiss kept records of these accounts, and in 1972 they were published as 'The Vestibule'.

This book almost didn't make it into my collection because the title meant nothing to me. (Why was a book on medieval architecture on a shelf about the afterlife?)

I eventually recognised that when one enters a vestibule or entrance hall, they have passed through the front door of the dwelling but not yet crossed the threshold into the house itself. When one substitutes the word 'house' with 'death', it becomes apparent this is what near-death experiencers describe. They pause at the vestibule of heaven!

What a clever title.

One of the experiences Weiss collected was by Burris Jenkins, who suffered horrific burns as a result of an explosion on his cruiser in 1957.

Jenkins was rushed to hospital where the surgeon calculated the odds of his survival as ninety-nine to one against.

Following a four hour operation, Jenkins left his body. "There was no sensation of warmth or cold," he recalled, "just complete comfort."

Another first-hand account in Weiss' collection was by E. L. Huffine, who survived a plane crash.

While the year was not stated, it would appear to have occurred in the 1930's based on the description of the small plane Huffine had purchased. With his wife Roselyn as passenger, he was taking it up for the first time when it shakily rose barely five feet and plunged through a hedge, ripping off the wings and flipping on its back.

Having left his body and taken up a position about fifty feet away, Huffine watched his wife struggle to unfasten the safety belt and roll free to the ground.

"There was another form on the ground, too," Huffine wrote. "I knew it was mine, but it did not contain the consciousness with which I was observing all that was happening. Roselyn was dragging the body away from the smoking plane, but I watched with indifference. It was such a clear revelation! I felt myself as clear as light. There was no sense of pain, only a feeling of completeness and well-being."

I referred back to 'Life After Life' and found many similar statements:

"There was no pain, and I've never felt so relaxed."

"...a momentary flash of pain, but then the pain vanished."

"I couldn't feel a thing in the world except peace, comfort, ease, just quietness."

"...the most extreme comfort I have ever experienced."

It appeared that the process of dying, or at least reading about it, was not as confronting as I had feared. I pressed on with renewed enthusiasm.

In 'The Waiting World', Matson related the story of a teacher who had been swimming in Lake Erie when he almost drowned. "The next thing I knew," he explained, "I was surrounded by deep darkness and a feeling of sublime peace."

Ten-year-old Herman Stultz' also faced the prospect of a watery grave in Germany in 1896. He had been warned by his mother to stay away from the water, but boys will be boys, even in 1896. He went too close to the edge near the waterfall and fell in.

Tossed about in the swirling waters, he fought in vain to keep his head above water while his sister ran to find their older brother, Hans. She later estimated that it had taken them around thirty minutes to locate their drowning brother.

In his autobiography — penned seventy-five years later — Herman clearly recalls the sense of calmness and serenity that suddenly engulfed him. (Herman Stulz, Autobiography, CLDS circa 1971)

Another youngster who almost met his end in deep waters was naval cadet, Francis Beaufort, who also experienced a sense of calm at the point of drowning.

In 'An Autobiographical Memoir of Sir John Barrow, Late of the Admiralty' (1847) Beaufort gives an account of the time he fell off a small boat in Portsmouth Harbour. Unable to swim, and struggling to make himself heard, he swallowed water and quickly sank below the surface.

Beaufort wrote: "From the moment that every exertion had ceased, which I imagine was the immediate consequence of complete suffocation, a calm feeling of the most perfect tranquillity superseded the most tumultuous sensations. It might be called apathy, certainly not resignation, for drowning no longer appeared an evil. I no longer thought of being rescued, nor was I in any bodily pain. On the contrary, my sensations were now of a rather pleasurable cast, partaking of that dull but contented sort of feeling which precedes the sleep produced by fatigue."

Young Francis eventually became Admiral Beaufort and presumably learnt to swim in the process! The wind scale he later devised was made mandatory by the Royal Navy in 1838 and is known to us today as the Beaufort scale.

It has often been said that drowning is not an unpleasant experience, but what about other causes of death?

Dr. David Livingstone (of "I presume" fame) was almost devoured by a lion! Now that could not have been pleasant.

In 'Livingstone's Africa: Perilous Adventures and Extensive Discoveries in the Interior of Africa' (1872) Livingstone wrote: "...I saw the lion just in the act of springing upon me... he caught my shoulder as he sprang and we both came to the ground below together. Growling horribly close to my ear, he shook me as a terrier does a rat. The shock produced a stupor similar to that which seems to be felt by a mouse after the first shake of a cat."

The intrepid explorer and medical missionary sustained severe splintering to his upper arm, along with numerous teeth holes as deep as gunshot wounds. A statue erected on the grounds of the David Livingstone Centre in Blantyre, Scotland in 2004, vividly demonstrates this dramatic incident.

Can you imagine anything more terrifying, or more potentially painful than being eaten by a lion? Well, you may be surprised by Livingstone's next words:

"It caused a sort of dreaminess in which there was no sense of pain, nor feeling of terror, though [I was] quite conscious of all that was happening." He added that "this shake annihilated fear and allowed no sense of horror in looking round at the beast."

Livingstone' stated that his only emotion was that of intense curiosity as to which part of his body the lion would have next.

Good heavens!

"The peculiar state is probably produced in all animals killed by carnivore;" Livingstone concluded, "and if so, is a merciful provision by our benevolent Creator for lessening the pain of death."

Another not-so-fun way to die would be to fall off a mountain, but Swiss Geologist and mountaineer Albert Heim survived such a fall and reported: "...everything was beautiful without grief or anxiety, and without pain... elevated and harmonious thoughts dominated and united the individual images, and like magnificent music, a divine calm swept through my soul."

As a result of his experience, Heim was compelled to conduct what was perhaps the first in-depth research into near death experiences.

He published his report in the year book of the Swiss Alpine Club in 1892 as 'The Experience of Dying From Falls' and described his own encounter, along with thirty other first hand accounts of near-fatal falls by mountain climbers and workers who fell of scaffolding.

He also gathered accounts of soldiers who sustained life-threatening injuries during wars, and from people who nearly drowned or almost died in accidents.

Heim learnt that "no grief was felt, nor any paralysing fright. There was no anxiety, no trace of despair, nor pain, but rather calm seriousness, profound acceptance and a dominant mental quickness."

His research on falls also revealed that "consciousness was painlessly extinguished, usually at the moment of impact, which was at the most heard but never painfully felt."

Albert Heim later became one of Einstein's lecturers at the Zurich Polytechnic School. In a letter to a friend in 1952, Einstein wrote that

Heim's lectures had been "magical".

Might Heim have shared the results of his research with his students? Perhaps Einstein read the published report by this lecturer he admired, and if so, could it have been Heim's influence that led Einstein to consider that time and space were not fixed and constant as was assumed by physicists at the time?

In 1930, Swiss minister Oskar Pfister who was also a lay psychoanalyst and friend of Freud's, published an interpretation of Heim's findings.

Pfister theorized that the victims of these near-fatal accidents were evoking infantile fantasies in order to evade the unacceptable prospect of death. (Otherworld Journeys: Accounts of Near-death Experiences in Medieval and Modern Times, Carol Zaleski, Oxford University Press, 1988)

I wondered how likely it was that an intrepid explorer and medical missionary, a Swiss geologist held in high esteem by Einstein, and a nineteenth century admiral who invented a wind scale still used almost two centuries later, had nothing better to do than make up 'infantile fantasies'.

Did this mean I was starting to believe?

***

Dying with "elevated and harmonious thoughts" was all very nice, but what happened next?

I recalled one woman in Dr. Moody's book who had decided she was "just going to wait until all the excitement died down and they carried my body away, and try to see if I could figure out where to go from here."

Apart from Dr. Ritchie who called into the local café, had anyone mentioned actually going anywhere or being anything other than calmly and serenely dead?

Charles John Lambert did. During his near-drowning, Lambert had been surprised to find that he was no longer in his body.

"My spirit was out of the water," he wrote, adding that he was delighted to find that he could "move about without the slightest effort and with great rapidity."

Lambert recalled seeing a friend searching for his body, but despaired that he "had no power to communicate with him." (A Curious Experience in Drowning, 1886)

We met Herman Stulz a few pages ago, when he almost drowned in Germany in 1896. In his autobiography, Herman wrote that while his

40

sister was searching for their older brother, he found himself "standing on the opposite shores watching 'little Herman' spinning around under the fall." (Herman Stulz, Autobiography, CLDS circa 1971)

From this vantage point, he observed his siblings running towards the waterfall. "Hans was already in high school," he boasted, "and had learned how to revive drowned persons."

He watched as his big brother dragged him out of the water, then rolled him over a log to squeeze the water out. "Of a sudden," he wrote, "my spirit walking towards Hans took possession of my body again."

After he recovered and was well enough to receive a whipping for playing near the waterfall, Herman began to ponder his strange experience. "I was bewildered and confused that I actually saw what happened to me. I told my parents and sisters, and they just laughed."

Canadian contractor George Godkin would have laughed too, until he died in 1948 as the result of a gas explosion and subsequent fire. With third-degree burns to sixty percent of his body, he was not expected to survive. Having always believed that death was "an end in blackest night" we can only imagine his shock when he realized he had separated from his physical body.

Godkin later declared that he had "travelled into that land beyond death, and returned," and expressed amazement at the vast differences between the two worlds.

One of the first things he noticed was "a sense of weightlessness," adding "it is the earthly body that gives the soul that heavy gravity feeling." (Voices From the Edge of Eternity, 1968)

No wonder people described feeling like feathers, handkerchiefs, or floating pieces of paper.

When seventy-six year old Betty Patterson died as a result of a burst appendix, she later stated: "At first I felt as if my spirit, my self, was separating from the husk of my body and floating up to the ceiling of the room. From there I could look down at my body on the operating table." (Glimpses of the Beyond, 1974)

Julia Phillips Ruop was also amazed to find herself leaving her body when she died during a thyroid operation in the 1930's. She, too, floated above the bed and looked down at her physical form and at the group around the operating table. Then she heard the nurse say: 'Doctor, her pulse is going.' (Guideposts Magazine, 1963)

I had no difficulty dismissing Julia's account. If she heard the nurse say that her pulse was going, then I concluded she was not yet dead, only close.

I silently congratulated myself for being so astute, while also wondering how I might justify the fact that she had also seen her own body and viewed the group from above their heads.

John Brown's account was not quite as easy to dismiss. He heard the doctor actually pronounce him dead.

Brown died of an unidentified illness. In his 1897 book, 'Mediumistic Experiences of John Brown, the Medium of the Rockies', he wrote: "It then became dark, my eyes could no longer see... my limbs were useless... my breath had almost stopped, but I heard and knew all that was said and done."

Brown's wife, son-in-law and four doctors (two of whom were his close neighbours) were at his bedside when he suddenly found himself "lying horizontally above my body and about two feet from it. With no effort on my part I moved off from over my body and stood upon my feet, about five feet from it."

Brown continued: "I could see it [my body] on the bed, and I saw Mr. Woodward... let go my head that he had been holding and straighten my body on the bed. I stood right there... I heard Dr. Dickey say to one he met on the stairs: you are too late; he is dead."

E. L. Huffine also heard the words of others, but these were strangers and they were certainly not gathered at his bedside.

You may recall that Huffine crashed his aeroplane in the 1930's. A crowd of strangers quickly gathered at the airfield to watch the unfolding drama. A few of Huffine's friends were also present, and they rushed to help him. When there was no response to artificial respiration, one of his friends began shouting at him.

"At the sound of my name," Huffine later wrote: "I felt as if a strong wire was tugging me back toward my body. I was reluctant to return and continued to look on, experiencing the most complete contentment (but)... the pull became stronger each time he called me, and suddenly I was looking up into their faces."

Staggering to his feet, he made a beeline to a woman standing at the edge of the crowd. "I heard what you said about me," he told her.

When the startled woman denied saying anything, he repeated her words: "Well, he must have been a wild one! It's no more than he deserved! Only birds are supposed to fly!" (The Vestibule)

The woman turned ashen and fled to her car.

A hauntingly similar account occurred to Stefan von Jankovich, who was a passenger in a sports car involved in a head-on collision in Switzerland in 1964. Stefan had been thrown out of the car and onto the pavement.

Fortunately, two doctors were driving on the same road at the time and were quickly by his side. One tried a cardiac stimulant drug, and when that had no effect, the other injected adrenalin directly into his heart. It is estimated that Stefan's heart was arrested for more than five minutes.

"I felt myself hovering; yes, I was really hovering." Stefan wrote in his autobiography. "I was above the site of the accident and saw my badly injured lifeless body lying there... people gathered around me... it was extraordinary that I could perceive not only the words spoken aloud by the people around my body, but also their thoughts."

Stefan recalled an older man who had negative thoughts about him. "Well, he is done for," the onlooker thought, "but it was certainly his own fault. He was just the sort of person who would rush thoughtlessly through this area in a sports car."

Stefan wanted to call down to him and say "Stop talking nonsense. I was not even driving. I was only a passenger."

Then, Stefan became aware of a woman with a young daughter who was "shocked when she saw my corpse... she silently prayed, first an 'Our Father' and then a 'Holy Mary'.

"This woman's unselfish prayer made me joyous," Stefan recalled, "and I felt radiated with love." (I Was Clinically Dead: My Death was my Nicest Experience, published 1985, title translated from German)

Author Leslie Grant Scott also became conscious of what was going on in the minds of others as she lay dying in Ceylon in 1918.

In her article, 'Dying as a Liberation of Consciousness: Record of a Personal Experience' *(1931)*, she wrote that she had been able to tune into the doctor's thoughts as he prepared a hypodermic shot, and she knew he was hopeful it would work. Then she heard those thoughts turn to disappointment when the doctor realized his treatment was having no effect.

How would doctors react, I wondered, if they knew their dying patients might be monitoring their every thought!

It would seem that it is not even necessary to be in the same vicinity as the dying person to have your thoughts overheard. One account described by researcher Robert Crookall in his 1972 book, 'Casebook of Astral Projection', involved a woman who, after dying in hospital, left her body behind in the bed and ventured into the corridor.

She saw her husband waiting, then wondered where her daughter was. Instantly she found herself standing in a gift shop where her daughter was looking through 'get well' cards.

"I could hear her read the verse," this woman stated. "She decided it would be disrespectful and bought another. Then I was back in my body. When my daughter came with the card, I repeated the verse she had read."

Did this woman really 'hear' her daughter reading a verse in a card?

Was it possible Stefan von Jankovich heard negative thoughts and a silent prayer?

Could it be proven that E. L. Huffine clearly heard a conversation at a distance while out of his body?

I would question experiences like these over and again in the years ahead, but would rarely find a motive for deception.

CHAPTER 8

WHERE IS SHE?

"Mum. Mum," I whispered, gently shaking her shoulder.

She muttered something into the pillow. "Mum. The doctor's here to see you."

"Don't want any today." She mumbled.

"Mum, come on," I coaxed. "time to wake up."

"Hmmmm? Wassa matter?"

"The doctor's here. He needs to examine you. Come on, sit up."

I put my hand on her back and tried to raise her into a sitting position. She was lighter than a feather and her sharply protruding shoulder blades dug into the palm of my hand.

"Hullo Phyllis," the doctor said jovially, "having a bit of a nap, were we?"

I glared at him. Patronising doctors irritated me.

My mother was a sixty-five year old woman, not a six-year-old child, and she was a 'you', not a 'we'. Furthermore, she wasn't having "a bit of a nap". She was doing what she did all day, every day – sleeping her life away.

I rearranged the pillows behind her and tried to make her comfortable. She looked up at me questioningly, trying to focus as the doctor sat on the foot of the bed and unrolled his stethoscope.

***

I retreated to my doorstep and sat hugging my knees, rocking back and forth in anger, fear, frustration and panic. I wanted to scream obscenities at anyone and no-one, at God, the doctor, even my mother.

"Where is she where is she where is she?" I chanted, fighting back tears.

Perhaps it was true that we only occupied a body but we weren't the body. No-one, it seemed, was currently occupying my mother's body.

"Mum, come back. Please. If you can hear me, wherever you are, come back. I need you! Where are you?"

***

Most of the examples in 'Life After Life' indicated a lack of interest in the physical body once it had been vacated. One woman commented: "I knew it was my body but I had no feelings for it."

Another experiencer had chosen not to look: "Oh I knew it [the body] was there all right, and I could've seen it had I looked... but I didn't want to look because I knew I had done my best in life and I was turning my attention now to this other realm of things."

Some expressed surprise at seeing themselves. One said: "Boy, I sure didn't realize that I looked like that! You know, I'm only used to seeing myself in pictures or from the front in a mirror, and both of those look flat... it took me a few moments to recognize myself."

An accident victim told Dr. Moody: "I could see my own body all tangled up in the car. But you know, I had no feelings for it whatsoever. It was like a completely different human, or maybe even just an object... I knew it was my body but I had no feelings for it."

My pre-Moody reading confirmed Dr. Moody's research.

When Earl Stowell died of an unspecified illness in the 1800's, he found himself just below the ceiling looking down at a body stretched out on the bed. "I didn't feel as if it were my body," he later stated. "It was just a body." (Biography of William Rufus Stowell, 1893, CLDS History Library)

Some reported a brief period of confusion until they realised they had died. I could certainly understand that. If I was ill or in pain, then suddenly leapt out of bed and began dancing around the room or bouncing off the ceiling, I'd probably need some convincing that I was dead!

Burris Jenkins was certainly confused following an explosion on his cruiser in 1957. "The patient tried to identify himself as me," he recalled indignantly when he left his body and looked back at the person occupying his hospital bed. "I shuddered away from the thought and ignored it. Slowly I circled the room... I went through the fourth floor window and into the hospital courtyard above New York City and above the clouds."

Jenkins' experience again put me in mind of George Ritchie who, according to the lady I met in the park, flew through the night air and landed outside a café in Mississippi.

Surely such bodiless escapades could not be part of the dying process. I concluded that these fanciful reports had to be hallucinations.

As if to debate with me from the pages of an old book, Jenkins insisted his experience was not hallucinatory. "It had absolute reality to it," he insisted, adding that he had the presence of mind to "...make a mental note of this courtyard."

As soon as he recovered sufficiently to get out of bed, Jenkins made his way to the window to look down at the courtyard. "It was right on target," he declared. "It looked exactly the same as when I went out the window, for I had never seen it before, having been rolled into the hospital on a stretcher as an emergency patient."

Peggy Raso also had difficulty relating to the patient in her hospital bed after she developed complications following childbirth in 1960.

She looked down at the bed from her vantage point near the ceiling and saw "a girl there who looked to be in a great deal of pain. Her lips were blue, she appeared to have a blue moustache... her hair was wet looking and strung out on the pillow."

Peggy watched doctors and nurses rushing in and out of the room in a frenzy of activity. One inserted an oxygen tube into the patient's nose, another was hitting her hard on the chest. Then she heard a nurse tell a doctor: "Peggy's dead."

Peggy found this confusing. She knew *she* wasn't dead. "I tried to tell them I was not down there," she later reported. She wondered why they were all looking down at the poor woman in the bed when she was watching them from above their heads.

Then she heard her aunt say to a nurse: "She was such a good little mother!" Those words startled her. She suddenly realized that the pale woman with blue lips was actually her!

Once she understood this, Peggy's confusion vanished. "I felt my face relax into a knowing smile," she stated, adding "well, maybe more of a smirk. I realized I was privy to something they were not understanding."

Peggy moved out into the hall and watched her husband crying while her aunt tried to comfort him. "I tried so hard to tell them I wasn't there any more and I wasn't in pain," she wistfully recalled. "I wished they could all be up there with me."

Back in her room, one of the doctors leaned close to her ear and began calling her name. "I knew I was Peggy," she confessed, "but I did not want to answer. I did not want to go back down there." The doctor said "You've got to make it," and she wondered why. "All of these people wanted me to come back and leave this wonderful place that I thought I alone had found."

Peggy looked at her husband again and thought "I must go back to tell them all about this. I could hardly wait to tell them... I gave a wistful look at the beauty of this other existence and started down. I hovered over the body for a moment and thought 'I will go back up there at another time.' I went back to the body and immediately felt all the pain."

Did Peggy "tell them all about this"? Apparently so, for she later confessed: "Little did I know how this news would be received in 1960."

As she provides no further details, we can only imagine how her husband, aunt and others reacted, even though it was difficult to dismiss the fact that she accurately described activities and conversations going on while she was 'out'. (Journal of Scientific Exploration, Vol.12, No.3.)

Mr. Bertrand's account was also hard to dismiss. The elderly teacher had accompanied a group of his students on a climb in the Swiss Alps in the late 1800's, but he grew tired and decided to stay behind as the guide led his group further up the mountain.

While he sat and waited alone, Mr. Bertrand suffered a stroke and left his body.

"Well," he thought, "at last I am what they call a dead man... how strange! I see better than ever, and I am dead, only a small space in the space without a body!"

Mr. Bertand was then "... astounded to recognize my own envelope." He found this intriguing. "There is the corpse in which I lived and which I called me as if the coat were the body, as if the body were the soul," he mused. "What a horrid thing is that body, deadly pale, with a yellowing-blue colour."

When his companions returned, the guide "administered to my body the well known remedy." He doesn't state what this was, but if I knew,

I'd buy a very large bottle of it because it was obviously successful.

Mr. Bertrand reluctantly returned to life and immediately admonished the guide for leading the students up the right hand path of Titlis Mountain when earlier he had insisted they go by the left. The guide asked how he could have known this when it was impossible to see the track from his vantage point... not to mention the fact that Bertrand had been dead.

"Dead! I was less dead than you are now," he remarked, and explained how he had left his body and watched them on their journey. (Journal of Scientific Exploration, Vol.12 No.3)

Mr. Bertrand's account interested me, because like Peggy Raso, he had been able to prove his experience through his knowledge of their actions while he was dead.

British army officer, Surgeon to the King in Scotland and Emeritus Professor of Surgery at the University of Aberdeen, Sir Alexander Ogston was also able to verify his experience.

In his 1919 memoirs, 'Reminiscences of Three Campaigns', he wrote: "I was conscious of the body as an inert tumbled mass near a door. It belonged to me but it was not I."

Ogston had fallen victim to typhoid fever during the Boer War (1889-1902), but while his feverish body was confined to a hospital bed "near a door" he spent very little time occupying it.

He later recalled: "Mind and body seemed to be dual, and to some extent separate... my mental self used regularly to leave the body... until something produced a consciousness that the chilly mass, which I then recalled was my body, was being stirred as it lay by the door. I was then drawn back to it, joined it with disgust, and it became I, and I was fed, spoken to, and cared for. When it was again left I seemed to wander off as before..."

I found this account particularly intriguing because Ogston was never declared dead. No-one had to resuscitate him each time they fed him or spoke to him, so who or what was the 'I' that returned each time it needed to occupy the body?

I had to assume it was merely his mind wandering as a result of fever, but an experience he had during this time made me second guess that assumption.

"I could see through the walls of the building," he wrote, "though I was aware that they were there, and that everything was transparent to my senses."

As a result, Ogston was able to watch an army surgeon, a man he had never met and who was in a different part of the hospital, grow ill and die.

"I saw them cover his corpse and carry him softly out on shoeless feet, quietly and surreptitiously, lest we should know that he had died."

When Ogston recovered, he told the nurses what he had witnessed. They confirmed it had occurred precisely as he described.

I wondered if this ability to leave the body at will also applied to those trapped in comas. As families gathered around beds, heads bowed in sadness, perhaps their loved ones were calling from above: "hey, that's not me, I'm up here! Why are you all looking at that thing in the bed?"

It certainly seemed that having left their bodies, people lost all interest in the shell (or 'envelope' as Mr. Bertrand called it) they left behind. "What a horrid thing is that body," he had remarked.

"It belonged to me but it was not I," Sir Alexander Ogston had declared of his "inert tumbled mass".

"I watched with indifference," E.L. Huffine had stated when his wife dragged his lifeless body away from his crashed aeroplane.

These were all fascinating observations, but none could beat the charming 'old-world' statement by Dr. Wiltse in 1889: "The body and I no longer had any interests in common."

CHAPTER 9

NO INTERESTS IN COMMON

The author of 'Human Personality and Its Survival of Bodily Death', (1904) which contained Dr. Wiltse's account was Frederic W. H. Myers.

Myers had been a Professor of Classics at Cambridge University in the late nineteenth century. In 1881, he joined with some of his Cambridge colleagues to set up the Society for Psychical Research in order to scientifically investigate and validate or disprove paranormal claims.

The first president of the SPR (as it came to be known) was Henry Sidgwick, Professor of Moral Philosophy at Cambridge. Other founding members included experimental physicist Lord Rayleigh, mathematician and principal of Newnham College Eleanor Sidgwick, physicist Sir William Barrett, and philosopher Gerald Balfour, who would later become prime minister of England.

These were hardly people whose opinions could be dismissed lightly!

The SPR collected and carefully analysed over seven hundred cases of survival and post-mortem communications. Among them was the account by Dr. Wiltse, who died of typhoid fever in 1889.

Dr. S. H. Raynes, the physician attending Wiltse, reported that while his patient had occasional small gasps of air, he was without pulse or perceptible heartbeat for about four hours, was clinically dead for half an hour and was "as fully as I ever supposed anyone to be dead."

Wiltse later stated that he briefly lost consciousness as he died, then returned after what may have been "a minute or a thousand years" to find he was still in his body, but that "the body and I no longer had any interests in common".

He observed that his living soul was intimately interwoven within his bodily anatomy and reasoned that "I have died, as men term death, and yet I am as much a man as ever. I am about to get out of the body."

A medical doctor himself, Wiltse paid careful attention to this process.

He watched the separation of the soul from the body with awe and wonder. He saw what he termed 'the Ego' slowly break away from the tissues of the body and heard the snapping of small cords, beginning at the feet, at which point he began to retreat from the feet to the head "as a rubber cord shortens".

As he reached the hips, he declared to himself: "Now, there is no life below the hips."

Dr. Wiltse later explained that his "whole self was collected into the head." He then emerged and experienced "floating up and down and laterally like a soap-bubble attached to the bowl of a pipe until I at last broke loose from the body and fell lightly to the floor, where I slowly rose and expanded into the full stature of a man."

A feather, a handkerchief, a piece of paper ... and now a soap-bubble!

Another who described the process of leaving the body was Arthur E. Yensen, a down-to-earth mine geologist with a strong scientific bent who wasted no time pondering the existence of souls or the possibility of an afterlife. Yensen knew, without doubt, that such beliefs were nothing more than fanciful imaginings.

In 1932, Yensen was a passenger in a car that crashed and rolled. He was thrown 60 feet (18 metres) through the air and deposited unceremoniously into a ditch by the roadside. He staggered into an upright position, but as he did, he felt "as if I was coming loose from my body."

He later wrote: "While I believed my body was me, I knew instinctively that if I separated from it I'd be dead. While the thought of dying didn't bother me at all, I tried to hold my body and soul together with sheer willpower... but the effort was too much, my soul and body started separating again and continued to separate until I felt a short sharp pain in my heart which felt as if something had been torn loose, then slowly and softly I rose out through the top of my head."

What happened next changed Yensen's entire outlook on life. I have included more about both his and Dr. Wiltse's fascinating experiences later in this book.

***

The last time I sat on the doorstep, I had demanded of the universe that it "show me the evidence."

Could I deny that it was doing as I asked?

How could these people all be saying basically the same things so long before Dr. Moody penned his ground-breaking book?

These were not people who nurtured aspirations to become rich and famous authors of sensational books.

Besides, I reminded myself, no-one became rich and famous in 1889 or 1932 by writing books about such strange experiences! Most of them didn't even talk about it.

The influence of religion had been considerably stronger in those days, yet none of these accounts contained religious overtones so they were not simply recycling church teachings.

Yensen had been a sceptical mine geologist with no interest or belief in the existence of an afterlife, yet even as he accepted there was no such thing as a soul, he knew that if 'he' separated from his body, he would be dead.

How?

All the same, I needed to keep my enthusiasm in check.

Accepting that we survive death on the strength of a few first hand accounts in some musty old books only made me gullible, and gullibility could very well lead me along a road to nowhere.

It was on such a road that dangers lurked.

If I accepted we survived death, would I have to accept reincarnation as a consequence of that belief?

Perhaps I would also start believing in ghosts. Then I might join up with those strange people who sneaked around so-called haunted house saying things like "is anyone here? Rap once for yes and twice for no."

What does one do when a ghost raps twice for no, anyway?

From there I might graduate to searching for fairies in my garden!

Even worse – I might find them!

I suddenly saw myself as one of those funny old ladies who owned a black cat, consulted her crystal ball, talked to invisible people and frightened little children who nervously passed by her front gate!

I longed to believe, but I knew I had to steadfastly refuse to indulge that longing.

I would continue to search for answers, but I was determined to remain rational.

I would question everything. I would accept nothing on face value.

***

In 'Stranger Than Life' (1955), author DeWitt Miller included a report by nurse Virginia Randall, who was tending Dorothy, a young polio victim confined to an iron lung.

Dorothy had slipped away but was quickly revived. She later confided to nurse Virginia that while unconscious, she had been delighted to find that she could walk again.

"My muscles could do what I wanted them to do," she rejoiced, "and I felt completely happy, no pain, no restrictions, all light and gay. I was so pleased to leave my worn-out shell behind me and be free."

These reports — if true — provided me with some comfort. Not long before her current illness, Mum had graduated from the walking stick she had used for over a decade to a wheeled walking frame. Even that became difficult for her to manage, as her arms were becoming almost as weak as her legs. She persisted bravely, unwilling to surrender to a wheelchair.

Now, she had been confined to bed for months and I doubted that even if she recovered from this mysterious malady, she would have enough strength to use the frame.

When I read about Dorothy's delight that in death her muscles became responsive, I considered that perhaps I was being selfish by constantly willing my mother to live.

Would dying mean she would be able to run and dance again? How I longed for it to be true!

Wait! How ridiculous was that? How could Dorothy have muscles if her body was dead? I tossed the book aside. Why was I reading this nonsense? My mother needed my help, not my death wish!

***

"She says she feels like she's being slowly poisoned." Dr. Simmons said quietly.

A 'traditional' doctor, David (as he insisted we call him) was the least intrusive of those who had visited my mother in the past few years, and one of the few still willing to make house calls. He was also friendly and approachable, and often extended his visits with coffee and a chat about Mum's health problems.

"I know," I nodded over the rim of my coffee cup. "she's said the same thing to me."

We sat in silence for a moment, then it suddenly occurred to me that David might be nurturing evil thoughts.

"Well, don't look at me!" I blurted out. "*I'm* not trying to poison her! But I know what she means, it's like she's allergic to everything. There has to be a reason. She's always worse on smog alert days, and she gets really dizzy if she talks on the phone and also after she tries to eat, especially if it's food from a tin can, like baked beans or canned soup, and..."

David sighed and stared into his coffee cup. "Frankly, I think she's just given up on life," he murmured.

"Well, I'm not about to let that happen, so what can we do?"

He shrugged. "I think... you need to come to terms with the possibility that her time..."

"No! There's got to be something we can do!"

"Sandy, your Mum's very weak. She's skin and bone and she's not eating enough to keep a bird alive. And she's not moving around. She's been laying there in her bed for months and she's never going to get better like this."

"So what do you suggest? That I make her get out of bed and run a marathon every day?" I asked sarcastically, wondering why I was directing my anger at David when he was only trying to help.

"She can barely stand, David." I said in a gentler tone. "I almost have to carry her to the bathroom."

"I know. I know. That's what I mean. I think it's time we considered admitting her to hospital."

"Hospital? Why?"

"Well for starters they can do tests we can't do here. And they can feed her through a tube so she doesn't get any weaker, and give her physio."

I shuddered at the thought of my mother being fed through tubes. It pained me to think of her being kept alive against her will, surrounded by strangers, dying alone. We'd always been there for each other. I needed to see this through, be there at the end to hold her hand and comfort her.

"David, if Mum's really dying then I'd rather she do it here in peace and comfort, and with some dignity."

"Well, as a friend, I say that's your choice." David shrugged. "But as her doctor, I'm not sure I can turn a blind eye and just ignore the fact that your mother needs to be in a place where she can be..."

He drifted off.

"Where she can be? What?"

He looked directly at me. "Properly looked after!"

His eyes showed a touch of defiance as they locked onto mine. He obviously expected a response, and he got one.

"Properly looked after?" I barked. "I have properly, as you so diplomatically put it, looked after Mum for most of my life. I know what she needs and wants far more than some giggling nurse or arrogant doctor in some hospital, I..."

"Hey, no need for all that." He held up one hand as though he thought I was going to slap him. "Look, you need a break too. And you need to know it may not be pleasant when, IF, the time comes. I'll arrange for nurses to call in regularly, but," he stood and reached for his case, then turned to look at me, "just think about it, OK?"

***

I thought about it.

I spent hours sitting on the doorstep, thinking about it.

I cried, berated God, cursed David and most of all, got angry with Mum.

Why did she want to die? Had life and her disability become too much for her to endure?

As long as she was home and I was close, there was still hope. In hospital, surrounded by strangers and feeling abandoned, she'd be far more likely to give up.

But... could I do it?

Could I take the chance she might die because I was too proud to admit defeat and allow her to go to hospital? Would my decisions and actions today lead to guilt and regret for the rest of my life?

At sixty-five years of age, my mother's body was no longer her friend. It had not been her friend for more than twenty years. Was it time for her to discard it?

Could I sit beside her when the time came and assure her she was going to a better place? Could I sound convincing, even if I didn't totally believe it myself?

Could I face the rest of my life alone, waiting for my own turn?

If anyone's up there, I need help. Please! I want to do the right thing but I don't know what the right thing is any more.

Someone, anyone, please, tell me what to do. Show me the way.

***

'Allergy Overload' had been an afterthought during my shopping spree at the TS Bookshop.

This book had nothing whatsoever to do with my search for answers about the afterlife. It 'just happened' to be sitting on the counter near where I stood as I waited to be served.

I had scanned the back cover merely to pass the time, then began reading the first page. What I read gave me hope that it might contain answers to other, more important questions.

I was right. This book that would change my life in more ways than I could imagine.

CHAPTER 10

WHAT THE HECK IS A VEGA MACHINE?

The author of 'Allergy Overload', Stephen Griffiths, was a middle-aged Australian man who had been so ill that he was convinced he was dying. His symptoms closely matched those my mother had been experiencing for over a year. The opening lines of this book were:

"Two years ago I became very ill... barely able to move around or think clearly... I ached and sweated continuously... my vision was often blurred... I suffered from continual bowel and bladder problems... I was constantly tired... exertion resulted in giddiness and exhaustion. My heart pounded and regularly missed a beat. I felt I was beginning to confront my own demise." (Allergy Overload, Fontana Books, 1987)

Griffiths' health had continued to deteriorate until he could barely walk from his office to his car. He even stated that he felt like he was being slowly poisoned!

Then he heard about a doctor in England who had invented a vega machine.

I turned the pages with growing anticipation. Was this, whatever this thing was, the answer we were looking for? Could I order one and have it posted, or would I need to get my mother on a jumbo jet and fly her to England? What a thought, when I had difficulty getting her to the bathroom!

Mr. Griffiths went on to explain that he had phoned the clinic in England and had been assured his symptoms were all due to multiple food and chemical intolerances and allergies, and that the vega machine could determine precisely what these were so he could avoid them or be treated for them.

This sounded feasible.

58

"Do you know anything about vega machines?" I asked Dr. David during his next visit.

"No. What are they?" he muttered as he scribbled in his notepad. I doubted he was writing "vega machine". David rarely took much notice of anything I suggested.

"It tests for allergies and intolerances. I was just reading this book about a man who had all the same symptoms and this vega machine revealed all the things he had to avoid. He's much better now."

David glanced up from his notepad and honoured me with a condescending smile.

"I'll put her on Stemetil, that should help with the dizziness." He returned to his notepad scribbling. "If it doesn't, at least it should stop the nausea," he muttered distractedly. "Oh and by the way, I have some sample pills in my case, they're supposed to increase appetite. Want to give them a try?"

"No thanks!" I snapped, taking the prescription from him. "But don't you think..."

"I'll call in and see her again in a few weeks and we'll see how she's coming along."

That evening I penned a plea for help to the book's author. His six page handwritten reply arrived a few weeks later.

He wrote that the vega machine had proved so successful, not only for him but for hundreds of others, that it was now being used around the world. He added that he was now his "old self" again and was sure my mother would soon be back on her feet.

When I phoned the Allergy Association, they confirmed that vega machines were now in use across Australia and provided details of trained practitioners.

One of these was a doctor at a medical clinic only a few miles from home.

The interesting part would be getting her there!

***

"I'm going to fall off." Mum cried out, bracing herself with her hands. "The bed's tipping."

"You're not going to fall. Trust me." I begged. "Just sit still while I get you dressed."

She sighed, and her voice caught in her throat. "Do we really have to go? He's just another doctor. I've seen so many."

59

I knew she was close to tears and I felt like a bully, but I was determined to at least give this vega machine a try.

I held her tightly as we slowly made our way through the house and out to the car, and her frail frame almost slid through my arms a few times.

It was a hot summer's day and smog hung in the air like a dirty fog as we drove through the busy suburban streets. I could almost cut the diesel and petrol fumes with a knife.

By the time I pulled into the clinic's car park, Mum was dry retching. I borrowed a wheelchair from the front desk and she slumped into it, then I wheeled her into the coolness of the waiting room. Her eyes glazed over and she came close to losing consciousness a few times. It was the most activity she had experienced for a year.

"Oh Mr. Stephen bloody Griffiths," I cursed the author silently as we waited to be called, "you'd better know what you're talking about!"

"Hullo!" A wide toothy grin greeted us in the waiting room. "I am Docker Wong. Welcome. Come, come!"

Dr. Wong was an energetic, small-framed oriental doctor with a smile that seemed bigger than his face.

I wheeled Mum into the room he indicated and took a seat. After discussing her symptoms and taking copious notes, he led us into another office where she was hooked up to a small machine.

An hour later, we emerged with a 3-page list. Mum's face was deathly pale. Almost every food had been ticked. Ticks were not rewards, they indicated an allergy or intolerance.

Her chemical intolerances included petrol, diesel, and phenol. Among other applications, phenol was used to line tin cans and coat telephones. Now the logic behind her dizzy spells after eating tinned soup or talking on the phone began to make sense.

We returned to Dr. Wong's office and he examined the list.

"Is this possible?" I asked him. "Can someone really be allergic to all these foods?"

"Yes, yes, yes." He smiled and nodded vigorously. "Many foods, very very common."

"But Doctor, there's nothing left for her to eat!" I pointed out in frustration as I glanced once more over the list. A few vegetables and some obscure grains remained unticked. She could hardly live on such a grossly restrictive diet.

Then I remembered that she'd already lived for a year on a restricted diet! Half a sandwich for lunch and a few mouthfuls of vegetables washed down with sips of tea in the evening had been her usual daily intake.

On the occasional good days, she sometimes managed to nibble on a small banana!

"No problem, we fix. Ok? We fix!" He smiled at me as he continued to scribble notes and nod vigorously. "Foods become problem because of chemical allergy, but we fix chemical, then foods OK. Soon she can eat all foods, but first we fix chemicals. No problem! I make homeopathic drops for chemicals, and also we do intravenous vitamin c, I think. That help!"

"Intravenous vitamin C? Does she need to go to hospital for that?"

"No no, we can do here." He shrugged. "No problem."

No problem? Was that all he could say? I fought the urge to scream at him that the problem was NOT "no problem". The problem was a BIG problem!

For over a year my mother had been slowly wasting away. Instead of allowing her to die with dignity, I had dragged her out of bed, poured her into a car, driven her through smog and smelly fumes to get her here, and for what? For an irritating, ever smiling, overly enthusiastic doctor to announce that she was basically allergic to all food, but that it was "no problem, no problem"!

What she needed was more food and better nutrition, not a mile-long list of foods to avoid.

This Docka Wong, as he referred to himself, was proving to be like all the doctors who had condescended to do house calls during the past twelve months, offered a dizzying array of prescriptions and sample pills and arbitrarily dismissed anything I said as inconsequential nonsense.

***

Amazingly, Mum began to feel a little better during the two weeks between each appointment. The nausea and vertigo eased and she began to spend a little time sitting up each day.

"As you can see," I explained to Doc David as I saw him to the door after his next visit, "she's making wonderful progress!"

"Hmmmm" was his unenthusiastic response. "She's not out of the woods yet. She still looks very frail."

"But she's up!" I announced. "She hasn't been out of bed for more than ten minutes at a time for a whole year and now she's sitting up for at least an hour every day. She's even eating, a little! You don't think that's progress?"

"I guess," he shrugged. "What can I say? These things happen sometimes, spontaneous recoveries. The body's an amazing thing."

"Spontaneous recovery after a year on the edge of death?" I laughed. It wasn't a friendly laugh, because I was using it as a means of swallowing my anger.

"Apparently you have all the answers," he smirked, "so tell me, to what do you attribute her recovery?"

I really wanted to push him out the door and slam it in his face. Instead, I sighed a long-suffering, trying-so-hard-to-be-tolerant sigh and said calmly: "Remember I asked you about a vega machine?"

"Ah, yes," he said with a dramatic flourish, "the miraculous vega machine! So, you plugged her into one and she got better?"

I took another deep breath and wondered if the time had come to say a final goodbye to Dr. David. Perhaps not. Who knew when we might need him again.

"No," I said quietly. "I didn't plug her in to anything, I took her to a doctor, yes, a real doctor, who uses one, and it showed up all the things she needed to avoid. He also made up homeopathic pills and gave her vitamin c intravenously."

David rolled his eyes. "There's no scientific evidence for homeopathy!" he stated emphatically. "It's just water. A placebo. And as for vitamin C, the body can only use what it needs. Introducing it into the body intravenously is useless."

"Tell that to Norman Cousins!" I snapped. If this conversation continued much longer, I'd soon lose the battle to control my temper.

He looked at me questioningly. He obviously didn't know who Norman Cousins was, and I doubted he even wanted to know.

Had he asked, I'd have told him that Cousins, a political journalist in the US, had been admitted to hospital in 1964 with a heart condition and Ankylosing Spondylitis, a rare disease of the connective tissues.

His doctor had given him a one in five hundred chance of survival and advised him that his joints would soon seize up. Cousins was advised that he would soon need to make a choice: did he want to spend his final days lying down, or sitting up?

What a choice!

Cousins, however, decided on a different route. He fired his doctor and booked himself into a hotel, insisting hospitals were not good for one's health. He rented a movie projector and a stack of funny movies and laughed every day until his stomach hurt. He also arranged to have regular injections of massive doses of vitamin c, even though doctors pointed out that this had never been tried and might kill him!

Cousins did die, but not until he spent a further twenty-six years living a very active and rewarding life. His book, Anatomy of an Illness, was later made into a movie, with Ed Asner playing Cousins.

I continued to smile sweetly as I closed the door gently behind Dr. Simmons, then I bit my fist to stifle a scream of frustration.

***

I sat in the waiting room during our fourth visit to the clinic.

With the help of a wheeled frame, Mum had walked to the car, and from the car to the waiting room. That was amazing progress. I still needed to support her. Muscular weakness combined with her anorexic frame meant she could fall over her own shadow!

Her growing alertness had freed me to enrol in a variety of courses including massage, kinesiology, polarity therapy, reiki and reflexology. Inspired by Dr. Wong's focus on alternative medicines, I also devoured books on homeopathy, flower essence therapy and colour healing.

Thoughts of the afterlife were relegated to the "too-hard basket" as I rejoiced in having my mother back. I packed my tower of books away in a cupboard. I didn't want her to know what had been occupying my mind and my time while she had been semi-comatose for a year.

During our initial visit, Dr. Wong had warned me privately that the new bottle of strengthened homeopathic drops he intended to make up every two weeks would probably exacerbate my mother's symptoms for a few days, adding that this was a good sign. It indicated the drops were working.

Mum had not been present during this warning, and I did not repeat it to her. She felt bad enough without being told she might soon feel even worse! Yet within hours of taking the strengthened drops each fortnight, she would be back in bed with vertigo, palpitations and nausea, and remain there for a few days.

For the rest of those two weeks, however, she made progress!

So much for homeopathy being a placebo, I silently told Dr. Simmons as I sat in Dr.Wong's waiting room. I was no longer concerned that I regularly had conversations with people who were not in the immediate vicinity.

In retrospect, I realize it was my way of struggling to come to terms with new ideas, and having one-sided conversations in my head was an essential part of the process. At the time, I simply accepted that I was losing my mind and was not entirely sure that I cared.

Half an hour later, the door opened and my mother appeared with the doctor by her side.

"She better, yes? Dr. Wong smiled broadly at me. "Going good, eh? No problems, no problems."

I smiled and agreed. While there were still "problems", I could not deny that my mother had made more progress in the past 3 months than I had even dared to hope. I was so relieved I could have hugged 'Docka Wong' right there in the waiting room.

As we drove home, those words came back to haunt me. "And so it begins."

***

Ah yes, I realized after Mum — exhausted after her outing — had an early night and I took up my usual position on my doorstep. Maybe it wasn't about Mum's health. Maybe it was about my delayed career.

Rhonda and Bill (or was it my flying matron?) had told me I would begin to realize the potential I had to give other people the help and remedies they needed. The voice was really saying: "and so [your career in alternative medicine] begins".

Yes, of course! It had been preparing me for that!

But wait! Who or what was 'IT?'

'IT' had been a voice in my head that knew something I didn't know. How was that possible?

People who heard voices were mentally ill, weren't they? Therefore 'the voice' had to be my imagination. Didn't it?

How could I justify what 'IT' said, while also dismissing 'IT' as imagination?

I was back where I started. Either a mysterious cosmic message had been sent to prepare me for my glorious mission. Or I was mentally ill.

I spent the rest of the evening staring into space and asking the universe important questions:

Did the voice really exist?

If it existed, who or what was it?

Was there more to life than simply being born and dying?

Could dead people really fly through space to distant planets, or even out-of-town cafes?

Did I have a dead nurse watching over me?

Was I destined to spend the rest of my life sitting on this doorstep, talking to myself?

Too many questions. No answers.

Then, something happened that would turn my world inside out and upside down.

CHAPTER 11

WE MEET AT LAST

"How old is she?" the vet asked as he examined Muffin.

"Almost fourteen." I replied through my tears.

She had been panting for most of the day, and I knew she was in pain. "Just a tummy bug" I told us both. "You'll be fine, we'll get you fixed up soon."

By the time we arrived for our vet's appointment, she could no longer stand. I requested a stretcher and the receptionist helped me carry her into the surgery. With great difficulty, Muffin swung her head around to ensure I was still with her.

"I'm sorry," the vet said gently, "but there's really nothing we can do at that age. She's old and she's obviously in great pain. The kindest thing would be to put her out of her misery."

My tears turned to audible sobs. "But it might just be something she ate." I pleaded. "How can you be sure…"

He gently placed his hand on my shoulder. "We'd need to do tests, keep her here for days," he said softly. "Do you really think she would want that? Would *you* want that?"

"No." I whispered, stroking her head. Apart from a few weeks with a surrogate mother, Muffin had been with me since I rescued her and her 3 siblings from the gutter that rainy night nearly fourteen years earlier. She had been my constant companion, my confidante, and the most intuitive animal I had ever known.

We'd played together with her precious red ball during those fourteen years because it was her ball and she'd have no other, even when it had lost its bounce and was covered with dry slobber.

66

She had protected me with her ferocious snarl when anyone she didn't know came to the door. Little did they know that this huge, snarling monster was a gentle giant.

She sat beside me during those endless, worrying nights on the back doorstep, leaning up against me as if to give comfort.

During those long, lonely nights, I occasionally noticed her wink at me.

At first, I thought I was imagining it, but it happened time and again. I began to wink back. When I did, she would immediately drop down beside me, slip one giant paw over my thigh, let out a long sigh of contentment and close her eyes. It was as if we shared a very special secret.

Now I was being asked to kill her.

My sobs became uncontrollable, and I looked down at her beautiful face. As I did, she winked at me one last time. It was all I needed to know.

"Go ahead." I said quietly.

"You will never be replaced, my darling." I whispered in her ear as the vet prepared the injection. I stayed with her, stroking her gently until she took her last breath. She was no longer in pain. I kissed her gently on the nose and drove home with tears streaming down my cheeks.

Once home, I gathered up her lead, her sheepskin rug and her beloved red ball. I didn't want to see them again but I couldn't bring myself to throw them out yet, so I put them in a plastic bag and secreted them in the back of a drawer in the garage.

Mum was asleep, and Muffin was gone. I wondered how much lonelier life could become.

***

"So, death, we meet at last." I growled at the universe from my think-step that evening. I buried my head in my knees, not sure if I wanted to scream abuse at the top of my voice or curl up in a little ball and make the world go away.

I had begun my search for evidence of an afterlife because my mother was dying. But as she slowly recovered and my world began to look a little brighter, my beloved dog had been snatched from me. Now I really knew the agony of losing a loved one.

Grief, I discovered, was an aching, gaping, nagging, unfillable void, somewhere or everywhere inside. It was a cavernous emptiness, raw and untouchable. My love for her stuck in my throat and welled up behind my eyes because it had nowhere else to go.

Countless dogs and cats had shared my life throughout the years. All of them had been special, but none quite like Muffin. We had communicated on some non-verbal level. I didn't kid myself into believing I was psychic and had tuned into her canine conversations, but over the years I had begun to suspect the reverse was taking place.

Muffin always seemed to know what I was thinking or how I was feeling. I had only to consider taking her for a walk and she would excitedly run to where her lead was kept.

If it occurred to me to give her a bath, she would hide under the table. When I was feeling down, she would adopt a sad expression, sit beside me and lean her huge weight against my side as if to provide comfort.

We had always pondered the big questions together on the think-step, Muffin and I. Now, I sat there alone and cried.

The pain of my guilt magnified the overwhelming emptiness of my grief. I hadn't personally administered the lethal injection, but I had given the nod for it to be done.

I had killed her, and I would to live with that forever.

I spent most of the following week slumped in a chair during daylight hours and staring into the vast emptiness of space from my doorstep when light faded to darkness.

Had she known what was happening as the vet prepared the lethal injection and I stroked her head, assuring her that everything would be ok? Had she understood my agony?

Did dogs survive death? If so, had she forgiven me? Could I forgive myself?

Where is she?" I begged the universe. "I need to know."

There would be no sympathy from the universe.

At least, so it seemed at the time.

***

Three weeks after Muffin's death, the colour slowly began returning to my bleak, grey world. I still missed her, but the pain was easing.

One night, I finished reading, turned the bedside light out and snuggled down to sleep.

Suddenly, I felt my bed move the way it always had when Muffin jumped on it.

My bed was antique and unusually high, and Muffin hadn't been able to lift her large aging frame up to it in her declining years. But I distinctly felt the shudder.

I raised my head and looked down the length of the bed, and there she was, illuminated by the moonlight streaming through the window. My beloved old dog stood proudly at the end of my bed with her tail raised and her eyes sparkling mischievously.

But she wasn't old! She was slimmer, about the size she'd been at her peak. She had that "hey, let's play ball, huh, huh?" look about her, as though she was ready to leap off the bed and chase her slobbery old deflated ball as far as I could throw it.

"Oh Muffin," I said out loud, somehow forgetting I'd left her old body at the vet's clinic three weeks earlier. How could I have forgotten? "Lay down!" I commanded.

The bed shuddered even more violently, just as it had when I'd said those words to her in the past. Ever anxious to please, she had always responded to "lay down" by dropping like a ton of bricks. And indeed, she had weighed close to that!

I lowered my head onto the pillow and closed my eyes, then the realisation of what had just happened hit me like the ton of bricks I had just felt. I sat bolt upright and peeked over the bedcovers.

There was no Muffin stretched across the bed, waiting for my next instruction or the toss of her ball.

I spent most of that night wide awake, trying to decide if I had actually seen her or had merely been dreaming. But I knew, without doubt, that I'd been awake. I was never one to drop off to sleep quickly. And unlike a dream, I had seen her clearly.

Eventually, I chose to dismiss it as grief-stricken imagination, but the following morning I second-guessed my verdict.

Why hadn't I seen her as fatter and older, when that was how she'd been in recent years?

Over the next few weeks the image faded, and again I began to doubt it had even occurred.

Months later, while flicking through a magazine, I came across the following item:

PEDIGREED BURMESE CAT ASTOUNDS ITS OWNERS BY LEAPING ON TO THEIR BED AND PURRING THREE WEEKS AFTER IT HAD DIED.

> "Our beloved Burmese, Mitzi, passed away of extreme old age in 1982," recalls Post reader (name provided). As she grew older, Mitzi had fallen into the habit of sleeping on our double bed. One night, about three weeks after we lost her, I got a real shock. I was lying wide-awake when I felt something very familiar– a cat leaping up and nestling at my feet. I immediately assumed a neighbour's cat had entered through our window, but when I looked, both the window and bedroom door were closed. And although I could feel the weight quite unmistakeably, no cat was visible. It was then, feeling rather silly, that I whispered "Mitzi?" and was answered by a familiar purring. My husband was asleep during the first visit and simply laughed when I told him next morning. But on the next two occasions he was awake, too. We're now both convinced that *our cat came back from the dead.*"

Three weeks later! Was this a coincidence? Perhaps. But I was beginning to recognise a pattern in these coincidences.

The lady in the park and Dr. Wong had both entered my life when I needed them.

Books I hadn't known existed found their way to my bookshelf, even if my credit card often had to assist them on their journey

Had Muffin visited me that night in my bedroom, or had my grief merely provided a comforting hallucination?

More questions. There were always more questions.

It was time to revisit Dr. Moody and his predecessors. I retrieved my books.

CHAPTER 12

OTHERS

Many experiencers in Dr. Moody's book became aware of the presence of others hovering nearby or standing beside them as they died.

Some recognised these as friends or relatives who had died in the past, while others had no idea who they were but felt they were guides helping them make the transition or preparing them for their return to life.

One woman died giving birth and noticed many people hovering around the ceiling of the room.

She later stated: "They were people I had known in my life, but who had passed on before. I recognized my grandmother and a girl I had known when I was in school, and many other relatives and friends. It seems that I mainly saw their faces and felt their presence. They all seemed pleased. It was a very happy occasion, and I felt that they had come to protect or to guide me. It was almost as if I were coming home, and they were there to greet or welcome me."

As one woman left her body, two beings identified themselves as "spiritual helpers."

Another detected the presence of beings all around her, and when she wondered what was going on she received the reply, in thought form, that she was dying but would be fine, and felt comforted by this.

Then I came to an account in 'Life After Life' that totally confused me.

A man described 'feeling' that as he left his body, his recently deceased friend, Bob, was standing right next to him.

"I could see him in my mind and felt like he was there," he explained, "but it was strange. I didn't see him as his physical body. I could see things, but not in the physical form, yet just as clearly, his looks, everything."

"Does that make sense?" this man on the page asked. I responded with a firm "No!" I continued reading.

"He was there but he didn't have a physical body," he explained, as though trying to help me understand. "And I could sense every part of it, arms, legs, and so on, but I wasn't seeing it physically."

But how? I asked the book, aware but unconcerned that I was now also conversing with inanimate objects.

The book replied. "I didn't think about it being odd at the time, because I didn't really need to see him with my eyes. I didn't have eyes anyway."

Oh dear! Would I, could I, ever understand this?

It didn't get any easier when I returned to my pre-1975 books.

In 'The Waiting World', author Archie Matson gave an account of Gene Albright, who described leaving his body when he died in 1960. He heard his wife praying, but when he looked closer, he realised something very startling. He later said: "I was hearing the words of her silent prayer."

Albright then noticed there were dozens of beautiful, radiant people in the room with him. He tried to alert his wife to this, but she was unable to hear him, so he asked the closest spirit person to explain what happened and where these people came from.

"It isn't possible to put into words," Albright explained, "the pure love and oneness I experienced as I turned my attention to this person. He spoke no words to me. I just knew, directly and exactly, the answers to my questions. I knew I was dead... time had ceased to be important. I could 'see' in either direction with ease. Yesterday and tomorrow were two parts of the same time. I could see energies, forms, and interlocking fields of the most beautiful colours and sounds greater than the finest music ever played by masters."

While out of his body, Albright also came to understand that energy is love, and he focused on the love of his wife. "As I did," he recalled, "everything else faded away. The pain returned and the long battle began again. I opened my eyes... I had lost something, something I had lived with most of my life: fear."

A prominent Virginian banker, Aubrey Eggleston, died of a heart attack in the early 1930's. His wife related that when he returned, he insisted that he had "gone into the next life where he was met by many of his loved ones who had passed over before him." (Voices From the Edge of Eternity, 1968)

Episcopal clergyman, Louis Tucker was thirty-six when he died of ptomaine poisoning in 1909. Thirty-four years later, in his book 'Clerical Errors' (1943) he described emerging into "a place where many people were being met by friends."

"It was quiet and full of light," Tucker stated, "and father was waiting for me. He looked exactly as he had in the last years of his life and wore the last suit of clothes he had owned."

Charles John Lambert was greeted by those he termed "spiritual persons" after being trapped under a log in a river in the nineteenth century.

"I seemed to be on the most familiar terms with them," Lambert recalled, adding: "My spirit friends took me away from the scene of the incident." (A Curious Experience in Drowning, Juvenile Instructor, 1886)

Was this the origin of the expression 'being spirited away'.

Polio victim Dorothy met her deceased grandmother, her aunts, and even her dog (which gave me much comfort), and was surprised to learn they had expected her, adding that her arrival seemed part of a plan. (Stranger Than Life, 1955)

When Lorenzo Dow Young left his body, a "heavenly messenger or guide" was by his side immediately. Young observed his sister and wife weeping bitterly over his death, and he tried to comfort them.

"I begged of [the guide] the privilege of speaking to them," he wrote in 'Fragments of Experience' (1882) "but he said he could not grant it."

I'm not surprised! I sincerely doubt that a tap on the shoulder or a disembodied voice would have done much to comfort the weeping women!

Percy Cole also wrote about meeting his guide and becoming aware of deceased loved ones in a book with the dubious title, 'Psychic Odyssey'. But in this case, Cole actually received proof!

A friend had given this book to me, insisting I'd enjoy it, and once again I had taken it to be polite. My recent interest in near-death experiences made me sufficiently weird to most people and ensured my social isolation if I dared speak of it, but books about hauntings and apparitions had never been on my list of bedtime reading.

It sat on my bookshelf, unopened, for months.

When I eventually glanced at the back cover, I noticed it was an autobiography. I opened it to find the author had personally signed it in 1959.

I doubted it would hold any interest for me, but just in case, I had taken it to bed with the intention of flicking through it before discarding it to make room for my ever-expanding collection of NDE books.

In the process of skimming through it, I came across a fascinating account of the author's own near-death experience! Percy Cole died when he was having all his teeth extracted in 1935.

A few nights before his appointment, Percy had a dream in which a lady came to him. She told him her name was Dorothea and explained that she was "no longer of this world". She warned him that the anaesthetic he was to have for the dental operation presented a major risk for him.

The dentist and the doctor arrived at Cole's home the following morning (as incredible as it may seem to us today, it was not unusual in 1935 for such an operation to take place at the patient's residence) and a mask sprinkled with ether was held over his mouth and nostrils.

"I found myself completely out of my body." Cole wrote. "There were others in the room now, besides the doctor and the dental surgeon. One of these was the lady of my dream, Dorothea."

Cole felt exhilaration and joy at being "out of his body", but Dorothea expressed concern that he would not be able to "get back in again."

"We warned you about this," she said.

There were two people standing near the door. He could not clearly see the couple's features, but had the impression they were his deceased parents.

The dentist was shouting at him to "breathe, Mr. Cole. Breathe!"

Dorothea insisted it was time for him to try returning to his body, although she added with a smile: "You can stay here with us if you like."

"It would have been lovely to have stayed," Cole wrote. "The world and its work seemed so very far away. But just at this critical moment, our dog Patch barked as she ran across the lawn below the open window. The sound of that bark from close at hand brought me back to a sense of my responsibilities. I thought of all the trouble I should bring upon my wife and son if I did not come back."

"You'll have to put up a fight for it if you are going to get back,"

Dorothea warned.

Obviously, Cole did fight to return. He awoke to find himself in bed, his wife sitting by his side.

Many years later, Percy Cole returned to his homeland, England, and visited a psychic artist. The resulting portrait of Dorothea was precisely as he remembered her.

Another who received proof of her brief sojourn in heavenly realms was French ballerina and choreographer Janine Charrat, who suffered third degree burns when her dress caught fire during the filming of a television show in 1961. Her account was included in the 1974 book, 'Glimpses of the Beyond' and was reported in newspapers at the time.

On leaving her body, Janine was met by "a woman in a silk dress who floated towards her."

"You don't remember me, then, Janine?" the ethereal woman asked. "I'm Isabelle, your grandmother."

Isabelle took her granddaughter tenderly by the arm. "At the moment you may feel lost," she explained. "Because of that, I'm going to show you something that I hope will restore your courage, for you're going to need all the courage and trust you can muster."

They walked together towards a clear pond and Isabelle encouraged Janine to look carefully onto its surface.

"It will be a long time before you are well again," her grandmother told her. "Keep on looking into the pool. You must use every opportunity you have here."

As Janine stared intently at the pond's surface, she began to observe images of her long and painful journey back to health.

She saw the treatments she would need to endure, the operations she would undergo, and the difficulties she would encounter as she struggled to walk again.

She also saw a wedding taking place on a South Sea island. On looking closer, she realized it was her own wedding, and it was to someone she did not yet know.

"I heard myself call him Michel," Janine later stated, "and was conscious that this other self of mine was radiant with happiness."

Janine had doubts that all this could be true, but when she turned back to speak to her grandmother, Isabelle was gone.

Janine's burns were so extensive that the odds of saving her had been slight, but with the help of painful treatments, skin grafts, physiotherapy and most importantly, the courage she gained from her visit to the other side, she returned to the stage a year later.

In 1969, eight years after her accident, Janine married Michel Humbert on the South Pacific island of Moorea.

CHAPTER 13

MOTHER MOVED IN

By 1991, I was still standing on the threshold of awakening, loaded down with a suitcase full of doubts and fears. The progress Mum had made since our first visit to Dr. Wong's clinic was amazing and had inspired me to gain qualifications in a variety of alternative healing techniques.

My life now revolved around my courses and study, along with weekly visits to my grandmother at the nursing home.

My grandmother (better known to everyone as Nan) was exceptionally bright for her 99 years. She watched cricket on her portable TV and understood the game far better than I did!

On Saturday mornings she studied the horseracing form guide and marked her selections in each race. She didn't invest any money on these picks. She had none. But listening to each race on her radio or watching them on TV gave her an interest and kept her mind active.

During our visit one wintry day in 1991, she seemed her usual, alert self as she related the latest nursing home gossip and complained about the luke-warm lunch she'd been served earlier that day.

Then, she said something that stunned us: "Oh and guess who lives here now! Mother! She moved into room 7. It was so good to see her again. We've been having lots of lovely chats."

Mum and I glanced at each other and shifted uncomfortably in our chairs. How did one respond to such a comment? Oh good, we'd love to meet her? Don't be silly, your mother's been dead for over 70 years?

Anything other than "that's nice" seemed inappropriate.

"She's hallucinating," Mum said later as we climbed into the car.

"It's a sign."

"I guess so," I sighed as I drove out of the car park. "We have to remember she's 99. The time had to come, sooner or later."

I heard a faint sniffle and turned to see Mum wiping her nose with a tissue. "Are you ok?" I asked.

Her face suddenly contorted into a sob and I pulled the car over to the gutter.

"Hey," I patted her arm, "it doesn't mean she's going to die tomorrow. She may just be losing some of her grip on reality. It could take years before she loses it altogether. She was fine for most of the time we were there, wasn't she? It was only that one statement."

"I know," Mum whispered through her tears. "But she's ninety-nine. I have to accept we're going to lose her soon and I feel so bad that I missed visiting her for so long."

"You were practically dying yourself!" I reminded her. "I visited her as often as I could. She knew you were unwell, she understood."

Mum took a deep breath. "I know. And thank you for doing that. But she's *my* Mum and I'll never have another one. I should have made the effort."

I reached for her hand, "And you're *my* Mum and *I'll* never have another one. She's ninety-nine and you're sixty-eight. Keeping *you* alive is more important. There's no way I'd have driven you across town when you could barely even sit up in bed!"

She smiled through her tears and squeezed my hand.

We sat in silence for a few minutes, then she turned to me and with a touch of surprise in her voice, said, "You know, I never thought about her actually dying. Isn't that silly?"

"Nope. Not silly at all," I said as I glanced at the rear vision mirror and prepared to drive away. I didn't want to expand her statement into a discussion, because then I might have to admit how completely I understood what she was going through.

Until a few years ago, I'd never thought about my own mother dying. I'd been trying to deal with it while she had been, at best, semi-conscious. She had no idea what God and I had been arguing about on the back door step.

On our next visit, everything went smoothly until Nan leant forward and said in a conspiratorial tone, "Dr. McCann came to visit me yesterday!"

Dr. McCann had been our family doctor in the 1950's, and had probably been past retirement age even then. It was highly unlikely he was still practicing, or even still alive.

Mum and I had agreed to play along if she started hallucinating again, so we smiled politely and said "how nice, and how is dear Dr. McCann?"

"Oh he looks so well..." she remarked, "...and younger than he was years ago when we used to go to him..."

Now there's a strange hallucination, I thought. She remembers we *used* to go to him years ago.

"... and he told me I was nearly dead. By the way, did you bring that book about Tasmania I asked you for?"

"Er... yes, I..." Mum tried to retain her composure. "Here it is."

"Good, I want to show the nurse." She took the book, placed it on the table, then continued relating Dr. McCann's message. "He said I was already dead from my head down to my chest, and from my feet up to my hips, and that when they meet in the middle he'll come back for me."

Many years later, while writing this book, I re-read Dr. Wiltse's account of leaving his body in 1889, and I gasped in amazement at the similarities to my grandmother's words that day.

Wiltse had "watched the separation of the soul from the body with awe and wonder... beginning at the feet," at which point he "began to retreat from the feet to the head as a rubber cord shortens". As his soul reached the hips, Wiltse declared: "Now, there is no life below the hips."

"And you'll never guess who else came to see me yesterday." Nan continued to prattle on. "Keith! Is that the right book?" she interrupted herself again, retrieving the book from the table. "I wanted the one with the photo of Beauty Point in it. Is it in here?"

"Um... Keith came?" I asked, not sure if I even if I wanted to know. I'd had a boyfriend called Keith over twenty years earlier, but doubted he would suddenly decide to visit my grandmother.

"Keith who?"

Nan either didn't hear or chose not to as she thumbed through the book. "Her nephew." Mum whispered. "I'll explain later."

"And oh he's grown into such a fine young man!" Nan announced, still thumbing through the book. "You wouldn't know him now! He's coming back to see me again soon! Oh good, here's the photo I wanted."

I was having difficulty following this conversation!

Later, Mum told me the story. Nan's sister, Lil, had given birth to Keith over seventy years ago. Nan often looked after him when Lil worked, and the two had formed a close bond. When Keith was six months old he became seriously ill and his condition deteriorated rapidly. Nan was contacted and advised to come quickly.

At the time, she was far from her sister's house and it took most of the day to travel the distance. When she arrived, Keith looked up at her from his basinet and smiled. A few minutes later, he died. Nan and Lil both knew, without doubt, that he'd waited for her to arrive.

Mum and I had another cry in the car park before we drove home.

My great grandmother, our old doctor, Nan's infant nephew. We agreed that this could only mean one thing. Nan was rapidly nearing death and her dying brain was conjuring up weird hallucinations.

What she said on our next visit, however, forced us to reassess our beliefs.

***

Shortly after Muffin's passing, I heard about a two-year old black and white Cavalier King Charles Spaniel that was being mistreated. I couldn't bear to know an animal was suffering when I could do something about it, so I drove across town to collect her and paid a hefty sum for the privilege of giving her a good home.

"Does she have any possessions?" I had asked the surly owner. "A lead? Collar, toys?"

"Nah, never took her for walks," he shrugged. "And she doesn't play with toys."

I lifted Nikki into the car and sat her on the passenger seat, and she looked up at me. Her enormous brown eyes locked onto mine. I scratched her head. "Don't worry sweetheart, you're safe now!" I turned to wave to the owner, but he had already disappeared inside, so we drove away.

As we turned the first corner, Nikki moved closer, then placed her paw gently on my leg, the way Muffin so often used to do when we sat together on the doorstep.

I parked the car on the side of the road and cried.

"Muffin, if you're there, somewhere, watching, forgive me. I know I promised I'd never replace you. This isn't a replacement. It's a rescue."

When I arrived home and carried Nikki into the house, Mum was out of bed and sitting in her recliner. "Oh let me look at the little darling!" she said as we entered the lounge.

I put Nikki on the floor. She immediately ran to the couch, jumped on it and began pawing at the cushion.

"Hey, there'll be none of that, little madam," I scolded as I walked toward the couch. "Come on, get away from..."

I froze in my tracks when she uncovered what she'd been seeking. A deflated, dirty red ball. Muffin's ball.

Mum and I looked at each other in amazement.

"Did you...?" I began to ask, well aware that she couldn't have retrieved it even if she'd known about it. Her unsteadiness combined with the three steep steps without handrails at the back door prevented her reaching the garage where I'd hidden the ball over a year ago.

"Of course not! I didn't even know you'd kept it!"

"Then how...?"

There was no answer. All we could do was sit in thoughtful silence as we watched Nikki playing happily with Muffin's old red ball. I silently thanked Muffin for her approval, wanting, longing to believe she heard me.

***

"We can't tell her," I insisted as we drove into the car park of Nan's nursing home a few days later. "She loved Muffin so much, she'd be sad to think we'd replaced her."

"Yes, I suppose you're right." Mum agreed.

Our visit passed without incident. Nan was in good form, chatting happily about the current cricket test and relating details of a recent rowdy argument between two elderly residents.

When the time came to leave, we were relieved there'd been no mention of ghostly visitors this time.

We kissed her goodbye and promised we'd be back to see her next weekend. As I reached for the doorknob, she suddenly blurted out: "Oh, and by the way, I love your new little black and white dog. She's so sweet."

We smiled and nodded.

The moment the door closed behind us, we turned to each other and spoke in unison. "But how could she...?"

No-one but Mum and I knew about our recently acquired little black and white dog. Even if they had, no-one but Mum and I ever visited Nan.

I thought long and hard about this comment. Without having physically visited us, how could she have known? We could not have inadvertently mentioned the new addition to our family on a previous visit, because we didn't even know Nikki existed until a few days ago. Besides, she had described Nikki as "so sweet", suggesting she had seen or interacted with her.

I was slowly coming to terms with the concept that when people died they left their bodies and travelled to distant horizons, but how could someone who was still alive achieve such an amazing feat?

It was time to learn more about these out-of-body experiences.

***

I had purchased Robert Monroe's 'Journeys Out of the Body' two years earlier on the recommendation of the sales assistant at the TS Bookshop, but had been discouraged by the dust jacket blurb.

Monroe claimed to be a "solid citizen" who had been 'out of his body' a thousand times, and had written his book so others could avoid the confusion and terror he'd initially experienced.

I'd tossed it aside.

The universe, however, had other ideas. It seemed that it kept challenging me to step over the line I vowed and declared was my 'absolute boundary' and beyond which no sane and self-respecting person would dare to venture.

Solid citizen Robert Monroe refused to play by my rules.

This New York radio-broadcasting president developed a strange malady in 1958. Whenever he tried to sleep, his body began to shake and vibrate for about five minutes.

Fearing he had developed epilepsy or a brain tumour, Monroe visited his doctor and was put through a series of tests. The results proved he was perfectly healthy. Confused but relieved, he took his doctor's advice to "stop trying to resist it and see what happens."

The vibrations continued intermittently for several months until one night, while waiting for them to pass, he tried to distract himself by thinking about his hobby. An avid glider, he was looking forward to the gliding trip he had arranged for the following day.

Lost in his thoughts, he felt something pressing against his shoulder, and when he reached behind him he felt a smooth surface. Had he fallen out of bed, he wondered. Looking around, he realised there was no furniture surrounding him. It wasn't the floor!

Monroe looked down (which he initially thought was up!) and saw

82

his bed. He was bouncing gently against the ceiling!

To his horror, he noticed his wife in bed with another man! Believing it was merely a strange dream, he willed himself to zoom in to take a closer look and discovered the "other man" was himself!

Convinced he was dying, Monroe desperately swooped back to his body and dove in. He immediately felt the comfort of the bed covers and was able to view the room from his usual perspective.

He returned to his doctor the following day and submitted himself to another series of tests. Again, nothing abnormal showed up, so he sought the advice of a psychologist friend, Dr. Bradshaw.

The advice Bradshaw gave him was to repeat the experiment if possible. Shocked, Monroe pointed out that he wasn't ready to die.

"Oh, I don't think you'll do that," Bradshaw stated calmly. "Some of the fellows who practice yoga and those Eastern religions claim they can do it whenever they want to."

He wondered why anyone would want to have such terrifying experiences, and asked his friend what "it" was.

"Get out of the physical body for a while." Bradshaw explained. "They claim they can go all over the place. You ought to try it."

Monroe experienced six more episodes of vibration before he felt brave enough to imagine himself rising upward. He floated over his bed and stopped in mid-air. Suddenly, the thought occurred to him that he might fall, which sent him immediately hurtling back into his body.

Still concerned that he may have developed a mental illness, Monroe kept his experiences to himself and searched libraries and bookshops for information. The only books he could find were religious.

I knew the feeling!

These books advised him to "pray, meditate, fast, go to church, absolve sins, accept the Trinity, believe in the Father, the Son and the Holy Ghost and resist Evil."

Religion had not played a major part in Robert Monroe's life, so this advice did nothing but add to his confusion. Did he qualify for sainthood, he wondered, or was this the work of the devil?

The next time it happened, he later recorded the following: "I smoothly floated up over the bed, and when I willed myself to stop, I did, floating in mid-air... after a few seconds I thought myself downward, and a moment later found myself in bed again."

Having found he had some control of this intriguing phenomenon,

Monroe began experimenting regularly and taking notes after he returned to his body.

In September 1958, he recorded the following: "Again, I floated upward, with the intent of visiting Dr. Bradshaw and his wife."

Aware that Dr. Bradshaw was ill in bed with a cold, Monroe expected to visit him in the bedroom. "Again came the turning in air," he wrote, "the dive into the tunnel, and this time the sensation of going uphill."

I was intrigued by his mention of a tunnel.

"Then I came upon Dr. and Mrs. Bradshaw. They were outside the house, and for a moment I was confused... I didn't understand this because Dr. Bradshaw was supposed to be in bed."

[Dr. Bradshaw] "...was dressed in light overcoat and hat, his wife in a dark coat and all dark clothes. They seemed in good spirits, and walked past me unseeing, in the direction of a smaller building like a garage. I floated around in front of them, waving, trying to get their attention without result."

Monroe phoned the Bradshaws later and asked where they had been between four and five that afternoon. Mrs. Bradshaw explained that she went to the post office, and added that Dr. Bradshaw, having decided that a little fresh air might make him feel better, dressed and went with her.

When Monroe asked what they were wearing, Mrs. Bradshaw described their clothing precisely as he had witnessed it.

There were numerous other verified examples of Monroe's travels throughout the book, along with his efforts to validate his experiences.

I had to acknowledge that if these accounts were true, this was an amazing talent.

Subsequent research revealed that Monroe's ability to leave his body at will was not unique. The term "out of body experience" (OBE) was initially used by G. N. M. Tyrrell in his 1943 book, 'Apparitions', although it has also been attributed to Charles Tart, a leader in the area of consciousness studies.

Monroe later collaborated with consciousness researchers including one of the founders of transpersonal pychology, Stanislov Grof, astronaut Edgar Mitchell (the 6th man to walk on the moon) and Dr. Elisabeth Kubler-Ross, and in the early 1970's he also sought out professionally qualified scientific and engineering people to help him conduct research acceptable to other scientists.

As a result, the Monroe Institute was established as a non-profit education and research organization. During its first thirty years, over 20,000 people attended its residential program. These included a group one might not immediately equate with consciousness research, the US military!

The former director of the Intelligence and Security Command of the US Army confirmed in the Wall Street Journal in 1994 that they had sent officers to the Monroe Institute in 1978 and 1983 for out-of-body experience training. The purpose of this would later become known as Remote Viewing, a form of distant surveillance.

Robert Monroe died in 1995, but his legacy lives on. Today, the Monroe Institute comprises several buildings over 1.2 square kilometres in Virginia (US) where it continues its research into non-physical realities and human consciousness.

While I found Monroe's accounts amazing, I could not make them fit into my grandmother's observation of our newly acquired dog. People came to the Monroe Institute from all over the world to learn how to achieve out of body states at will. My grandmother was 99 years old and living in a nursing home.

Where was the connection?

CHAPTER 14

NOODLES DON'T HAVE RAINBOWS

The next element of the near-death experience Dr. Moody described was the sensation of travelling rapidly along or being pulled through a dark space. While most described this as a tunnel, others used words like cave, well, trough, passageway, enclosure, funnel, vacuum, void, valley or cylinder.

One man reported moving through a long dark place "like a sewer or something", while another said it felt like being on a roller coaster because he was travelling at a tremendous speed.

Another stated: "It was just like a swoooooosh and I felt like I was drawn through a limited area, a kind of funnel, I guess. It was dark and black in there, and I moved through it quickly."

In later reading, I came across a charming account by Chris, a boy who died at the age of four.

Two years after his experience, Chris explained to paediatrician Melvin Morse: "When I died, I went into a huge noodle. It wasn't like a spiral noodle, but it was very straight, like a tunnel. When I told my mom about nearly dying, I told her it was a noodle, but now I am thinking that it must have been a tunnel because it had a rainbow in it, and I don't think a noodle has a rainbow." (Parting Visions, 1994)

While the image of travelling to heaven through a tunnel (although rarely a noodle!) had become popular over the years, I could not recall coming across any references to it in my pre-Moody books, apart from Robert Monroe's out-of-body experiences.

Was the tunnel an urban myth, an image introduced in 'Life After Life' that people had grasped and ran with, a symbol with no basis in fact?

No basis in fact? How silly that sounded. After all, what could possibly be based on fact when researching the afterlife?

I re-read all my pre-Moody books again and was surprised to find references to tunnels I had missed the first time around.

In 'The Waiting World' *(1975)*, I read an account by a doctor's widow who nearly died after the Caesarean birth of her youngest child. She told Reverend Matson she had "gone down a long tunnel... being propelled forward. The tunnel was wide and light and there were many people around."

I found it a little disconcerting when she described this tunnel as "white-tiled like the old Illinois Central tunnels to the trains at Chicago" and she was concerned about having no money and no ticket. But at least it was a pre-Moody tunnel.

Julia Phillips Ruop wasn't concerned about buying tickets. Following a thyroid operation in the 1930's she described starting through "...what seemed to be a long, dark passageway... and as I went along I thought calmly, this must be what they call dying." (Guideposts magazine, 1963)

In 'Glimpses of the Beyond' (1974), author Jean-Baptiste Delacour included an account by Mrs. Frances Leslie, an American woman who lived in Paris and died unexpectedly in her apartment. The doctor injected adrenalin directly into her heart, and when she was able to speak, Mrs. Leslie told the doctor:

"...all of a sudden I was hearing a very faint, light humming sound. Or was it the colours all around me that were making the sounds? I was floating in a long shaft that seemed very narrow at first and then became wider and wider, always getting wider and with brighter and more radiant colours the farther I floated forward in the passageway."

I found it interesting that Mrs. Leslie initially described the area she was travelling through as a shaft, then as a passageway, and later stated "... I couldn't be sure what was up and what was down in that tunnel, that shaft-like place."

Describing her journey back to the body, she said: "This tunnel-like place... got narrow around me. I suddenly realized I was becoming a physical person again."

When she appeared to be out of danger, Mrs. Leslie declared: "I'm in a hurry to get back again."

She lived for a further twelve hours, then died again and could not be revived.

When Andy Petro drowned in Lake Michigan in 1956, he told Phillip

L. Berman (The Journey Home) that he suddenly found himself in a tunnel.

"It was dark and spherical," he explained, "and as I entered it I could see myself at the bottom of the lake. So I knew the Andy now entering the tunnel was the same Andy that was stuck on the bottom of the lake."

Initially, Andy found this frightening, but his next thought was "boy, it sure is great to be warm... I could see this light at the far end of the tunnel feeding warmth to me... and the closer I got to the light, as I shot down the tunnel, the warmer I got."

Following a heart attack, James Lorne described how he was "floating in air and could clearly see my body lying down there." Then he "landed in a long corridor filled with soft twilight."

He later described seeing a bright light shining at the end of it. "I could also hear voices coming from there," he stated. (Glimpses of the Beyond, 1974)

I found another mention of a pre-Moody tunnel, a most unusual one, in Percy Cole's 'Psychic Odyssey'.

As you may recall, Cole died in 1935 while having his teeth extracted. What I found particularly intriguing about his experience was that when it was time for him to return to his body, he had to turn *away* from the light and into the darkness of what he described as "a kind of tunnel".

"I fought my way against the stream," he wrote, "for a stream of shadows pressed against me as they passed on towards the light. How long this kept on, I do not know, but at last I saw in the distance a tiny light, just a mere glimmer far away. Struggling against the stream, I pushed my way towards it."

Here was an account from 1935, published in 1959, in which the experiencer travelled through a tunnel not in order to *reach* the light, but to return from it, fighting valiantly against those passing *towards* that light.

This tunnel, it would seem, is a two-way street.

As intriguing as this was, I was disappointed not to have found further tunnel references in my pre-Moody collection.

Months later, after scouring shelves and tables at library sales, fetes and markets, I was fortunate to find two books by British geologist and botanist Robert Crookall. 'The Supreme Adventure' had been published in 1961, and 'Intimations of Immortality' in 1965.

A meticulous researcher, Crookall spent a lifetime collecting accounts of out-of-body experiences and wrote numerous books on the subject during the 1960's. These also included accounts by those who left their bodies in situations we would now term NDE's.

Their words were chillingly reminiscent of those in 'Life After Life':

"I was not lying in the bed but floating in the air, a little above it. I saw the body stretched out straight."

"I saw about me those that had been dead for a long time... then I seemed to rise up out of my body."

What really excited me, however, was the number of times tunnels (or words similar to it) were mentioned in Crookall's books:

"I seemed to float in a long tunnel. It appeared very narrow at first but gradually expanded into unlimited space." (This one occurred in 1952)

"I was rushing along through a pitch black tunnel" (Mrs. Bounds, who had an NDE in 1954)

"...proceeding along a straight black tube with hardly any room to move." (This one happened in 1894)

One hapless experiencer in Crookall's research recalled falling into, rather than travelling up the tunnel:

"I was falling... down a dark, narrow tunnel or shaft... the speed is so tremendous that one gets the effect of tumbling through a hole into a new sphere."

Tumbling through a hole into a new sphere? Was this Alice in Wonderland?

French ballerina Janine Charrat had a similar experience:

"I was overcome by a dizzy, whirling feeling, and I thought I was falling into a deep well. The fall never seemed to end, and all my attempts to catch hold of something were in vain." (Glimpses of the Beyond, 1974)

Another who "fell" into heaven was Allan Lewis, an industrial chemist in Australia. Allan had died three times as a schoolboy in 1946, and later stated that on one of those occasions, he and his ethereal companion reached heaven by "travelling at incredible speed down a bottomless pit." (And When I Die Will I Be Dead?)

More about Allan Lewis later.

Narrow shafts, deep wells, bottomless pits! It seemed there was no end of routes to heaven.

Many years later, I read 'Science and the Near-Death Experience' by Chris Carter in which he quotes Apache chief Geronimo, who dictated his memoirs to S. M. Barrett shortly before he died in 1909.

Geronimo tells the story of an Indian who died on the battlefield and slid into a dark cave which gradually grew lighter as he travelled through it. When he emerged, he found himself in a forest. Further on, he came to a green valley.

"He said that he saw and recognized many whom he had known in this life," Geronimo related, "and that he was sorry when he was brought back to consciousness."

Could a cave be considered a tunnel? Certainly! Even Dr. Moody had pointed out that while many spoke of a long dark place, they had used numerous words, including cave, to describe it.

However, I had difficulty accepting the description one man had related to author Robert Crookall in the 1960's. This man had died in 1955 and recalled travelling through "...an avenue of trees, slowly moving farther and farther from my body."

As he advanced along this avenue, he found himself heading towards "a brilliant light at the end of it."

While an avenue of trees vaguely suggested a tunnel, and a brilliant light at the end was consistent with other accounts, I arbitrarily dismissed it. I was becoming very adept at drawing a line in the sand and presuming that anything beyond that line of credibility was not worth my consideration.

How much I still had to learn!

What I encountered next suggested that tunnels, and even tree-lined avenues, were not the only routes to heaven!

CHAPTER 15

OTHER ROUTES TO HEAVEN

An autobiography called 'Bring Yourself to Anchor' (1941) was brought to my attention by a friend who knew about (and was surprisingly tolerant towards) my interests.

The author, Commander Archibald Bruce Campbell, (Royal Navy) also "walked along a road to heaven".

During a sudden serious illness, Campbell found himself standing by his bed and gazing down at his physical form. He later remarked that he looked "pinched and grey" adding "... the stubble on my chin was about four days' growth."

Feeling an urge to get out of the house, Campbell passed through the closed doors of the bedroom and front door with ease. "It did not astonish me," he wrote, "I just wondered why it was not necessary for me to open the doors."

As one would!

"No sooner had I stepped outside the garden gate," Campbell continued, "than I found myself in a strange country. A wide moor stretched as far as I could see. Then I came to a narrow but well-worn track... I saw that it led to a road. I came to it, and was amazed to see it thronged with people."

As they reached the crest of the hill, Campbell saw a vision of ethereal beauty: "Golden browns, reds and oranges chased each other across the scene," he wrote. "As the colours intermingled they seemed to diffuse warmth and love around us all. The comfort of it was wonderful."

Campbell spoke to a man nearby. "What road is this?" he asked. "Where does it lead?"

"Why, this is death." the other man replied. "Isn't it lovely? If only the people on earth would realize it. They are really the dead. We are just beginning to live."

Thinking only about the grief this would cause his beloved wife, Campbell decided to return, prompting a pitying look from the other man.

He made his way back through the "seemingly endless mass of people" until he reached the narrow trail again.

This homeward journey was hauntingly familiar. In 'Psychic Odyssey', Percy Cole had written: "I fought my way against the stream, for a stream of shadows pressed against me as they passed on towards the light."

Campbell then found himself back in his own front garden. "I walked to the bed, and there I was lying snugly between the sheets."

"There I was?" What an interesting comment. It reminded me of the lady in the park, oh so long ago, telling me about George Ritchie and how, when he returned to the hospital after his excursion to the 'afterlife café', he had to search the wards looking for himself!

"I seemed a lot better." Campbell wrote. "Gone was the drawn look on my face, and I could hear myself breathing quietly and evenly."

He heard his wife crying and he opened his eyes. "What is the matter, darling?" he asked. His wife screamed in shock, which was hardly surprising. The doctor had declared her husband dead the previous night and had arranged to return that morning to make further arrangements.

"I did all in my power to prevent you from slipping from us," his doctor later explained, "but as we watched we saw and heard the last breath leave your body. I know it too well to make a mistake. When I saw you [the following morning], I knew a miracle had happened."

Campbell's experience also brought yet another to mind. While reading the account by Dr. Wiltse's (who had declared: "the body and I no longer had any interests in common") in the 1904 book, 'Human Personality and Its Survival of Bodily Death', I had come across a similar description, another one I had casually dismissed because it didn't fit within my boundaries.

Perhaps it was time I started paying attention!

Extremely ill with typhoid fever, Dr. Wiltse had eventually been pronounced dead. He then regained consciousness to find himself floating down onto a narrow roadway which inclined upward and appeared to be built of milky quartz and fine sand. Below the roadway he observed the treetops of a forest.

Although there was no apparent support for this road, Wiltse felt no fear. He described leisurely wandering along it and stopping often to admire the mountains, trees and river.

Two roads, and an avenue of trees! Could these *all* be dreams or hallucinations? Having asked this question of the universe, I was soon provided with more accounts of people walking to heaven.

It seemed the universe and I were getting on well lately.

An obscure book called 'Hawaiian Folk Tales' was a real surprise. The compiler, Thomas G. Thrum, had gathered stories from various historians including the Reverend A. O. Forbes, Mrs. E. N. Haley and King Kalakaua. This book was published in 1907 and found its way to me eighty-five years later.

Mrs. Haley contributed a report about a young woman named Kalima, who died after a long illness. I presumed a book about Hawaiian folk tales would simply be what it implied — folk tales — so was initially ambivalent when it was brought to my attention. Another surprise awaited me.

"The grave was dug," Mrs. Haley wrote, "and when everything was ready for the last rites and sad act, husband and friends came to take a final look at the rigid form and ashen face before it was laid away forever in the ground."

Fortunately, before Kalima was buried, she moved, took a long breath, and opened her eyes. A few minutes later she said "I have something strange to tell you."

It took several days before Kalima was strong enough to say more. She called her family and friends to gather around and told them the following story:

"I died, as you know. I seemed to leave my body and stand beside it, looking down on what was me. The me that was standing there looked like the form I was looking at, only I was alive and the other was dead. I gazed at my body for a few minutes, then turned and walked away."

My attention was assured. Here was a hundred year old account of an out-of-body experience in which the subject showed disinterest in the physical body. It was just as so many modern-day experiencers had described.

What I read next, however, was even more fascinating.

"I left the house and village, and walked on and on to the next village, and there I found crowds of people, oh, so many people! The place which I knew as a small village of a few houses was a very large place, with hundreds of houses and thousands of men, women, and children. Some of them I knew and they spoke to me, although that seemed strange, for I knew they were dead, but nearly all were strangers."

Kalima continued: "They were all so happy! They seemed not to have a care; nothing to trouble them. Joy was in every face, and happy laughter and bright, loving words were on every tongue. I left that village and walked on to the next. I was not tired, for it seemed no trouble to walk. It was the same there; thousands of people, and every one so joyous and happy."

Kalima spoke to a few people in the second village, then continued on her journey. "I seemed to be on my way to the volcano, to Pele's pit, and could not stop, as much as I wanted to do so. All along the road were houses and people, where I had never known anyone to live. Every bit of good ground had many houses, and many, many happy people on it. I felt so full of joy, too, that my heart sang within me, and I was glad to be dead."

As we now know, Kalima eventually returned to life. I have included more of her story later in this book.

There are over seven thousand kilometres of ocean between Hawaii and New Zealand, yet a Maori woman called Ngakahikatea, who was born 'sometime in the 1850's' and had little contact with Europeans, related a story eerily similar to Kalima's when interviewed by author and historian Michael King.

As a young girl, Ngakahikatea became very ill and eventually, her breathing ceased. She left her body and hovered nearby, watching her family prepare her funeral. Then she set out on her journey north.

Ngakahikatea was heading for Rerenga Wairua, a place also known to the Maori culture as the Leaping-Off Place of Spirits.

I found it fascinating that Ngakahikatea lived in the southern hemisphere (New Zealand) and headed for a sacred place on the north tip of the north island, while Kalima resided in the northern hemisphere (Hawaii) and walked towards South Point.

When Ngakahikatea reached Rerenga Wairua, she ascended to a ledge and called to her ancestors to let them know she was ready to enter the land of the dead, then prepared to slide into the entrance, but she found it blocked by a curtain of seaweed.

Then Mahuta, the Maori god of the forests, advised her that her ancestors did not want her yet and instructed her to "go back where you come from until they are ready. Then I shall send for you."

"I rose and returned to my body and my people in Waikato," she told Michael King in the late 1960's, at which time her age was estimated to be well over a hundred. She still dressed in traditional costume and only spoke the Maori language.

"I passed over all the places and things I had seen on the way," she recalled.

Not surprisingly, Ngakahikatea's family were surprised when she took a breath and sat up.

"So it is that I live on," she explained to King, "because the spirits of my dead will not claim me. I shall not die until they do."

The spirits of her dead were certainly not in a hurry. They eventually called her home in 1975, when she was around one hundred and twenty years old. Michael King included her account in his book, 'Being Pakeha Now', in 1985.

In yet another part of the Pacific, in an area encompassing the north and northeast of Australia, lays a group of islands known collectively as Melanesia. These include Vanuatu, the Solomons, Fiji and Papua New Guinea.

Modern-day Canadian anthropologist Dorothy Counts spent many years working in Melanesia, and among other data, collected reports of near death experiences among the people of these islands.

In 'Experiences Near Death', sociologist and senior university lecturer Allan Kellehear quotes Counts: "...in no case was a tunnel experience identified. All informants report the early part of the NDE as walking on a road."

Wow!

One account documented by Counts during this time was the story of Andrew, a young man who was dead for several hours in the 1960's: "When I died everything was dark," Andrew said, "but I went through a field of flowers and when I came out everything was clear. I walked on along the road and came to a fork where two men were standing... [one] man took my hand and we entered a village."

After exploring the village, and one hut in particular, it was time for Andrew to return. He saw a beam of light. "I walked along it," he later told Mrs. Counts. "I walked down the steps, and when I turned to look [back] there was nothing but forest. [I walked]... through the forest and along a narrow path. I came back to my house and re-entered my body and was alive again."

An interesting aspect of this account was that while he was in this 'heavenly village', Andrew saw the local lay minister's wife. He knew her, because she often took food to the young boys who resided in the men's house. What Andrew did not know at the time was that this woman had collapsed and died in the village square shortly after Andrew died, but before he returned.

I contacted Dorothy's Counts' husband and colleague, David, who had accompanied his wife during this field research in the 1980's and he had no hesitation confirming this account.

Drythelm's experience, as reported by Saint Bede's in 'An Ecclesiastical History of the English Peoples', occurred long before any of those above and provided another walk to heaven.

Drythelm fell ill and died one night, then returned to life at daybreak. "A handsome man in a shining robe was my guide," he later reported, "and we walked in silence. As we travelled onward, we came to a very broad and deep valley of infinite length... he soon brought me out of darkness into an atmosphere of clear light... [beyond] lay a broad and pleasant meadow."

***

A broad and deep valley, a well-worn track, a narrow roadway made of milky quartz and fine sand, a deserted road and another road that was thronged with people. These experiencers reported travelling through forests, valleys and fields of flowers. They saw mountains, trees, rivers, wide moors, pleasant meadows and populated villages.

Such heavenly ambles were not only reported in ancient times, nor were they restricted to non-western experiences. Even a nineteenth century American medical doctor and a twentieth century English Navy Commander had walked to heaven.

Of course, all these accounts were from people who had died and returned to tell their stories. The following words, however, were spoken by a king on his deathbed, and suggest that the 'permanently dying' may also take similar routes to heaven!

In 1964, King Paul of Greece lapsed into a coma. He was not expected to regain consciousness, but he rallied briefly.

"I thought I'd already gone off" he told his wife. "I still feel far away... I must have already been on the other shore."

Then the dying king added: "I had a vision of a long dark road with a light showing at the far end. It gave a wonderful feeling of peace and happiness, a great uplift of the spirit." (Glimpses of the Beyond, 1974)

In an effort to provide comfort for the bereaved people of Greece, Queen Frederica wrote down her husband's last words and published them as 'A Gift From Heaven'.

***

While I was pondering what to make of these accounts, I found one more route to heaven!

As you may recall, when Burris Jenkins died as a result of an explosion on his cruiser in 1957 he floated through the fourth floor window and into the hospital courtyard. But then, he felt "...this great sense of acceleration through intergalactic space, the curvature of the earth, the clouds."

"As I passed the orbit of the moon," Jenkins wrote, "suddenly I realized I had passed through the Solar System itself. My passing view was the earth, several planets, the sun, the Milky Way, and the edge of the galaxy. As the acceleration increased, the density of the stars began to become less and less. Even the galaxy appeared as a star itself. It was at this point that I first became concerned."

I suspect I'd be concerned, too! Surely this was a 'one-of' account.

Not so.

Mary Grohe "died" of a heart attack two days after an operation, and also reported that she had "seemed to be hurtling like a projectile through space." (The Waiting World)

Earl Stowell also "went out into the sky" when he died. "Our speed of travel increased," he wrote, "until it seemed we caught up with rays or beams of light and passed them as if they were standing still." (Biography of William Rufus Rogers Stowell, 1893)

Then, I found two accounts in 'The Light Beyond', a later book by Raymond Moody that appeared to support these intriguing claims.

One child stated that during his dying experience he "felt himself rise above the earth, passing through the stars and finding himself up with the angels."

Another NDEer who took part in Dr. Moody's research described himself as "zooming up and seeing the planets all around him and the earth below like a blue marble."

The most fascinating 'astronaut' account to find its way to me, however, was by renowned psychiatrist, Carl Jung, who described his experience following a heart attack in Switzerland in 1944.

In his autobiography, 'Memories, Dreams, Reflections' (1963), Jung wrote: "It seemed to me that I was high up in space. Far below I saw the globe of the earth, bathed in a gloriously blue light. I saw the deep blue sea and the continents... its global shape was plainly distinguishable and its outlines shone with a silvery gleam through that wonderful blue

97

light."

Jung continued: "Later, I discovered how high in space one would have to be to have so extensive a view — approximately a thousand miles! The sight of the earth from this height was the most glorious thing I had ever seen."

In 1944, it had not been possible to view our planet from such a distance. It would take a further seventeen years before the first human, Yuri Gagarin, travelled far enough into space to gain such a perspective, describing earth as being "surrounded by a light blue aureole".

A decade after Gagarin's flight, the sixth man to walk on the moon, Edgar Mitchell, wrote about looking upon "a sparkling blue and white jewel, a light, delicate sky-blue sphere... like a small pearl in a thick sea of black mystery."

These more recent descriptions were uncannily similar to Jung's 1944 observations: "I saw the globe of the earth, bathed in a gloriously blue light."

***

I glanced through the kitchen window again. It was still there.

Why would a pigeon squat on our back lawn for over an hour? There was no protection, no safe escape from predators. I decided to investigate.

"Shoosh! Shoosh, silly bird" I yelled, waving my hands a few inches from its beak. It gave no indication it cared. Its eyes were open but it didn't flinch.

It occurred to me that perhaps it was dying.

I had never thought about birds dying naturally. Birds got eaten by cats or run over by cars. They didn't simply drop out of the sky mid-flight, or die on suburban back lawns.

This one, it seemed, was doing precisely that.

I sat on my thinking step and watched. It made no movement. I felt powerless to help the poor creature, but felt there must be something I could do.

Then I remembered rescue remedy, an amazing mixture of flower essences that helps alleviate stress and fear. I rushed inside and grabbed the little dropper bottle, knelt beside the bird and squeezed a few drops on its beak, then returned to my doorstep.

A few moments later I was relieved to see the pigeon raise its head and look skyward. "Ah, must have had a shock," I thought. "Maybe it had flown into a window or been chased to the point of exhaustion by another bird, and the rescue remedy fixed the problem! Wonderful."

I was about to return inside when the bird unfolded its wings and stretched them out. Still looking skyward, it made three strong flaps. I paused, wondering why it had not become airborne.

Instantly, its head dropped to the ground. Its outstretched wings collapsed. The bird was dead.

My knees turned to jelly and I allowed myself to flop back onto the step. I tried to put into perspective what I had just witnessed. Why would a dying bird, moments before death, suddenly look skyward and flap its wings as if to fly away?

Had this bird seen its own 'route to heaven' in the last moments of its life? Did its physical body automatically react to the flight of its soul during those few seconds they were still joined?

Did birds even have souls? I didn't know. But the experience had a strangely profound effect on me, and I knew I would remember it forever.

CHAPTER 16

WE MEET AGAIN

Nan lapsed into a coma on September 19, 1991. She died two days later, a few weeks after her comment about our new dog and a mere five days short of her hundredth birthday.

Was it possible that our old doctor's comment that she was dead from her head down to her chest, and from her feet up to her hips, had been spookily accurate? If there had been so little of her left alive, perhaps she had been free to leave her body whenever she chose.

Had she come to visit us? Did she travel in the car with us each time we left the nursing home? The implications of this possibility sent shivers up and down my spine. Had my grandmother been 'haunting' us before she died?

Even if she had, I missed her. Now, Mum and I were all there was.

The funeral was held a few days later. Five people came. Nan's nephew (the brother of her beloved Keith, who had died in infancy), and a married couple we had known in the 1960's, all sat near the back as though being too close to a coffin might be dangerous. Mum and I chose the second row.

After fourteen years in the nursing home, Nan had known everyone there. She often patted hands and gave advice to heart-broken nursing assistants, provided a sympathetic ear for stressed kitchen staff, and sat beside ailing patients. Visitors for other patients would often call in to see her for a chat on their way to another room.

We waited. No-one else came.

The minister stumbled over the notes I had scribbled out the previous day.

"Lucy Grace Harding, who you all know lovingly as Nan, loved to knit and crochet, and many of you here today will have something she made. She also loved to watch cricket, and...."

I cringed. "You *all* know? *Many* of you?" Was this what life was about? You're born, you live, you die, and no-one really gives a damn?

With quivering voice, I stood to read a poem I had recently and coincidentally (there's that word again!) come across. It had no reason to be included in a book about flower essences, yet I had just happened to read it a few days before the funeral and I knew I had to read it on the day!

> I sprung up from my body
> For all the world to see
> But they looked down with tear-filled eyes
> At that which wasn't me.
> I shot up to the heavens
> And then swooped down again.
> I shouted out in sheer delight
> With all my might and main.
> I wrapped my arms around them
> Those ones who mourned me so.
> I said "Oh, know my happiness.
> Do try, do try to know."
> Then one looked up from mourning
> O'er that which was not I
> And said in breathless wonder
> "I feel that she is nigh.
> I heard a little whisper,
> I know it was her voice.
> She said Oh know my happiness,
> Rejoice with me. Rejoice!"

(Mary Tabor, reproduced in 'The Medical Discoveries of Edward Bach Physician', 1973)

Had I believed the words I read? Oh, how I longed to say I did. I wanted to hear that little whisper, feel a brush of cold air against my face, catch sight of a misty form hovering over the coffin.

Then again, would I have believed it if it happened, or would I still find a way to justify it or dismiss it, as I had when Muffin jumped on my bed three weeks after her death?

If watching Nikki playing with Muffin's deflated old ball had not convinced me, then what could? (Although I confess, that incident brought me closer to acceptance than anything else to date!)

We left the funeral parlour and drove home in silence. I had wanted to celebrate Nan's life, not send her off with a shrug and a feeling of "who cares?" The other three joined us at home for a "nice cup of tea, thanks" and we shook off the sadness as we exchanged stories about Nan. We laughed at the many humorous anecdotes, smiled at the happy memories.

Mum was in the midst of telling a story when suddenly the lights in the room dimmed. She stopped mid-sentence and we all looked up at the ceiling. A moment later, they brightened, then dimmed, brightened, dimmed, and brightened.

"You're welcome, Nan!" I addressed the light globes.

Mum chimed in with "Glad you're enjoying it, Nan!"

"They left suddenly!" I commented a few minutes later as I gathered up our visitors' half empty cups.

"Hmmm," Mum agreed. "Funny about that." We both laughed.

***

Later that evening, I sat on my think-step and pondered beloved pets appearing on beds or retrieving hidden toys, and lights dimming.

Had Nan really dimmed the lights in gratitude? I hoped so. It was comforting to imagine loved ones watching over us, trying to communicate.

But I also knew it was too easy to mould an incident into something meaningful.

Perhaps a car had crashed into a nearby power pole at that moment, or there had been some other interruption to the power supply.

I simply couldn't allow myself to be gullible.

When I was 28, the prospect of my own mortality had briefly sent me spiralling into depression, but when the answers didn't immediately appear in big letters across the sky, I filed my questions in the too-hard basket and went back to enjoying life.

When Mum's health rapidly declined ten years later, the question of mortality had shifted gears. It was no longer about me. It was about someone I loved dearly.

I asked questions, then played at finding answers. Is there, isn't there?

I bought books, read them, then tossed them aside. Maybe, maybe not.

I had experiences, then second-guessed them. Could it be, can't it be?

Now, my grandmother was gone. The previous year, I stroked the head of my cherished dog as she took her last breath. I missed them both very much, but I also had to consider the possibility that both may have tried to contact me, tried to reassure me.

I could go on dismissing these incidents, keep my head in the clouds and pretend none of it mattered.

It mattered.

CHAPTER 17

LET THERE BE LIGHT

There's always a light at the end of the tunnel. At least, so we're told. The only tunnels I'd encountered until now were during train trips, so whenever I had heard this expression I presumed it referred to railway tunnels. I often cynically added "but it's probably the headlights of an oncoming train!"

Now, I wondered. Had this expression originated in historical near-death accounts? Participants in Dr. Moody's research also reported seeing the proverbial light at the end of the tunnel. Some described it as a mere pinprick of light, but added that it grew brighter and larger as they progressed towards it. Others were immediately surrounded by a bright light that illuminated everything around them.

Most said this light had an unearthly brilliance, although it did not hurt their eyes. Dr. Moody presumed that this was probably because they no longer had physical eyes. That made sense.

Of course, as they had no physical eyes, I still had to question *how* they were seeing *anything*!

Had anyone who survived a close call with death prior to the publication of 'Life After Life' described seeing an incredibly bright light? My pre-Moody books provided the answer. It was a resounding YES!

A painting displayed in the Palazzo Ducale in Venice, Italy, shows angels assisting the departed through a long tunnel towards a bright light. Entitled 'Ascent of the Blessed', this stunning artwork is part of a group of four paintings called 'Visions of the Hereafter' by Dutch artist Hieronymus Bosch.

It was painted in the fifteenth century!

One of the most interesting aspects of this painting is that while angels and a bright light were part of religious beliefs at that time, a 'tunnel to heaven' was not. One can only wonder where the artist might have found his inspiration.

Eight hundred years before Bosch transferred his vision to canvas, Saint Bede wrote about the monk Drythelm, who had died and journeyed to the other world. On returning to life, Drythelm spoke of a light "flooding all this place that it seemed greater than the brightness of daylight or of the sun's rays at noon."

Even before Drythelm's otherworld journey, 6th century priest Salvius returned from death after spending an entire evening lifeless on a funeral bier. "...I went through a gate that was brighter than normal daylight," he reported. "The light was indescribable, and I can't tell you how vast it was."

Salvius described a cloud that was "more luminous than any light and yet no sun was visible, no moon and no star, indeed the cloud shone more brightly than any of these and had a natural brilliance of its own. (History of the Franks by Gregory of Tours, 6th century)

While I was reluctant to include mystical religious experiences in this book, I could not resist the description of the light by sixteenth century Carmelite nun, Saint Theresa of Avila, who not only had a near-death experience but is also reported to have regularly left her body, visited other realms and conversed with her departed parents and other spiritual beings while deep in prayer.

In her 1565 autobiography (written to allow her superiors to assess her spiritual journeys) Saint Theresa described suffering: "a paroxysm in which I remained for four days... without any feeling."

Although her body was prepared for burial, Saint Theresa survived. Her attempt to describe the light she saw at this time could just as easily have been written by a modern-day near-death experiencer:

"I wish I could give a description of at least the smallest part of what I learned, but when I try to discover a way of doing so, I find it impossible, for while the light we see here and that other light are both light, there is no comparison between the two and the brightness of the sun seems quite dull if compared with the other."

More recently, but still long before Moody's ground-breaking research, Robert Crookall's 'The Supreme Adventure' (1961) featured numerous examples of brilliant light illuminating the end of the tunnel.

An account from 1935: "I was in a long tunnel with a light at the end... I knew that if I could only get to the light at the end I should understand everything."

Another from 1935: "Have you ever looked through a very long tunnel and seen the tiny speck of light at the far end? Well, I found myself... hurrying along just such a tunnel or passage."

And in 1950: "Suddenly there appeared an opening, like a tunnel, and at the far end, a light. I moved nearer to it and was drawn up the passage."

Marba Peck Hale recalled her grandfather telling her the story of how her grandmother, Flora Ann Mayer died of diphtheria at the beginning of the twentieth century, and then returned. "She said she felt herself being drawn into a whirlpool-like tunnel," he told her. "Then she saw a very bright light." (Marba Peck Hale papers, CLDS, circa 2000)

In 'The Waiting World', Reverend Archie Matson wrote about a teacher who had been taking a swim at a private beach when he almost drowned. The teacher told Matson: "The next thing I knew... I became aware of lights glowing from the edges of the darkness. The lights came closer... or I came closer to the lights."

Norman Vincent Peale's friend, John Clarke, had also described "lights all about me, beautiful lights."

Percy Cole became aware of a bright light while out of his body during dental surgery in 1935. "Although the summer sun was shining in at the window from a cloudless sky," he wrote, "it was not nearly as bright as that other light."

When it was time to return, Cole had to "turn away from that light and travel back into darkness."

Polio victim Dorothy's attention had also been drawn towards a bright light as she died. "As I slowly approached it," she recalled, "I found myself in a new world. A soft diffused light, not like harsh sunlight, glowed and everything was joyful."

Describing his close call in his 1897 book, 'Mediumistic Experiences of John Brown, the Medium of the Rockies', the nineteenth century medium wrote: "...it seemed to me that I was moving slowly through a warm atmosphere; and in the distance I began to perceive a lighter or whiter spot in the darkness. As this light gradually increased in size, it came nearer to me, till finally it filled the room, and all outside. It was not like the light of our sun, it was more white, more still. It appeared to carry with it a life principle."

Many years later, just when I thought I had exhausted all references to pre-Moody NDE's, another one, this time even older than most, actually made the news!

In 2004, Dr. Phillippe Charlier was browsing in a Paris bookshop when he came across an old medical book. Published in 1740, 'Anecdotes de Medecine' had been written by French military physician Pierre-Jean du Monchaux.

Dr. Charlier purchased it for the equivalent of one dollar.

This battered old book had held its secrets for almost three centuries. One of these was an account of a man the author referred to as M.L.C and who he described as "one of the most famous apothecaries of Paris." Perhaps, like many NDEr's today, M.L.C's fame prompted him to request anonymity for fear of ridicule.

Monchaux wrote: "M.L.C. had a bad fever in Italy and he was cured by French doctors and surgeons using bleedings. After the last bleeding, which was very abundant, he remained unconscious for such a long time that the doctors were worried."

According to Monchaux, the patient later declared that "after losing all external sensations, he saw a light that was so pure and strong, he thought he was in paradise. He perfectly remembers this sensation, the most pleasant and beautiful he ever felt in his life."

Monchaux added: "In the twelfth century, a theologian maintained that all men are illuminated by a ray of primordial light when the soul and the body separate: luminofitas lucis prima." (Latin, translation: first or prime luminous light).

The author also related an account of an Irish knight from the French regiment who "fell into a river; they all thought he drowned. A marshall of same regiment pulled the unconscious man out of the water. However, he claimed that... deep under the water, he felt a quiescence and an indescribable peace."

Almost three hundred years ago, Monchaux compared these accounts with those reported by others who had similar experiences as a result of drowning, hypothermia and hanging, and stated: "Many people of all ages and gender claim to have felt a similar sensation in the same conditions."

The purchaser of this book, Dr. Charlier, was intrigued. A medical doctor himself, he followed Monchaux's example and compared these accounts to modern-day reports.

Like the original author, Charlier discovered many similarities, such as indescribable peace, a light so pure and strong that it seemed like paradise, pleasant and beautiful sensations, and a clear recall of the event.

He published his findings in the peer-reviewed Journal of Resuscitation.

***

I subsequently discovered there was more to this light than meets the eye, if you'll excuse the pun.

Many experiencers in Dr. Moody's research insisted this light was an actual being with a distinct personality. While no features had been seen, participants in the study agreed that incredible love and warmth emanated from it, and each said they were drawn irresistibly towards it.

I tried to get my head around such a concept. How could light be alive?

Once again, I found examples of others perceiving a being in or of the light, long before such a concept was described in 'Life After Life'.

When Julia Phillips Ruopp travelled through a long, dark passageway during an operation in the 1930's, she "emerged into an overwhelmingly wide space of light," adding that it was "a pulsing, living light which cannot be described in words." (Voices From the Edge of Eternity, 1968)

During Burris Jenkins' 1957 near-death experience, he became aware of "countless beings [who] were in great harmony with a light that was off to my right and all around me."

"The light is indescribable, Jenkins wrote. "It is a light that generates everywhere, yet it is not a light like our sunlight or anything like it. It is a Living Light and all these beings are in harmony and in communication with it."

A confirmed atheist, Jenkins was surprised to find himself acknowledging that "this must be God, the Ultimate Being, only I am not with it. I can't talk to it, communicate with it, and it isn't talking to me."

Confused and disoriented, Jenkins screamed "God help me!" Suddenly, he found himself back in bed.

Was this God, as Burris Jenkins believed? Some of those interviewed by Dr. Moody said yes, others identified it as Jesus or an angel, while some simply referred to it as a "being of light". No doubt one's religious beliefs, or the absence of them, determined their perception of this light.

During an address at the UN, Professor Bruce Greyson told the audience: "When Star Wars came out, many nder's said 'Yes! That's it! It's the Force!'"

This light has a profound effect on all who experience it. One child explained to paediatrician Dr. Melvin Morse that "it's a light that has a lot of good things in it." Another said joyfully: "Life is for living, the light is for later."

Perhaps the most intriguing statement Dr. Morse heard was from a young boy who said "I see pieces of that light everywhere I go now."

Occasionally, this light spoke to them. Whoever or whatever the light was, Moody's research revealed that it occasionally communicated a question.

"What do you have to show me that you've done with your life" one woman reported in 'Life After Life'.

At this point, and perhaps to help each find their answer, the 'light being' provided a rapid, panoramic review of the life they had just lived.

Each person who experienced this review (and few made it this far into the experience) remarked that their entire life flashed before their eyes. In an instant, every experience, action, thought, conversation and emotion was perceived and remembered with absolute clarity, along with the repercussions of their thoughts, words and actions on others.

CHAPTER 18

WHAT HAVE YOU DONE WITH YOUR LIFE?

How often have we heard the expression "my life flashed before my eyes" when someone came close to dying? Here were people confirming that this really did occur.

Dannion Brinkley's life certainly flashed before his eyes. He was clinically dead for more than twenty minutes after he had been struck by lightning during a telephone conversation in 1975.

The electricity entered through his ear, travelled down the length of his body, then exited through his feet. The nails in his shoes welded to those in the floor. When Brinkley lifted out of them and flew across the room, his shoes remained where he'd been standing.

He briefly wondered if an aeroplane had crashed into the house, then watched as his wife tried to resuscitate him. He observed the paramedics arrive, declare him "gone", place him on a stretcher and cover his face with a sheet.

Then he visited a spiritual realm and had a harrowing life review.

"I was faced with the sickening reality that I had been an unpleasant person," Brinkley wrote in his book, 'Saved by the Light' (1994), confessing he had been self-centred, mean and angry throughout his life. He had been a school bully who had grown into an adult bully.

During his life review, Brinkley found himself exchanging places with all the people he had harmed. He felt every punch he had ever thrown, cringed at every insult he had ever used to humiliate others, and experienced every ounce of physical and emotional pain he had caused each person.

Did I dare to keep reading?

Was Dannion Brinkley going to hell?

Was *I* going to hell?

I may not have been the bully that Brinkley confessed to being, but I wasn't perfect. Then again, who was?

I recalled the pamphlet I had been handed in the street once. *"God will ask us to give account of what we have done."*

I shuddered at the implications, then fled to my think-step and began to mentally list all the things I had done or said, or even thought, that would require "giving an account of myself."

I ran out of brain cells before I completed my list!

***

No! No! No! I silently yelled at the night sky. If this is true, then surely we'll all be spending eternity in hell.

Well at least I'd be in good company!

Was there really an angry and petty God sitting on some heavenly throne waiting to condemn us all to eternal hell because we didn't live perfect goody-two-shoes lives?

If God did exist, what kind of ego would this God have that it needed to be worshipped by all?

But wait. Did Dannion Brinkley describe an enraged being condemning him for his dastardly deeds? Or even, for that matter, praising him for any charitable ones? No!

Did he mention a furious God pointing an accusatory finger at him and declaring in a booming voice that he must burn forever in the flames of hell? No!

OK, I told myself. Let's try to be calm and logical about this. Let's consider the possibility that the words: "God will ask us to give account of what we have done" wasn't actually meant as a ploy by religions to make us behave, but an opportunity to review our own failures and successes, just as we might have been encouraged to do by our parents after a day at school.

Were any of us saints? Perhaps we were all just sinners trying our best. How I hoped my Irish grandmother was busy at some heavenly task and wasn't listening to my thoughts!

***

When I found the courage to return to my research, I was relieved to learn that all subjects in Dr. Moody's book insisted that the question "what have you done with your life?" was not asked in condemnation, but simply to make them think about their lives.

One woman pointed out that "there wasn't any accusation by this 'being of light'," and added: "when he came across times when I had been selfish, his attitude was only that I had been learning from them, too."

After hundreds of interviews, Dr. Moody developed a deeper understanding of this form of self-punishment. In 'The Light Beyond' (1988) he wrote:

"...if I see myself doing an unloving act, then immediately I am in the consciousness of the person I did that act to, so I feel their sadness, hurt, and regret. On the other hand, if I do a loving act to someone, then I am immediately in their place and I can feel the kind of happy feelings."

This made perfect sense. How better to understand our faults and failings than to experience their effects on others?

***

If this was our judgement, then it seems it was our own judgement of our own selves, provided for us as an opportunity to understand the repercussions of our words, actions, and probably even our thoughts.

Was that comforting? Or did that make it more terrifying?

***

As usual, further research revealed that this life review certainly did not begin with Dr. Moody's book.

In 'Deathbed Observations by Physicians and Nurses' (1969), I found a comment from a nurse who had experienced a panoramic life review during a near-drowning:

"It appeared before me," she wrote, "as a film depicting the pictures of my own life from the current time (I was in my thirties) down to the days of my earliest recollection when I was two years old."

Over two thousand years earlier, Greek philosopher Pythagorus taught that at the time of death, the soul "sees over and over again its earthly existence, the scenes succeeding one another with startling clearness." (The Supreme Adventure, 1961, and Intimations of Immortality, 1965)

German physicist and philosopher, Gustav Fechner wrote in 'The

Little Book About Life and Death' (originally published in 1836):

"[At death] we shall be able at a glance to take stock of everything that has ever interested us, everything we have stored in our memory. During the moments just before death we already have an inkling of that. As we look back on life, memories return that had seemed completely lost."

"Everything I had ever done passed before me as though it were a flying picture on a screen," George Albert Smith recalled with amazement. "Quickly the vivid retrospect came down to the very time I was standing there. My whole life passed before me." (Your Good Name in The Improvement Era, CLDS, 1947)

Swiss geologist and mountaineer Albert Heim had a similar experience. After surviving a near-death experience as the result of a fall, he wrote (in 1892) that he saw his "whole past take place in many images, as though on a stage at some distance from me. I saw myself as the chief character in the performance... the memory of very tragic experiences I had had was clear but not saddening. I felt no conflict or strife, conflict had been transmuted into love."

Charles John Lambert was a thirteen-year-old lad when he became trapped under a log while playing in a river.

"No human power could describe my condition," Lambert wrote in 1886. "Every action, and even every thought of my life, good, bad and indifferent, was clearly before my comprehension. I could not tell by what process this effect was produced, but I knew that my whole life in detail was before my view with terrible clearness." (A Curious Experience in Drowning, Juvenile Instructor, CLDS, 1886)

As author Leslie Grant Scott lay dying in Ceylon in 1918, she watched her life 'unrolling' to reveal her purpose. She later wrote that her mind had been "unusually active and clear" and that while she viewed the process impersonally, she understood everything.

In 1895 in a series of articles for 'The Present Truth', E. J. Waggoner wrote:

"Those who have come very near death, as by drowning or otherwise, and have been rescued at the last moment, have frequently described the strange action of the mental faculties, by which the events of the past life were brought in review before the mind in an instant of time."

Waggoner then used Admiral Beaufort's experience as an example.

We met Beaufort earlier in this book as the young sailor Francis, who drowned in Portsmouth Harbour in the early part of the nineteenth century and described "a calm feeling of the most perfect tranquillity".

Beaufort's memories of dying did not end there, however. He also experienced a life review:

"Though the senses were thus deadened, not so the mind;" Beaufort wrote, "its activity seemed to be invigorated in a ratio which defies all description — for thought rose after thought with a rapidity of succession that is not only indescribable, but probably inconceivable, by anyone who has not been in a similar situation."

Beaufort continued:

"Thus travelling backwards, every past incident of my life seemed to glance across my recollection in retrograde succession; not however in mere outline, as here stated, but the picture filled up with every minute collateral feature; in short, the whole period of my existence seemed to be placed before me in a kind of panoramic review, and each act of it seemed to be accompanied by a consciousness of right and wrong, or by some reflection on its cause or its consequences; indeed, many trifling events which had been long forgotten then crowded into my imagination, and with the character of recent familiarity."

The eventual publication of Beaufort's near-death experience took a complicated route, and while it may be an exaggeration to suggest it involved a cast of thousands, the process certainly included some of the cream of nineteenth century British society.

When naturalist Dr. W. Hyde Wollaston initially heard of his friend's experience, he had been so fascinated that he urged Beaufort to commit it to paper.

Beaufort obliged, and sent a copy to Wollaston in a letter which also included his reflections on the cause of such phenomenon:

"May not all this be an indication of the almost infinite powers of memory with which we may awaken in another world and thus be compelled to contemplate our past lives? Or might it not in some degree warrant the inference that death is only a change of modification of our existence, in which there is no real pause or interruption?"

Wollaston later shared Beaufort's letter with another close friend, Lady Lavinia Spencer, who described it as "most interesting and extraordinary".

Lady Spencer begged Wollaston for a copy, and he assured her he would provide one. Alas, Wollaston died suddenly (in 1828) before he had a chance to honour this promise.

Having heard about the account from Lady Spencer, Sir Henry Halford was also keen to acquire what he termed "this valuable document".

As physician to King George IV (and prior to that, to George III, and later, to William IV and the young Queen Victoria) Halford wrote to Lady Spencer, pointing out that he was also "...pursuing a peculiar subject to which this very curious statement of facts relative to the human mind while struggling with death, would be of invaluable assistance". (Lady Spencer, in a letter to Sir John Barrow)

Sir Henry Halford strongly urged Lady Spencer to assist in this matter.

Lady Spencer then contacted naval administrator Sir John Barrow and begged him to help her obtain a copy for Sir Halford, which he subsequently did.

Before sending it to Halford, however, Barrow read it himself and was so impressed that he included it in his own book, 'An Autobiographical Memoir of Sir John Barrow' (1847).

Had it not been for Barrow, we may never have known about Beaufort's nde, which made me ponder on how many more had occurred throughout history that were not recorded.

Another admiral, this time intrepid explorer Admiral Richard Byrd, also experienced a life review when carbon monoxide poisoning caused him to have a near-death experience during his Arctic expedition in the late 1920's:

"I saw my whole life pass in review... [and] I realized how wrong my sense of value had been and how I had failed to see that the simple, homely, unpretentious things of life are the most important." (Alone, 1938)

In his 1845 book 'Suspiria De Profundis' (translation: Sighs From the Depths), British author Thomas De Quincey recounted the testimony of a relative (many suspect it was his mother) who almost died when she was nine:

"I was once told by a near relative of mine that having in her childhood fallen into a river, and being on the very verge of death but for the critical assistance which reached her, she saw in a moment her whole life in its minutest incidents, arrayed before her simultaneously as in a mirror."

De Quincey continued: "A mighty theatre expanded within her brain. In a moment, in the twinkling of an eye, every act, every design of her past life, lived again, arraying themselves not as a succession, but as parts of a co-existence. Such light fell upon the whole path of her life backwards into the shades of infancy... [and] poured celestial vision upon the brain."

He adds: "Eventually, but after what lapse of time nobody ever knew, she was saved from death by a farmer, who, riding in some distant lane, had seen her rise to the surface, but not until she had descended within the abyss of death, and looked into its secrets, as far, perhaps, as any human eye can have looked that had permission to return."

As often happens today, the incident De Quincy related was treated with scepticism. However, he pointed out that this experience had "since been confirmed by other experiences essentially the same, reported by other parties in the same circumstances who had never heard of each other."

What a pity he hadn't recorded those as well.

I wondered how anyone could see their "whole life pass in review" when they were probably 'dead' for mere seconds, or at the most, a few minutes.

Then I read the following comment in Moody's 'Reflections on Life After Life' by a woman who was asked how long she was 'there'.

"You could say a minute or you could say ten thousand years. It doesn't make any difference."

That statement certainly confused me until I read another account by a man who had been trapped in an explosion. He floated above his body and watched as another man ran to rescue him. Then he had a review of his entire life and discussed it at length with those on the other side.

When asked how long the review seemed to take, he said it would have to have been at least an hour.

Had it taken an hour for the man to be rescued? Not at all.

On returning to his body, he saw that his rescuer was still heading towards him but was frozen in motion in precisely the same position he had been when the review began.

Wow!

CHAPTER 19

FANTASY FICTION

"Do you believe we survive death?" I blurted out as I peered into the refrigerator. I hadn't completely lost my mind, I was addressing Dr. Simmons while fetching milk for our coffees.

As a result of Dr. Wong's treatments, my mother had continued to make progress. She still suffered occasional stomach upsets, but at least she spent more time out of bed than in it these days.

Doc David still called occasionally, probably because he expected a spectacular relapse when what he believed to be the psychological effects of the homeopathic drops wore off. We never again discussed his insistence that my mother was dying, or his earnest recommendation that she be hospitalised.

When there was no response to my question, I turned to see him observing me with a combination of mirth and bewilderment.

"Survive death?" Just two small words, but he repeated them with such incredulity that I thought he was about to deliver a diagnosis of severe mental illness.

I placed his coffee on the table and sat down. "Well, you don't need to look at me like that!" I chided. "I've been reading about people who had near death experiences and there's some really interesting cases."

David smirked at me over the rim of his coffee cup, then sighed. "Hallucinations of a dying brain!" he said, dismissing them with a wave of his hand.

"But these people aren't dying!" I pointed out. "They're dead! Their hearts have stopped, they aren't breathing. They're literally flat-lining, and they're all saying the same things about what it's like to die! If they were hallucinating, wouldn't they all be having different experiences?"

I expected him to look at me with newfound admiration and beg me to tell him more. How easily we fool ourselves.

"And tell me," he said with a patronising smile, "just what *is* it like to die?"

"Well..." I searched for words that might convince him. "they get out of their body, and they see themselves on the bed, and they hear what the surgeon is saying or see what the nurse is doing and..."

"While they're being resuscitated!" he interrupted. "They've already been returned to consciousness and they think these things happened while they were dead."

"And..." I emphasised with a stern glare, "they go through a tunnel, and there's a light and people meet them, dead relatives or friends or guides, and they feel joy and love and peace, and..."

He leant forward and assumed the expression of a doctor about to deliver a terminal prognosis. "Do you know what happens to the brain when your heart stops beating? It gets starved of oxygen within a very short time. When the brain is starved of oxygen, it does some very strange things. It..."

"Yes!" I interrupted, aware I was almost shouting. "It stops functioning!" I was surprised to notice I was getting angry. "So how can people think and see and hear when their brain isn't even functioning?"

"They can't, once it stops altogether," he agreed, a little too calmly, "but it takes a while to die. Death doesn't happen in a single moment. It's a process. In the meantime, the brain can conjure up all kinds of strange hallucinations. Even this tunnel you mentioned, that's just the vision growing narrower..."

"But if that was the case," I interrupted again, even more impatiently, "then the light they see at the end of that tunnel would get smaller, not larger!"

Then, in a more subdued voice, I added: "Wouldn't it?"

I thought it prudent not to mention that one woman travelled through a tunnel lined with white tiles and a young boy mentioned seeing rainbows inside a noodle!

David drained his coffee cup, smiled again, reached for his bag and stood to leave. "I think" he winked, "you've been reading too much fantasy fiction."

"How much have you read about these near death experiences?" I asked as I accompanied him to the door. "Would you like to borrow one of my books, just to..."

"I can make time for a quick coffee now and then," he smiled in a patronising way, "but I'm afraid I don't have time to read fiction. I'll call in again next month. Bye!"

I smiled politely, closed the door gently behind him, then clenched my fists and pretended to thump the door in an effort to suppress a scream of frustration.

Why was I angry? It was me who still had difficulty embracing the concept of post-mortem survival. I was the one who needed proof, proof, and more proof.

Didn't I?

I had asked for his expert opinion with genuine sincerity, then had chosen to argue against his response. Was it simply because it wasn't the response I had wanted to hear? Had I wanted him to confirm everything I'd read so I could feel more comfortable about accepting it? Was I afraid of losing any hope of being convinced because a doctor had told me it was all nonsense?

***

After a long debate with Dr. David on the back doorstep (as usual, it mattered not at all that he wasn't present during this encounter) I realised my anger was not about whether we did or did not survive death.

I was irritated by the way he arbitrarily dismissed the subject, and me, in the same way he dismissed any contributions I made regarding my mother's health problems or her gradual return to life.

I would encounter this close-minded attitude many times in years to come.

"Do you know anything about Dr. Moody's work?" I would ask the agitated person who scowled at me if I dared to introduce the topic.

"Have you ever talked to anyone who had a near-death experience?" I'd try again, if and when they paused to take a breath.

Alas, it would always be to no avail. If they replied at all, it would be a response similar to Doc David's. In other words, total dismissal, either patronisingly or angrily.

"Of course not!" they would shout or smirk.

"I'm not into all that religious hocus-pocus nonsense" one acquaintance told me.

"Neither am I" I replied, but he was no longer even pretending to listen.

If I was going to dismiss the prospect of an afterlife, I was determined to do it from a place of knowledge.

This was a minor breakthrough for me. It took me one step closer to overcoming my nagging scepticism.

Just one step, you understand. But even the longest journey begins with just one step.

***

Years of exacting research convinced Canadian Professor Ian Currie that visions at the point of death were real and not merely the hallucinations of a dying brain.

Currie won ten scholarships and fellowships during a distinguished academic career in sociology. For many years prior to the publication of 'Life After Life', he had studied personal stories and medical reports of near-death experiences occurring over the past hundred years.

In Currie's own words, he "invited and tested other explanations including hallucinations, self-delusion, delirium and cerebral anoxia or oxygen deprivation."

"Hallucinations are not objectively real," he wrote, describing them as "things that aren't there except in the mind. [Hallucinations] are extremely variable for different people, whereas death experiences are... highly similar, often virtually identical."

He found that many experiences occurred "among people who had no drugs (medication) prior to these events." When he compared the experiences of those who were given medication with those who weren't, he found their accounts did not differ in any discernible way.

The longer he spent researching, the more Currie became convinced that "the inhabiting soul is simply a tenant of the body for as long as that body exists."

Professor Currie worked in collaboration with colleagues in the field of medicine, theology, psychology and geriatrics to prepare and teach courses on death and dying.

"Few people are aware" he wrote, "that death, man's most ancient, mysterious, and relentless adversary, has been studied systematically over the past century by research scientists working in a variety of fields."

Were there such people as research scientists a hundred years ago, I silently asked.

Currie politely ignored me, and I couldn't blame him. His open-minded approach to the subject humbled me sufficiently to ensure that I was ready and willing to sit at the feet of someone wiser and more experienced on the topic than I was.

In his 1978 book, 'You Cannot Die', Currie wrote: "Had only a few death experiences been gathered by one eccentric and presumably deluded researcher," (and hopefully he wasn't referring to Dr. Moody!) "they would be relatively easy to dismiss, or at least ignore. But instead we are confronted with the fact that some or all of the phenomena... have been discovered independently by no fewer than eight researchers... and gathered from hundreds of people of highly diverse religious, educational, and social backgrounds. Their stories are uncannily repetitive."

"These conclusions are stupendous," he stated. "Their implications are awesome. And they are solidly based on scientific research."

"Who are they, these eight researchers?" I asked him excitedly, although I was already resigned to the fact that somehow, it was up to me to find answers to my own questions.

Ian Currie departed this world in 1992. What he described in his book as "one of the best-documented secrets of modern times" is no longer a secret for this fearless academic.

CHAPTER 20

THERE IS A TIME

"...very suddenly a light appeared," Dorothy said after she had been snatched back from the edge of death. "A great Golden Glory that was so dazzling I couldn't look at it." (Stranger Than Life, 1955)

Then a voice Dorothy described as "the sweetest I have ever heard" spoke from the light. It said: "No, Dorothy, I am sorry but it is not time yet. You have more to do down there."

There was only one place for me to go after I read those lines.

***

How many times have we heard the expression "it wasn't their time" when someone had a close call?

Was there a specific time for each of us to die?

Did we get sent back if we tried to jump the queue?

Could we survive anything if it wasn't our time?

Did we beat ourselves up for not doing enough to save a person when they weren't supposed to be saved because it was their time?

The implications of this were mind-boggling!

But why hadn't anyone in Dr. Moody's study suggested "a time to die"?

Or had they?

***

For days after reading Dorothy's comment, a popular 1960's song by The Byrds kept playing in my head, endlessly and maddeningly. Doesn't that just drive you crazy?

To everything, turn, turn, turn,
there is a season, turn, turn, turn,
and a time to every purpose under heaven,
a time to be born, a time to die…

How many 'children of the 60's' knew that the lyrics of this popular song had been adapted by Pete Seeger from the biblical Book of Ecclesiastics?

Certainly not me!

A time to be born, a time to die. This also put me in mind of an ancient parable which was retold as a scene in a 1933 play (Sheppey) by W. Somerset Maugham, and later included in John O'Hara's first novel, 'Appointment in Samarra' (1934).

A merchant in Bagdad sent his servant to market to buy provisions. The servant returned pale and trembling and told his master that he had seen Death.

"She looked at me and made a threatening gesture," he whimpered. "Now lend me your horse and I will ride away from this city and avoid my fate! I will go to Samarra and there Death will not find me."

Outraged that Death should attempt to steal a trusted servant, the merchant lent him the horse and the terrified man left as quickly as he could. The merchant then went to the marketplace and found Death lurking in the crowd.

"Why did you make a threatening gesture to my servant when you saw him this morning?" he asked Death.

"That was not a threatening gesture," Death replied. "It was only a start of surprise. I was astonished to see him in Bagdad, for I had an appointment with him tonight in Samarra."

I could see how this concept would be reassuring. It suggested that regardless of age or circumstance, we don't die prematurely, yet we can't avoid it when our time is up.

Many would argue this point, and rightly so! They might ask: "what about children, what about babies? How can it be their time to die when they have barely even started to live?"

I'm not qualified to answer these questions. I'm still trying to come to terms with the purpose of life and death.

Then again, can any of us truly know why we're born in the first place, why we live, or why we die?

***

It had been four years since I read 'Life After Life', so I spent another intense afternoon re-reading it. I was starting to wear the type off the pages, but I still continued to discover much I had missed on the first and subsequent readings.

One woman Dr. Moody interviewed had died of a heart attack, and while 'out', met her deceased uncle who blocked her path, saying: "Go back. Your work on earth has not been completed. Go back now."

Four years ago, I hadn't even been ready for deceased uncles speaking!

This was a lesson in itself. Did we only see what we expected to see, could we only believe what we already accepted as truth, and did we only notice what we were ready to accept?

In previous readings, I had probably dismissed this woman's statement and assumed her dying and befuddled brain had conjured up a reason for not being welcomed into heaven. Now, as I re-read it again, I was finding other accounts of people who were told it was not their time, or that they still had work to complete.

I returned to my sagging bookshelves and once again, re-read my pre-Moody books.

***

You may remember that earlier in this book we left Kalima walking through Hawaiian villages over a century ago. She was on her way to Pele's Pit but had no idea why she was going there, only that she was being compelled to do so.

Kalima walked through South Point, the promontory where, according to legend, Polynesians first arrived in the islands. It is revered as a sacred place by Hawaiians.

"The barren point was a great village," Kalima said. "I was greeted with happy alohas, then passed on. All through Kau it was the same, and I felt happier every minute."

Eventually, Kalima reached her destination.

"There were some people there, but not so many as at other places. They, too, were happy like the others, but they said: You must go back to your body. You are not to die yet."

She begged to be allowed to stay, but they insisted.

124

"If you do not go willingly," they threatened, "we will make you."

"Over sixty miles I went, weeping," Kalima recalled.

Maori woman Ngakahikatea had also been refused entry. Her ancestors had not wanted her yet and she was told to "go back where you come from until they are ready."

I found another example in the enduring classic, 'Black Elk Speaks' (John G, Neihardt, first published in 1932), in which Black Elk tells the story of his flight into the other world.

This journey was initiated by a ghost dance at Wounded Knee in which participants saw and communicated with dead relatives. Black Elk joined in, hoping he might see his recently deceased father again.

During the dance, Black Elk left his body, later stating that he had flown to a beautiful land where he saw many happy people camping in a great circle.

Then, two men walked towards him and one said: "It is not yet time to see your father, who is happy. You have work to do."

I wondered if I could give any credence to this account, since it appears to have been a mystical experience, not an NDE, but the words were there — "it's not yet time... you have work to do."

Then I came across nineteenth century medium, Mrs. Conant, who died as a result of an overdose of medication which had been incorrectly prescribed by a doctor who was "...at the time, unfortunately, under the influence of stimulants."

In 'The Biography of Mrs. J. Conant' (1873), author Allen Putnam wrote: "When she regained full consciousness, she remembered that she seemed to have been in some beautiful place... here she met the mother who left her in earlier years, and when she wept and begged to be allowed to stay with her, her parent gently but firmly told her that she must return to earth life, that she had yet a mission to perform."

Work to do. A mission to perform. Your work on earth has not been completed.

How eerily close were these phrases?

Years later, a friend in Atlanta, US, heard I was researching NDE's and excitedly told me of a conversation she'd heard in the 1960's when she was a child of about ten.

"The Governor's mother, Mrs. Maddox, was a regular customer of Mom's hairdressing salon," she told me. (Lester Maddox was Governor of Georgia from 1967 until 1971).

"One day after school I was sweeping the floor of the salon and heard her telling my mother that she had died and then came back. My mother was a very spiritual person and they talked at length, and I was so intrigued. I don't remember all she said now, but I do recall her saying that someone told her she had to go back because it wasn't her time yet."

On hearing such a tale in the 1960's, one might be inclined to take it with a grain of salt. Now we can recognize that it fits comfortably within the emerging pattern.

Even more intriguing was my friend's recall of how Mrs. Maddox had been returned: "She said that this person who was with her in heaven turned her around and blew on the back of her neck, and then she was back, and not only back but healed of whatever she had that had killed her!"

Percy Cole didn't have someone "blow him back to earth". He appears to have been offered a choice. As you may recall, Cole's spirit guide, Dorothea, had insisted it was time for him to try returning to his body, but she also added "You can stay here with us if you like."

Clergyman Tucker was also presented with a choice. While a doctor and two others had pronounced him dead, he was having a wonderful time greeting his deceased father and plying him with questions.

In his 1943 autobiography, 'Clerical Errors', Tucker wrote: "Someone behind us called out. What he said was in ideas, not words: if I were to go back at all I must go at once. Until then, the idea that I might go back had not occurred to either of us. I did not want to go back."

In the 1969 academic report, 'Deathbed Observations by Physicians and Nurses', Dr. Karlis Osis' reveals that some revived patients insisted they had been commanded back to life by a voice they heard during their "excursion in the other world."

I wondered what might have happened if these people had dug their heels in and refused to return, or had made a frantic run for it. Was there any place to hide in heaven?

Then I encountered another way souls were prevented from entering the spiritual realms before their time.

"In front of me, in the distance, I could see a grey mist," one of Dr. Moody's research participants recalled, "and I was rushing toward it. It seemed that I just couldn't get there fast enough to satisfy me... yet it wasn't my time to go through the mist."

A mist?

Throughout history, there have been numerous beliefs about the entrance to heaven. For example, the ancient Greeks believed we paid the ferryman to take us across the river Styx, while Christians expected to enter through a gate guarded by St. Peter. But I had never heard of emerging through a mist.

This entrance, it would seem, doubled as a border or boundary that prevented access to those who still had work to do, and it seems it could take many forms. People returned to describe how they had encountered rivers, mountains, doors, fences and even lines in the sand.

As the dying person (or ball of light, as the case may be, who knew?) approached such a boundary, they either knew instinctively, or were told by someone beyond it, that they could not cross it.

"I looked ahead of me, across the field," one woman told Moody, "and I saw a fence. I started moving towards the fence... but I felt myself being drawn back, irresistibly."

Another participant in Moody's research travelled headfirst down a v-shaped trough (another interpretation of the proverbial tunnel?) and described coming to a "beautifully polished door with no knob."

"Lord, here I am" this person said. "If you want me, take me." During the interview, the experiencer added: "Boy, He shot me back so fast it felt like I almost lost my breath!"

I was doubly intrigued by that statement. Did we also have breath in the afterlife?

Would I find any borders or boundaries in my collection of pre-Moody material? Of course!

In St. Bede's story of Drythelm in his eighth-century book, 'An Ecclesiastical History of the English Peoples', Drythelm reported that as his guide led him towards bright light, "we saw before us a tremendous wall... [beyond which] lay a broad and pleasant meadow."

A tremendous wall could certainly be a boundary!

In the late 1920's, Explorer Admiral Richard Byrd also encountered a wall when he died from carbon monoxide poisoning during his Arctic expedition. His struggle to get over it "went on interminably in a half-lighted borderland."

Byrd later wrote in his autobiography, 'Alone': "several times I was nearly across the wall into a field flooded with a golden light but each time I slipped back into a spinning darkness."

Boundaries, it would seem, come in many shapes and sizes, and

Heaven Knows

even a variety of materials. When Maori woman Ngakahikatea approached the Leaping Off Place of Spirits and crouched down to view the entrance to the Underworld, she had encountered a curtain of seaweed.

***

Earlier in this book I used excerpts from an account provided by Dr. Wiltse in 'Human Personality and its Survival of Bodily Death', but I believe readers will be as fascinated as I was with the rest of Wiltse's account, which also describes a boundary, along with instructions from a most unusual source!

You may recall that Dr. Wiltse had been pronounced dead in 1889 after contracting Typhoid Fever.

"How well I feel", he congratulated himself as he passed through the closed door, crossed the porch, descended the steps, then walked down the path and out into the street.

"Only a few minutes ago I was horribly sick and distressed. Then came that change called death, which I have so much dreaded. It is past now, and here I am still a man, alive and thinking, yes, thinking as clearly as ever, and how well I feel; I shall never be sick again. I have no more to die."

Wiltse walked a few steps before losing consciousness again. When he awoke, he found himself on a narrow roadway.

Life was considerably slower in those days, and so, it would seem, was death. Wiltse leisurely wandered along this highway in the sky, pausing often to admire the mountains, trees and river.

Suddenly he noticed three large rocks blocking the road some distance ahead and paused to consider what he should do. Instantly, a large cloud moved into position over his head and he became aware of an awesome presence within it. Thoughts entered his brain which he knew were not his own.

In the re-telling of his experience later, Wiltse confessed he could only translate these thoughts as meaning:

"This is the road to the eternal world. Yonder rocks are the boundary between the two worlds and the two lives. Once you pass them, you can no more return into the body."

The cloud-communication continued:

"If your work was to write the things that have been taught you, waiting for mere chance to publish them, if your work was to talk to private individuals in the privacy of friendship, if this was all, it is done, and you may pass beyond the rocks."

Wiltse was relieved and moved to pass beyond the rocks. Alas, there was more to come.

"If, however, upon consideration you conclude that it shall be to publish as well as to write what you are taught, if it shall be to call together the multitudes and teach them, it is not done and you can return into the body."

Again, here was another element, the nineteenth-century version of the question "what have you done with your life?" and the equivalent of "you must return, you still have work to complete."

Wiltse peeked through an opening between rocks and was greatly impressed by what he saw: "The atmosphere was green and everything seemed cool and quiet and beautiful." He also noted that "beyond the rocks, the roadway, the valley and the mountain range curved gently to the left, thus shutting off the view at a short distance."

All the same, it appeared to be a wonderful world beyond, and Wiltse reasoned: "I have died once and if I go back, soon or late, I must die again. If I stay, someone else will do my work and so the end will be as well and as surely accomplished, and shall I die again? I will not, but now that I am so near I will cross the line and stay."

Again he began to step past the large rock, but as he put his foot across the line, a smaller cloud appeared in front of him and he instantly knew he was going to be stopped. He found himself growing weak and unable to move. Then he lost consciousness.

Dr. Wiltse's experience was published in the St.Louis Medical and Surgical Journal in November 1889, and sworn depositions by five witnesses to his death were also provided.

CHAPTER 21

HEAVENLY TANTRUMS

"After I came back, I cried off and on for about a week because I had to live in this world after seeing that one," a woman confessed to Dr. Moody. "I didn't want to come back."

I was surprised to find so many pre-Moody accounts of people who were told they must return. Even more surprising was the discovery that most who took a glimpse through the veil had not wanted to return. Some even put up a valiant fight to stay.

Sixth century monk, Salvius, was not at all pleased to find himself back in his body. His lifeless corpse had spent a night awaiting burial, but the following morning he found himself awake and back in the physical realms.

"Merciful Lord," he pleaded, "why have you done this to me? Why have you decreed that I should return to this dark place where we dwell on earth?" (The History of the Franks by Gregory of Tours, 6th century, translated by Earnest Brehaut, 1916)

Describing his brief sojourn in heaven to the other monks later, Salvius said a voice had "come out of a luminous cloud and announced: let this man go back into the world."

A cloud? Salvius' experience occurred thirteen hundred years before Dr. Wiltse chanced to chat with a heavenly cloud which told him he must return to complete his work!

Amazing!

"Why have you shown me these things," Salvius begged, "only to take them away from me again [and]... send me back to a worldly existence which has no substance."

130

Apparently, the cloud was not interested in bargaining, so Salvius threw himself flat on the ground and wept."

Arthur E. Yensen also tried to resist when told he must go back after dying in a motoring accident in 1932.

Yensen met a group of loving beings on the other side. He expressed joy at being back in his "real home" and confessed to them that back on earth, he had felt like "a visitor, a misfit and a homesick stranger." (I Died and I Went to Heaven, 1955)

"Your earthly life is not supposed to be happy," one of Yensen's new friends explained. "We call it a miserable preliminary. If you find any joy in it you are just that much ahead."

Then, he was told he must return. "You have more important work to do on earth and you must go back and do it," one of his ethereal companions explained. "When your work on earth is done then you can come back here and stay."

"Back to earth? Oh no, not back to that horrible place!" Yensen begged his companions.

He later wrote: "Like a kid having a tantrum, I kicked and screamed 'let me stay, let me stay.' But all my protesting did no good. I would have stayed, but someone bigger than I was running the universe."

That same "someone bigger who was running the universe" also told Kalima in Hawaii that she must go back to her body. "You are not to die yet," it had said.

"I wish I could have stayed with those happy people." Kalima confessed. "It was cruel to make me come back. My other body was so beautiful, and I was so happy, so happy!"

Once home, Kalima stood beside her body and was repelled. "Was that my body?" she wondered. "What a horrid, loathsome thing it was to me now, since I had seen so many beautiful, happy creatures! Must I go and live in that thing again? No, I would not go into it."

Like others who had begged to stay, Kalima was given no choice, and she returned to that "loathsome thing" she called her body. You may be surprised later to learn how she re-entered it!

Initially, however, not everyone was pleased to be out of "that loathsome thing". In 'Glimpses of the Beyond' (1974), French actor Daniel Gelin recalled how horrified he was in 1971 when he was admitted to a clinic after a heart attack and found himself floating out of his body. He noticed the needle recording his heartbeat was totally still, and he watched the nurse drape a sheet over his face.

He called out in despair, begging someone to save him. No-one heard.

Then, Gelin's deceased parents appeared to him and he began to relax. His mother led him into a fairy garden where his son, Pascal, who had died after just fourteen months of life, was playing happily with other children.

"Tears of joy streamed from my eyes," Gelin recalled, "and a deep warm feeling of happiness flowed through me." Then his mother said: "Go now, Daniel, it's time, life is waiting."

"But what did I want with life now?" Gelin asked himself. "Just as earlier in the clinic I had fought against death with all my might, now I put up a fierce battle against returning to the living. I wanted to stay where I was. I ranted and raved like a madman... all in vain. An inexorable force bore me away."

He let out a final scream, opened his eyes, and knew he was alive once more.

Gelin later mused: "If at times I feel weak or depressed, I think back on the kingdom of the dead. I shut my eyes and the luminous life that was revealed to me comes back as an unforgettable reality."

I found Gelin's account particularly telling, because it suggested these experiences were not hallucinations. How many people who hallucinate during a severe illness later seek comfort by recalling them? How many use words like "unforgettable reality" to describe them?

I was also delighted to find a few near-death experiences hidden within the pages of the 1969 academic report, 'Deathbed Observations by Physicians and Nurses' by Dr. Karlis Osis.

While this report mainly dealt with the process of dying permanently, some patients included in the report had been revived at or after the point of death.

Many of these later admitted trying to resist returning to the body and once back, had asked questions like "why did you bring me back, Doc?" adding that "it was so nice there," or insisting: "I want to go back, let me go back."

Distinguished psychiatrist Carl Jung was another who was profoundly affected by returning to life. His story is one of the more unusual in my collection, and if ever there had ever been an account to challenge my credulity beyond my self-imposed boundaries, his was certainly the one!

You may recall that after his 1944 heart attack, Jung wrote in his memoir, 'Memories, Dreams, Reflections' (1963): "Far below I saw the globe of the earth, bathed in a gloriously blue light."

While gazing in awe at the universe around him, Jung became aware of a nearby temple with an entrance that led into a small antechamber where a Hindu man in a white gown sat silently in lotus posture on a stone bench.

"As I approached the steps leading up to the entrance," Jung recalled, "a strange thing happened. I had the feeling that everything was being sloughed away; everything I aimed at or wished for or thought, the whole phantasmagoria of earthly existence, fell away or was stripped from me..."

"Nevertheless," Jung continued, "something remained: it was as if I now carried along with me everything I had ever experienced or done, everything that had happened around me... it was with me, and I was it... this bundle of what has been and what has been accomplished..."

Was this Jung's version of a life review?

"There was no longer any regret that something had dropped away or been taken away," he wrote. "On the contrary, I had everything that I was, and that was everything."

Approaching the temple, Jung had no doubt he was "... about to enter an illuminated room and would meet there all those people to whom I belong in reality. There I would at last understand... what historical nexus I or my life fitted into. I would know what had been before me, why I had come into being, and where my life was flowing."

Jung had many unanswered questions. "Why had [my life] taken this course? Why had I brought these particular assumptions with me?" He felt sure he would receive answers on entering the temple, for there he would "meet the people who knew the answer to my question about what had been before and what would come after."

Suddenly, an image of his doctor floated before him.

"Aha, this is my doctor, of course, the one who has been treating me." Jung observed. "But now he is coming in his primal form. In life he was an avatar of the temporal embodiment of the primal form, which has existed from the beginning."

I paused again to consider the plausibility of this account. In all the reading I had done to date, I had only read accounts of the dying meeting spirit guides and deceased loved ones during their 'heavenly' experiences. Now, here was Jung not only encountering a Hindu man sitting in lotus position outside a temple, but also a living doctor.

And a floating one at that!

133

The doctor stood before him and in a mute exchange of thought, told him he had "no right to leave the earth and must return."

Jung was profoundly disappointed when he realized he would not be allowed to enter the temple to join the people in whose company he was so certain he belonged.

"Now I must return to the box system again," he thought sadly, "for it seemed to me as if behind the horizon... a three-dimensional world had been artificially built up, in which each person sat by himself in a little box."

Jung had to convince himself once more that life was important.

"Life and the whole world struck me as a prison," he wrote. "I had been so glad to shed it all, and now it had come about that I, along with everyone else, would again be hung up in a box by a thread."

During the three weeks it took Jung to regain his health, the view through his sickbed window of the city and mountains brought him no joy. He described them as being like "a painted curtain with black holes in it, or a tattered sheet of newspaper full of photographs that meant nothing."

"What happens after death," he later wrote, "is so unspeakably glorious that our imagination and feelings do not suffice to form even an approximate conception of it."

Jung initially felt anger towards his doctor for bringing him back, but then he began to intuitively recognize that the doctor would have to die in his stead.

"He has appeared to me in his primal form. When anybody attains this form it means he is going to die, for already he belongs to the greater company."

He tried to discuss this with the doctor, but his words fell on deaf ears.

I wasn't surprised.

Carl Jung was indeed this doctor's last patient. On the day Jung was able to sit up for the first time, his doctor "took to his bed and did not leave it again."

Soon after, the doctor died of Septicemia."

What was I to make of this?

If this account had not been by a world-renowned, scientifically trained and highly respected psychiatrist, and had it not been recounted in his own words, in his own autobiography, I would probably have dismissed it. I had become extremely good at doing so.

If Jung had heard the account second-hand, I suspect he may have been inclined to react in the same way, but having gone through the experience himself he was later able to declare:

"I shall not commit the fashionable stupidity of regarding everything I cannot explain as a fraud."

Was Jung addressing this statement to me personally from across the years?

CHAPTER 22

COMING BACK

The actual process of returning to the body was also fascinating.

One person in Dr. Moody's study reported: "My being seemed to have a small end and a large end, and at the end of my accident, after it had just hung suspended over my head, it came back in. When it left my body, it seemed that the large end left first, but coming back in, the small end seemed to come in first."

Another described being "sucked back" and said "it seemed that the suction started from the head, like I went into the head, I didn't feel that I had any say-so about it at all, not even any time to think about it. I was there, yards away from my body, and all of a sudden, it was over with. I didn't even have time to think I'm being sucked back into my body."

Some had no difficulty with the process of returning. Louis Tucker simply "swung into the darkness again, as a man might swing on a train, thoroughly disgusted that I could not stay, and absolutely certain that it was right for me to go back."

When John Brown died, he stood near the centre of the room. "[I] did not move when others would pass where I stood. They seemed to go right through me and still not interfere with me in the least."

Not sure where to go next, Brown decided he would "... stay with my family until something occurred to call me away; when all at once I was raised by a power, unseen by me, and moved directly over my body... I then lowered down and seemed to soak back into the body which all had pronounced dead."

A Native American Chippewa leader related an intriguing experience in the book, 'Travels in the Central Portion of the Mississippi Valley'

(1825).

Having been shot in a battle, he had watched his warriors mourn him, then he leapt up to follow them as they departed. Although he kept trying to attract their attention, they paid him no heed. Frustrated, he returned to his camp and tried to communicate with his wife. Again he was unsuccessful.

It eventually occurred to him that he had left his body on the field of battle, so he returned in the hope of reclaiming it. He described taking a long journey back to his body and leaping into it through a moving fire. He woke up alive!

While Percy Cole did not have to leap through fire, he did need to struggle to get back. As you may recall, he had to push against the stream of oncoming shadows as he made his way towards the glimmer of tiny light. "When at last I got there," he wrote, "I found myself in bed, with my wife sitting by my side."

Unlike Cole, Dr. Wiltse had returned to his room but not yet to his body. Here he observed his wife and his sister sitting by his bed, weeping. He then came into contact with the arm of a gentleman who was also at his bedside and was surprised to notice that his own arm passed through the other man's without apparent resistance.

Initially, I felt uncomfortable about the prospect of living people walking through dead ones, but Wiltse reached out from the pages to assure me it was not at all a frightening experience: "The situation struck me as humorous," he wrote, and added: "I laughed outright."

Surprised that no-one heard such a hearty laugh, he reasoned that "they are watching what they think is I, but they are mistaken."

He glanced at his body on the bed and noticed how pale he looked. "That is not I. This is I and I am as much alive as ever."

When Wiltse opened his eyes again, he was back in his bed. He looked down at his hands and realised, with regret, that he was also back in his body. "What in the world has happened to me?" he exclaimed in astonishment and disappointment. "Must I die again?"

Others endured a more difficult or painful process during the act of returning, perhaps because their bodies had been damaged.

After his car accident, Arthur E. Yensen recalled: "as I moved back into my body there was a painful prickly feeling all over, similar to a foot waking up, also a crowded feeling as if the real me was having to compress itself to get back into its hateful prison."

"Going back to earth was a sickening experience," Yensen added, "mostly because I thought I was through with it forever."

137

Yensen suffered the same frustration many do today. He tried to tell others what had happened, but their ridicule silenced him for twenty-three years. Eventually, prompted by the few friends who did believe him, he penned his account. His book, 'I Died and I Went to Heaven', was published in 1955, two decades before the worldwide success of 'Life After Life'.

Earl Stowell found himself hovering over the roof of his house for a moment, and in the process even noticed a few damaged shingles that needed attention! Then he sank back into his room and re-entered his body.

"It was painful," Stowell recalled, "and took quite a bit of effort to work myself back into the cold and stiff body... more than a few minutes passed before I could drive the cold out of it." (Biography of William Rufus Rogers Stowell, CLDS, 1893)

The love of a friend brought author Leslie Grant Scott back to life. In 'Dying as a Liberation of Consciousness: Record of a Personal Experience' (1931) she wrote: "From the next room came great, engulfing waves of emotion, the sadness of a childhood companion. My increased sensitiveness made me feel and understand these things with an intensity hitherto unknown to me."

This process of re-entering her physical body was equally difficult for Scott. "The effort to return to my body was accompanied by an almost unimaginable sensation of horror and terror," she wrote. "I had left without the slightest struggle. I returned by an almost superhuman effort of will."

During her slow recovery, Scott felt anger and frustration at being "compressed, caged in a dull stupid prison of flesh." How similar those words were to Jung's: "Life and the whole world struck me as a prison."

Charles John Lambert also described the agony of returning as "fearful." Lambert had left his body while it was pinned underwater by a log. Two friends had located it and dragged it out. "I was then informed that I might return to it." Lambert explained.

"In an instant, almost as quick as thought, I was at the spot where the drowning occurred and saw my body lying on the bank." He watched as his friends worked to get the water to flow from his mouth, and commented: "it looked loathsome to me." He re-entered his body and later described feeling: "as if every sinew of my physical system was being violently torn out."

"What I have described," Lambert later insisted, "was as real as anything could be, and was not imaginary. While my spirit was separate from its earthly tenement I saw and understood all that took place, as afterwards verified by the parties whom I have named." (A Curious Experience in Drowning, CLDS, 1886)

Remember that I suggested you might be amazed to learn how Kalima re-entered her body when she died over a century ago in Hawaii? Well, so intent was she on not occupying what she described as "that horrid, loathsome thing", those accompanying her had no choice but to force her back into her body.

"They took me and pushed me head foremost into the big toe," she explained.

The big toe?

"I struggled and fought," Kalima confessed, "but I could not help myself. When I passed the waist, I seemed to know it was of no use to struggle any more, so went the rest of the way myself. Then my body came to life again."

She moved, took a long breath, and opened her eyes. A few minutes later she said to those gathered around her: "I have something strange to tell you."

Now there was an understatement!

Australian schoolboy Allan Lewis was a little more co-operative than Kalima. He made four attempts to return to his body!

"Oh well," he conceded after his third attempt, "that's the end of me".

'And When I Die, Will I Be Dead' was a 96 page transcript of a radio program broadcast on ABC radio many years earlier. This obscure little paperback began with the testimony of industrial chemist Allan Lewis, who had a near-death experience in 1946 at the age of fourteen.

Due to an earlier bout of Scarlet Fever, Allan had developed a rheumatic heart, and suffered three heart attacks in one day while attending Devonport High School in Tasmania, Australia.

Unaware of the seriousness of his condition, he was taken to the sick room where three teachers gathered around to offer support. Suddenly, the excruciating pain in his chest disappeared and Allan experienced a feeling of great peace.

He could see his body from behind, and a little above, his own head, and from this vantage point he noticed one of the teachers massaging his legs. He tried to get her to stop.

"I'm dead. Don't bother with me, Miss Brown," he said.

She took no notice. He tried to grab her arm, but, as had occurred to Dr. Wiltse, John Brown, Dr. Ritchie and others, Allan's hand went straight through his teacher's arm.

Wondering what he should do next, Allan tried to open the door, but he could not get a grip on the handle. It didn't matter. He floated up to the ceiling and went straight through it, floating back down to the playground where girls were shooting hoops.

He noticed an elderly spirit lady trying to speak to one of them. "It's no good," he told her, "you can't get in touch with them," but she replied: "I've got to tell her. If I don't tell her she'll do the same thing as her mother did."

Allan noticed other spirit beings, but none took any notice of him so he returned to his body. As he did, one of the teachers announced that he now had a pulse. Instantly, the pain returned.

When the doctor arrived, he began to push on Allan's chest. Once again, Allan left his body and found himself looking down at the back of the doctor's head. He heard the words: "I think we've lost him."

"This is the second time," Allan thought philosophically, "I must be dead."

He floated through the window this time. He wandered around the school's tennis court, then through the streets surrounding the school. He saw many other spirits moving about six feet (180 centimetres) above the ground. He was intrigued that they looked "quite human and seemed to be clothed" and also that "they definitely didn't have wings like the typical image of angels."

When he returned to the sick room, he found the doctor still thumping on his chest, so he went back into his body, and again, the pain returned.

The doctor (Allan described him as a 'semi-senile elderly gent') suggested he rest and avoid activity for three weeks, then commented to one of the teachers that "chaps like that don't last much past twenty."

Less than an hour later, and while alone, Allan suffered his third heart attack. This time the pain was so excruciating he wanted to die and have it over.

"The pain went again and a beautiful feeling of peace came over me," Allan told the interviewer. "This was the peace that just passes all understanding. I can't explain it to you because there are no words in my vocabulary that could explain this absolute beautiful peace."

Accepting that he was now permanently dead, Allan returned to the tennis court and approached one of the spirits, explaining that he had just died.

"You're not supposed to be here," she said. "Go back to your body, there'll be someone there to tell you what to do. Just go back to it and wait."

Allan did as ordered and found two men waiting for him. One, Mr. Wright, had been a teacher at the school a few years earlier but had joined the RAAF and was killed in Kenya. Mr. Wright introduced Lucas and explained that he had brought him to "fix your heart up".

The stranger was dressed in ancient clothing and Allan argued that people of his period wouldn't know anything about heart surgery, to which Mr. Wright replied: "You'd be surprised what people have known and what people have forgotten."

A typical fourteen year old even then, Allan asked Lucas if he would also give him a "great big set of muscles so I could be a great athlete," but Lucas said "no, we don't do that kind of stuff. We're only going to repair your heart."

Leaving Lucas to work alone, Allan accompanied Mr. Wright on a "journey of heaven" which they reached by travelling at incredible speed down a bottomless pit.

Here he met up with Eric, a boy from school who had drowned a few years previously, and from conversations with him Allan gained many insights into the purpose of life.

Before he left, Allan received one final instruction: "Don't forget to breathe when you get back into your body."

Suddenly, he was back in the sick room. He noticed his body was blue. He stepped into it and heeded the warning to start breathing, which initially caused considerable pain.

"I was full of things that I was going to do when I got back." Allan said wistfully. "I was going to alter things. I was quite confident that ministers of religion and world leaders would listen to me and do the things that I told them because I could make life on earth so much happier and so much more pleasant."

Alas, it was not to be. After his return to health, Allan tried to discuss his experiences with his scoutmaster, who thought he was being macabre. He tried to talk with his minister, who showed no interest either. He then confided in his mother, but she dismissed him with a wave of her hand and said "oh, don't be silly".

Allan didn't talk about it again for thirty-three years.

In the mid 1970's, Dr. Elisabeth Kubler-Ross came to Australia and Allan happened to see an interview with her on television. When she described a typical near-death experience, he was amazed at how similar they were to his own, and realized for the first time that he wasn't unique.

Aware the doctor had predicted his death by the age of twenty, Allan had avoided marrying, but when he surpassed this mortality expectation by six years he consulted two heart specialists. Both agreed his heart was fine.

He married at the age of twenty-nine, and twenty years later told his story in a radio interview.

"When death comes, I know it may come with a lot of pain" Allan said, "but I do know that at the last few moments there'll be great peace and I'll slip over and it'll be easy."

I wanted to believe him, but seriously, an ancient ghost doctor "fixing" his heart? This was asking too much of me. Perhaps Dr. David had been right after all. Fantasy fiction!

Allan Lewis ended his radio interview with the following advice: "There is nothing to be frightened of. Everybody is born and that is a fairly traumatic experience. Death is nothing to be feared. The only bad thing about death is the grief it leaves behind. The people that stay, they are the people that suffer, not the person that dies.

***

Was that what I was most afraid of, being left behind?

If my mother died, who would share my joys. Who would take pride in my accomplishments?

Who would cry with me over my disappointments and comfort me after my failures?

Who would encourage me to dust myself off and try again?

When the only one you really matter to is gone... do you still matter?

CHAPTER 23

A FATEFUL DAY

During the five years since I first visited Rhonda for a psychic reading, we'd developed a close friendship. She regularly called in for a coffee, and while there would often "pick up" on something I needed to know.

On one occasion, Nikki trotted into the kitchen to greet her, and Rhonda suddenly blurted out "You know what? She's going to protect you from a burglar!"

Nikki was a Cavalier King Charles Spaniel! She would have been more likely to lick a burglar to death!

"A burglar?" I laughed. "Now come on Rhonda, how would a little bitty dog like this protect me from anything bigger than a cockroach?"

"She's going to bark like crazy. He comes over the fence and she sees him and she barks and barks, and you wake up and he gets frightened and runs away."

Nikki had already endeared herself to us days after collecting her from her disinterested previous owner. I had been sitting beside my mother's bed during one of her 'off' evenings when Nikki ran into the room and barked incessantly. My orders to "sit down and be quiet" had no effect.

As I stood up, she ran towards the hall, then stopped at the door to wait for me. Intrigued, I followed her as she led me into the kitchen. Once there, she stood in front of the stove.

I discovered I'd forgotten to turn the gas off and the kettle had almost boiled dry. Nikki faced the gurgling monster bravely as she barked her alarm, turning regularly to ensure I was watching.

She proved her worth many times, but none more so than a few nights after Rhonda's prediction when she leapt from her sleeping place at the foot of my bed and barked loudly at the window, waking me from a deep sleep.

Presuming she'd caught sight of a cat, I tried to pull her away, then noticed a hooded prowler loitering in the front yard. I shouted at him through the open window. He leapt the fence and scurried off down the street.

Score another one for Rhonda. She was uncanny.

***

The progress Mum had made under the care of Dr. Wong had been a great relief to both of us. She now spent most of every day awake! His vega testing, dietary recommendations, nutritional supplements and homeopathic remedies got her back on her feet, but she was still a long way from healthy.

There was nothing more he could do. Her appetite had improved a little, but not greatly, and she still suffered regular bouts of bloating and nausea.

Occasionally, she became so bloated that even district nurses could do nothing for her. An ambulance was the only option, as getting her into the car was awkward even when she felt well.

Once at the hospital (usually in the early hours of the morning) I would sit beside her and hold her hand as she tried to find a comfortable position on the cold, hard trolley. Then I would pace the corridors, sipping bitter coffee from a paper cup as the dawn broke, or munching stale chocolate bars from the slot machine for breakfast.

Then we'd return home. I'd help her into bed, wondering how long it would be before we did it all over again. My only consolation was knowing, each time, that she would be coming home.

Then came the fateful day in July 1993.

"Have you had a burglary here?" Rhonda asked, glancing around the kitchen.

"Rhonda!" I almost spat my coffee out. "Not another burglar! We had someone sneaking around two years ago and Nikki frightened him off, as you predicted. Is that what you're picking up?"

She thought for a moment, then said "No, it's definitely future, and this one gets in! It's not too far away either. Sorry, I'm just warning you so you can take evasive action. Nothing's set in stone, you know. You can change things if you know in advance."

I didn't really want to have this conversation, but I knew it was important. "What can I do?" I asked.

Rhonda shrugged. "Lock all the doors and windows if you go out. It's in the daytime, and it's on a weekday. He's a big man, and he comes in through a small window. I can see him squeezing through it. Not easy, he has big shoulders and the window's narrow."

"Ah well, this house doesn't have any narrow windows." I pointed out. "Look, they're all..."

"Sorry love," she interrupted, "but I can see it as clearly as I see you. I don't explain what I see, I just *say* what I see."

I took another sip of coffee and noticed my hands were shaking. Rhonda had been accurate too many times for me to doubt her.

"And he's writing on the wall." She added. "Probably something dirty. I don't know, I can't see what it is. Just make sure you lock doors and windows if you go out, ok?"

"Ok" I said quietly, and shuddered at the prospect of Mum being in the house if and when an intruder broke in.

She still wasn't ready to go out into the big world. I doubted she would ever be strong enough. Her walking frame was cumbersome, and it was difficult, even painful for her, to get into the car. Facing the stress of people and noise and activity was too much for her to cope with after years of suffering and isolation.

The last time she'd been out of the house was for her mother's funeral two years earlier, and she'd slept soundly for two days afterwards.

However, her slowly improving condition provided more opportunity for me to leave the house and visit my favourite city bookshop occasionally, and I wasn't about to change that because of something Rhonda said. She couldn't be right all the time, I told myself.

All the same, I took care to lock every door and close every window before I left the house a few weeks later.

***

When I arrived home at around 5pm, I vaguely wondered why the plants in hanging baskets on the back veranda had been lifted off their hooks. I didn't dwell on it. Perhaps Mum had been feeling better and had decided to do some re-potting. She loved gardening ("nothing can beat getting your hands in dirt" she would say) and she missed being able to sit on the ground in a garden bed and pull weeds.

As I opened the back door, Nikki greeted me frantically. While she

145

was always enthusiastic, she had never been so happy to see me. The kitchen was a mess. Vegetables and dirty dishes covered the table, spilt gravy stained the stovetop, and worst of all, Nikki had lost control of her bowel, in a most alarming way, all over the floor.

"Mum?" I called out frantically. "Mum, are you there? Mum?"

I searched the rooms, my heart thumping in my throat, my stomach churning.

"There's a note here!" Barry called from the kitchen.

I had met Barry a year earlier when I attended a writing course he was teaching, and he had since become part of our family.

"A note?" I called back, stumbling in an effort to reach the kitchen quickly and understand what was happening.

My mind was in a whirl. My mother was not here! My mother was always here. My mother didn't just go out and leave a note. Other people's mothers and wives and sons did that.

I snatched the note from Barry's hand and tried to comprehend the jumble of words I was reading.

"Your Mum had a fall but she's ok. She's in the Monash hospital. Constable Davies."

"Oh my God. Oh my God. We have to get to the Monash. Oh my God. Come on."

"Wait a minute..." Barry cautioned as he cleaned up Nikki's mess on the kitchen floor.

"NOW! We have to get to the Monash. Now!" I yelled.

"But what about Nikki?" Barry reminded me. "Does she need to be fed? And is there anything you should take? Nightdress, toiletries?"

I was thankful one of us had a cool head. I ran around the house gathering up essentials, took Nikki outside for a few minutes and waited impatiently for her on my back doorstep while I pondered the situation. Then I put her dinner on the floor and assured her we'd be back soon.

When we arrived at the hospital, Mum was still in the emergency room.

"Oh, thank goodness you're here." She greeted me. "I've... er... I've broken my hip. I'm so sorry."

"Don't be sorry!" I leant over to kiss her cheek. "I'm sure you didn't do it on purpose!"

Her face began to crinkle, and tears flowed. I tried to comfort her.

"Hey hey, it's ok. It's ok."

"Can I come home?" She looked at me pleadingly.

"Home?"

Did she seriously believe I could smuggle her out of the emergency room with a broken hip? Perhaps they had given her painkillers and she wasn't thinking clearly.

"Of course you can't come home, silly! You need to stay here until they mend you!"

"No, I mean... after. When they fix my hip." Her tear-filled eyes were still fixed on me.

"Well where else would you be going?"

She sighed deeply and her face relaxed. "Thank you. I thought... well, I thought you might send me to a nursing home."

"Oh Mum! Don't be so damn silly. Of course I wouldn't!" I squeezed her hand and she cried again, this time more from relief.

"Now, tell me what happened." I said.

"I was so stupid. I was cooking a stew and Nikki wanted out, so I went to the back door and unlocked it. She was in such a hurry, you know what she's like, jumping up and trying to get out before the door's open. She got under my feet and I fell against the door."

I listened as she described the pain she felt in her hip as she hit the floor, and the hour or more she spent laying awkwardly against the door while in excruciating pain, unable to move.

"How did the police find out?" I asked, silently beating myself up for not having been there.

"I had that big old cordless phone in my apron pocket," she explained.

Cordless telephones had only recently become available, and I was grateful I had purchased one so she could answer the phone without moving out of her chair or bed. It was a big brick of a thing and needed re-charging every night and I often wondered why I bothered. Now I knew.

"I don't know why I had it in my pocket," she said, "it's so heavy, I always leave it on the table. Then I didn't know who to call. The only number I could remember was the doctor's surgery, so I called that. They phoned the police."

"How did the policeman get in?" I asked.

"Oh that was a real fiasco," she sighed. "The only door not locked was the back one I'd opened for Nikki, and I was up against it. We talked through the door and he said he'd find a way, even if he had to break a window. I told him to try and not do that because you couldn't afford to replace it."

"For heaven sakes, Mum!" I scolded. "You're lying there with a broken hip for hours and you're worried about me having to pay for a window?"

"Well anyway, he didn't have to. The bathroom window wasn't locked so he got in there."

My mind suddenly went into overdrive. The bathroom windows! I had completely forgotten about those. On either side of the cabinet was a small, narrow window, each no wider than half a metre.

"Was he... did he happen to be... um... was he a big man? With big shoulders?" I asked hesitantly.

"Yes, poor man. He had to squeeze through it. He didn't break something, did he?"

"No, no, of course not. But... did he also..." Nah! I dismissed my theory as preposterous.

"Did he what?"

"Did he happen to write on the wall? I know that sounds silly, but did he..."

She thought for a moment. "Well, sort of, I guess. Not the wall. But he had to leave you a note and I had things all over the table, so he leant his notepad against the wall and scribbled on it. Why?"

"Don't worry," I smiled with relief, "I'll tell you about it when you're feeling better!"

Rhonda had been right again! But this time, she had misinterpreted what she'd obviously seen so clearly — a big man squeezing through a narrow window during a weekday, then writing on the wall.

It could have been worse. If she hadn't put the cordless phone in her pocket, the stew would have boiled dry. Who knows what might have happened as she lay propped against the back door waiting for me to arrive home, which had been about four hours after her fall!

Thank heavens for the big man!

***

My mother spent two weeks at the hospital, then a further three months at a rehabilitation hospital where she celebrated her seventieth

148

birthday.

I visited her daily and watched her progress, or rather, her lack of it. Try as they did, the therapists were never able to get her back on her feet. Her muscles were too weak to respond to exercise.

She returned home in a wheelchair in November 1993. Dr. McCann had been right all those years ago when he said she would eventually be wheelchair-bound, but instead of the five years he had predicted, it had taken twenty-five years.

Life would never be the same, for either of us. I needed to become an amateur occupational therapist and district nurse, mastering the technique of safely transferring between chair, toilet, and bed.

From her wheelchair, Mum would never again be able to reach far enough to cook a meal, fill her hot water bottle, or even make herself a cup of tea.

My visits to the outside world were reduced to half hour snatches.

Neither the rehabilitation hospital nor the doctor thought to tell us about subsidized council sitters. It would be more than six months before I discovered this service was available. I knew I could hire nurses, but my enquiries suggested I'd need full-time employment to afford them, which defeated the purpose.

My life began to spin in ever-decreasing circles.

I reviewed my bookshelf one lonely afternoon and was surprised to find it still held a large selection of books about the afterlife. I had put them aside a year earlier. Daily trips to the hospital, then later to the rehabilitation centre had left me little time or energy to research.

Then Mum had returned home and her immediate needs had demanded my full-time attention.

Besides, some accounts I read had challenged my credulity to the point that I was almost afraid to continue.

I had begun my journey as a sceptic. I had been determined to keep an open mind while not allowing myself to be gullible, and I had made considerable progress. The line over which "I must not step" had continued to move until it threatened to become a distant blur on the horizon.

So often during those years I had confessed to heaven that I was very close to believing in it. Then, as if to mock me for being so pompous, it would provide me with details of an ancient ghost "fixing" a schoolboy's heart while he romped in heaven, a Hindu man sitting in the lotus position outside a celestial temple, or a highway in the sky blocked by a talking cloud.

I had turned my attention back to books about health and my shelves were once again bulging. Books about homeopathy, flower essence therapy and a variety of other forms of alternative health were demanding more and more space on the shelves, so I had intended to remove the afterlife books.

Why hadn't I?

It was time to offer them to a local second-hand bookshop. Perhaps someone who needed them more than I did could find comfort in them.

I began to take all my 'death-books' from the shelf and place them in a box.

I paused when I came to Raymond Moody's 'Reflections on Life After Life', the second in his series, and a thin paperback called 'Return From Tomorrow' by Dr. George Ritchie, who had been the catalyst for Moody's research.

I smiled as I remembered that sunny day in a park five years earlier, when a sweet old lady had explained NDE's to me and I had politely written those book titles and Ritchie's name on a paper bag.

***

During time out on the doorstep, I reflected on how much had happened since that day in the park.

Thanks to Dr Wong and the miraculous vega machine, Mum had survived her year from hell.

I had qualified in a variety of healing techniques, passed exams in anatomy and physiology and treated patients in my small study at home.

I had written and conducted a correspondence course on nutrition for pharmacy assistants around Australia, given lectures and taught classes.

I became so immersed in the causes and treatment of allergies, I had been nominated to serve on the committee of the Allergy Association, which unfortunately, I'd had to decline.

"Because of the things you know about healing, you will be asked more of and more of in the future," Rhonda had advised five years earlier.

At the time, I thought that was utter nonsense. What had I known about healing?

"You will begin to realise the potential which you have to give other people the help, the remedies which they need." Bill had added independently.

What remedies?

As with so many accounts I read over the years, I had dismissed these statements at the time. How could I realise a potential I didn't possess?

When the treatments by Dr. Wong came to an end after twelve months, I treated Mum with reflexology, aromatherapy, flower essence therapy, massage, reiki, Bowen therapy, kinesiology and nutrition. She had responded well.

We still had the occasional rush to hospital when her stomach bloated and caused her pain and nausea, but these were becoming less frequent. Her eyes now revealed there was someone at home.

"And so it begins."

It had taken five years of questioning and soul-searching, but now I was sure I knew what the cryptic message had meant. My mother's mysterious illness had served to catapult me into years of study, and now I was on the right path.

"I'm right, aren't I?" I asked deep space.

Silence!

I pushed just a little harder.

"Couldn't you just give me a sign? Please? Just a little one?"

CHAPTER 24

THE DEATH DOCTOR

"I'm not sure I know enough, Jan! I might totally screw up."

I had met up with Jan at a café to discuss her upcoming and extended trip to Fiji, and to my surprise, she also asked me to take over her classes during her absence.

As my Polarity Therapy teacher for a number of years, I respected Jan's opinion. I just didn't agree with it. I had been teaching classes at neighbourhood houses and adult education centres, but the Southern School of Natural Therapies was a school for naturopaths-in-training. These would be serious students who had enrolled with the intention of creating a career for themselves, not merely to pass the time.

Jan dismissed my fears with a shrug. "You know almost as much about the technique as I do. I've taught you well. And besides, you're an excellent teacher."

"Hmmm, thanks." I offered a weak smile. "But I've never taught at such a prestigious place."

"Well, I've already told them you'll do it, so get over it and go get 'em!" she mocked, pretending to punch my arm.

Then the thought hit me: Here it is! It's the sign I asked deep space to give me a few weeks ago. Yes! I'm on the right track. Thank you, universe!

But could I do it? Did I really know enough yet?

Yes, I could do it! I began to relax, content in the knowledge that I had found my true calling. If the universe had as much faith in me as Jan had, there was no doubt this was why I was here.

"By the way," said Jan as she reached into her oversized handbag. "You like reading books about death, don't you?"

I laughed at the incongruity of teaching people health while reading about death. "Well, I used to. And not exactly death," I pointed out. "More specifically the afterlife. Why?"

Jan passed a book across the table. "I've had this one for years and I was having a clean-out. I thought you might find it interesting."

I slumped back in my chair as I looked at the cover of the book.

'On Life After Death' by Elisabeth Kubler-Ross. Hers was a name I had come across so often in my research!

What was the universe playing at? Was it trying to re-ignite my interest in the afterlife, or was I merely the chance benefactor of Jan's spring cleaning?

I chose to suspect the latter. After all, I was about to become a teacher at a prestigious naturopathic college! This was my true calling.

Wasn't it?

***

That evening, I retrieved the book from my handbag and read the back cover. It promised 'in-depth research on life after death'. The cover of Dr. Moody's first book had made a similar claim, although he had freely admitted that what he had done had not constituted a scientific study.

Would Kubler-Ross' work be any different? Probably not.

Was her research based on solid science? Doubtful.

Was it even possible to scientifically study the existence of an afterlife? Highly unlikely.

Then I paused, sighed, conceded defeat and took the book to bed. After all, this was a woman who had haunted me through the pages of other books for five years. Perhaps it was time I learnt more about her. Besides, it was only a thin little paperback containing a few short essays. It was ideal for a ten minute read before settling down to sleep.

Dr. Elisabeth Kubler-Ross catapulted me so rapidly into the next stage of my learning that I emerged from between the pages feeling like a cartoon character that had just been thumped on the head. I was literally seeing stars!

***

"Many people say: Of course, Doctor Ross has seen too many dying patients. Now she starts getting a bit funny."

These were the opening words of 'On Life After Death'. I could relate to them.

This little book, transcripts of three lectures given by Kubler-Ross between 1977 and 1982, truly marked the beginning of my journey of wonder.

Born in Switzerland in 1926, a very young Elisabeth Kubler set out to walk to Poland and Russia after world war 2 to set up first-aid stations, assisting at other aid stations along the way.

In her 'Death Does Not Exist' lecture in 1977, she recalled: "I personally saw the concentration camps. I personally saw trainloads of baby shoes, trainloads of human hair from the victims of concentration camps being taken to Germany to make pillows. When you smell the concentration camps with your own nose, when you see the crematoriums when you are very young like I was... you will never ever be the same again."

On her return to Switzerland she trained as a medical doctor in Zurich where she met and married an American fellow-student, Manny Ross. After moving to the U.S. with him, she accepted residency as a psychiatrist at the Manhattan State Hospital.

Dr. Ross, as she was now known, was horrified at the conditions of this hospital and the treatment the inmates received. She set about making radical changes. By listening closely and showing respect and compassion to these patients, she eventually won their trust. Those who rarely talked, and even some who had not spoken for years, began to open up and share their feelings with her.

At the end of her two-year residency she had succeeded in bringing an end to the most sadistic punishments, and the discharge rate of patients previously considered hopeless was 94 percent.

Dr. Ross then transferred to another hospital. "After a few months on the job," she recalled, "I noticed that many doctors routinely avoided the mention of anything to do with death. Dying patients were treated as badly as my psychiatric patient... they were shunned and abused."

"During my consultations," she added, "I sat on beds, held hands and talked for hours. There was, I learned, not a single dying human being who did not yearn for love, touch or communication."

She listened as the dying verbalized their fears, recalled their joys, and confessed their regrets.

"Tell me what you're going through," she would say to them "it will help me to help other people."

In her lectures years later she would advise students that "the best teachers in the world are dying patients. When you take the time to sit with them, [they] teach you about the stages of dying."

What was considered in those days a radical bedside manner preceded Dr. Ross to the next hospital in Denver in 1963, where she was asked by the University of Colorado to deliver a series of lectures for medical students on the subject of death and dying.

Aware that medical students had little interest in psychiatry, and even less in death, she invited one of her terminally ill patients to the lecture podium. She then encouraged the audience to ask questions about how it felt to face imminent death. This was a resounding success and became the catalyst Dr. Ross needed to begin her life's work.

After she moved to Chicago, Dr. Ross instigated a course at the University of Chicago and began weekly seminars on the treatment of terminally ill patients, reminding these future doctors that the dying needed to talk and deserved to be listened to so they could die with dignity and not merely be dismissed as medical failures.

During one of these early seminars, Dr. Ross did something so controversial that it almost destroyed her reputation.

She brought a woman to the stage who had been declared dead but was resuscitated, and who related that she had floated out of her body and watched the nurse rush out of the room to summon help.

Mrs Schwartz related that from her vantage point above the bed she had observed the doctors frantically working on her and was later able to report which members of the team had wanted to give up. She was even able to repeat a joke one attendant had told in an effort to relieve the tension.

While this was nothing new to Dr. Ross, the reaction of students at the seminar surprised her.

She later wrote: "They all leaped on me because I refused to label the woman's story as hallucination. They all wanted me to give this woman's experience a convenient psychiatric label so they could forget it." (There Is Life After Death by Kenneth L. Woodward, article in McCall's August 1976, page 134)

The cynical reaction by the medical students prompted Dr. Ross to begin an in-depth study of experiences reported by patients who had been resuscitated after having been declared dead.

After documenting hundreds of these reports, she had no doubt there was an afterlife.

After the publication of her first book, 'On Death and Dying' in

1969, Dr. Ross received international recognition and acclaim. This book remained on the US non-fiction bestseller list for over a decade and is still regarded worldwide as the classic work in its field of thanatology. Today, those who need to understand how to best care for a dying loved one are just as likely to have a copy on their bookshelves as the hospice nurse or the psychiatrist.

Even with such glowing accolades, Dr. Ross continued to attract criticism. Her seemingly outlandish statements irritated medical professionals who viewed death as the ultimate enemy, particularly after she stated in a lecture in San Diego in 1977:

"When our cocoon is in such a condition that the pulse and brain waves can no longer be measured and we have become unresponsive, our "butterfly" has already left its cocoon. The medical profession call this a coma, but we are still aware of everything going on in the immediate vicinity and even know what those nearby are thinking."

The medical profession was not impressed.

Dr. Ross stubbornly held her ground, and in 'On Life After Death', reminded us that despite the negative opinion of some, she had been honoured with twenty doctorates for her work with the dying.

What neither of us knew then was that years later she would be inducted into the National Women's Hall of Fame and be named by *Time* as one of the hundred greatest thinkers of the 20th century.

This wasn't an industrial chemist in Tasmania recalling a childhood near-death experience. This was a medically qualified doctor/psychiatrist and internationally recognised expert in the field of death and dying. I was now eager to learn what this ground-breaking doctor had to say.

One line, a few pages into the book, sent my mind spinning: "The dying experience is almost identical to the experience at birth. It is a birth into a different existence, which can be proven quite simply."

Wow!

I closed the book, turned out the light, and snuggled down to sleep, but my brain kept spinning. It was one thing to state that death was a birth into a different existence. It was entirely another matter to prove it.

I switched on the light to read a few more pages.

"At the time of transition" Dr. Ross wrote, "your guides, your guardian angels, people whom you have loved and who have passed on before you, will be there to help you. We have verified this beyond a shadow of a doubt, and I say this as a scientist."

My 'early night and a ten minute read' became a late night and a two hour read! Propped up in bed, eyes straining in the dim glow of my lamp, my enthusiasm for the subject was gradually renewed.

***

When Dr. Ross sat at the bedside of a dying child, she would explain to the child that the human body is like a cocoon, and that it is only a house to live in for a while.

"As soon as the house is in an irreparable condition," she would say, "it will release the butterfly. After the butterfly leaves its material body, you will experience some important things which you simply ought to know in order not to be afraid of death any more."

To Dr. Ross, this was no fairy tale. Throughout the 1960's she had interviewed over five hundred terminally ill patients, sat beside countless numbers who were going through the dying process, and listened intently to the stories of many who had died and been resuscitated.

One case was particularly poignant for her. A twelve-year-old girl had confessed to her father that she had an experience she'd never told anyone. A few years earlier, the girl had been deathly ill. She had left her body and had not wanted to return. As she explained to her father: "I don't want to tell my mummy that there's a nicer home than ours."

She also told her father that she had travelled to the "other side" where she had been lovingly held by her brother.

But she was confused. She didn't have a brother.

Her father was shocked. Her brother had died only a few months before she was born, and neither of her parents had ever mentioned him to her.

In the early 1970's, together with hospital co-worker Reverend Gaines, Dr. Ross began collecting accounts of near-death experiences from around the world.

To be certain the results contained no religious or cultural bias, they collected data from a variety of cultures including Eskimos, Hawaiians and Australian Aboriginals, and from people with various belief systems such as Hindus, Buddhists, Protestants, Catholics, Jews, agnostics and atheists.

Both Ross and Gaines were astounded by the results. The similarities to those they had heard from their own patients could not be ignored.

She shared the results of her worldwide study in her 1977 lectures:

157

"They are all fully aware of shedding their physical body, and death, as we understand it in scientific language, does not really exist."

"There is no time or distance. If we are separated from a loved one [as we are dying] we have only to think of them and we will be wherever they are in an instant. We may try to communicate with those we leave behind, but soon realise they can neither see nor hear us."

"We become aware that departed loved ones are awaiting us on the other side."

"We may travel through a tunnel, pass through a gate, cross a bridge, or travel through something else familiar to us. At the end of this journey, we will be embraced by an indescribably loving light."

"If we are meant to return, we are permitted to see this light only briefly. If this is the end of our earthly journey, however, we will experience understanding without judgement as we stand in the light, and will come to understand that life on earth was nothing more than a school."

"We will be shown our life from the first to last day and will re-experience every thought we had, every deed we did, and every word we spoke. In the light of unconditional love and non-judgement, we will come to understand the consequences resulting from those thoughts, words and deeds, and recognise how many opportunities we missed to grow."

"...many of our patients... are not always grateful when their butterfly is squashed back into the cocoon."

"Not one of the patients who has had an out-of-body experience was ever again afraid to die."

***

In the foreword to Dr. Moody's first book, Dr. Kubler-Ross had written: "This [the contents of 'Life After Life'] very much coincides with my own research... patients have experienced a floating out of their physical bodies associated with a great sense of peace and wholeness. Most were aware of another person who helped them in their transition to another plane of existence. Most were greeted by loved ones who had died before them."

Then she added: "It is enlightening to read Dr. Moody's book at the time when I am ready to put my own research findings on paper."

But she had not done so until much later, had she? She had published books on death prior to 1975, but these were about the process of dying and the five stages of grief, not about out-of-body experiences, tunnels, lights, boundaries, or the reluctance to return to life after a brief romp in heaven.

The afterlife lectures in this book had taken place two years after 'Life After Life's publication. By then, people around the world had become conversant with the elements of the near-death experiences as Dr. Moody had described them.

As much as I tried to resist, that irritating old scepticism briefly nagged at me again. It was time to re-visit my doorstep.

***

Could Kubler-Ross have merely been 'cashing in' on Moody's success? No! That just didn't make sense. This was a world-renowned expert on death and dying.

She had taught in colleges, universities, seminaries, medical schools and hospitals. Why would she and Reverend Gaines, who assisted her in collecting accounts from around the world, risk their reputations by copying someone else's research?

Besides, I had read first-hand accounts by saints and sinners, by admirals and doctors who lived and died long before 1975, as well as by geologists, an industrial chemist, an intrepid explorer and an engineer. These were hardly people who might be prone to flights of fancy.

These people had, to their amazement, left their bodies, travelled through tunnels towards a light, met loved ones, had life reviews and returned, albeit reluctantly, to tell of their experiences.

Most of them were not believed, so what did they have to gain? And all of them, without exception, had their experiences prior to the publication of the breakthrough book that many sceptics insisted was the catalyst for a spate of near-death fantasies.

I was no longer arguing with non-present people on my doorstep. Now I was engaging in full-scale debates with myself.

I needed to find more accounts like the one by the girl who met a brother she didn't even know she had, accounts that could somehow be proven.

I didn't know it then, but such accounts were so common, they even had a name.

CHAPTER 25

VERIDICAL ACCOUNTS

VERIDICAL (Oxford Dictionary definition):

Truthful (of visions, etc), coinciding with realities.

The 'shoe on the ledge' story is a veridical account, but it is an oft-repeated one, and such repetitions can result in minor distortions.

Over the years, this account surfaced again and again in numerous books, but sadly, details often differed with each re-telling. Each time I read a variation, I was alerted to the possibility this had just been another urban myth, particularly as it purportedly occurred in the year immediately following publication of 'Life After Life'.

Years later, however, I watched a documentary in which one of the two major participants in the incident, social worker Kim Clark Sharp, described what happened.

Sharp's first-hand account was also faithfully transcribed and included in Jeffrey Iverson's 1992 book, 'In Search of the Dead', and in 1995, Sharp's own book, 'After the Light' was published. I am therefore able to present the story without embellishment or conjecture.

Kim Clark Sharp was on duty at Harborview Medical on the day in 1976 when 50-year-old Mexican crop-picker, Maria, was brought into the trauma center. Maria had collapsed while visiting Seattle, and had been rushed to the hospital by ambulance.

Three days later, Kim saw the emergency team rush past her office to Maria's bedside, and from the doorway she watched the 'crash' team go into action. Maria's heart had stopped beating. Members of the medical team took turns pounding on her chest, then the paddles were applied and the display monitor eventually registered a blip. Maria was back.

A few hours later, Kim was asked if she would try to calm the patient, as Maria was so agitated the nurses feared she would suffer another cardiac arrest.

What happened next would change Kim's life forever.

"I saw it. I saw it all." Maria insisted, explaining that she had been up at the ceiling watching what was happening. "The doctors and nurses were running around and shouting. They punched my chest. Paper was running out of a machine and made a big pile on the floor. A man pushed something over my face."

"Maria didn't remember seeing me in the doorway," Kim explained, "but I was at a distance from her bed. She had everything else completely right, she knew who was in the room, what the equipment was doing. I didn't believe her. This was at a time when the phrase 'near-death-experience' had not been coined and literature about the subject was not widely available as it is today."

Then Maria said she had been distracted by an object on the third floor of the building, but in a different part of the hospital. She desperately wanted someone to go and find this object, a tennis shoe, that she had seen sitting on an outside window ledge.

In broken English, Maria had explained that "the shoelace of the shoe was caught under the heel," and she begged Kim to find it so she could prove to others that she really had been out of her body and wasn't crazy.

While Kim wanted to believe the patient's story, her rational, academic side refused to accept that it was possible. All the same, she tried to humour Maria by going to the car park and looking up at the hospital.

She saw nothing on any window ledge, so decided to try from inside the building. "I went from room to room." Kim stated. "I started on the east side of the north wing. I saw nothing."

Kim continued her search on the north side. "The windows were narrow and so I had to really press my face against the glass to look down and see the ledge at all. I was thinking I wasn't going to find the shoe."

Kim was four rooms along on the west side of the building when she looked down and saw the shoe! "It was an incredible, jarring experience," she recalled. "I felt my heart go thunk."

Kim tried to rationalise the event to her own satisfaction. She asked herself how Maria could possibly have known about this shoe, but nothing she came up with made any sense.

Maria was hardly likely to have gone to a tall building nearby, gained access to an upstairs office, looked through high-powered binoculars or a telescope and spotted the shoe just in case she had a heart attack and was admitted to that particular hospital.

Alternatively, she could not have disconnected herself from life support after admittance, wandered up to the third floor, pressed her face against the window and noticed the shoe.

Kim decided there was only one logical explanation. Maria had seen the shoe on the ledge while she was dead.

"After I got over my shock," Kim continued, "I reached out the window and pulled the shoe up. I high-tailed it back to the coronary care unit, but I put the shoe behind my back. I walked into the room more calmly than I was really feeling and asked Maria to describe the shoe again. For the first time, I asked what colour it was."

Maria replied immediately that it was blue! Then Kim again asked about the shoe's appearance. Maria again described the shoelace caught under the heel, and stated that the shoe was well worn and scuffed on the left side where the little toe would go.

"And then, rather dramatically, I pulled the shoe from behind my back." Kim related, adding that it was precisely as Maria had described it.

"She was elated and so grateful. We were just swept away by the emotion of it and embraced in sheer joy. I had no choice but to believe that this woman, by all accounts dead, had been out of her body that was no longer functioning. Right then my whole perspective about life and death shifted. Maria was really my great teacher." (direct quotes from: In Search of the Dead, and After The Light)

Kim Clark Sharp later became the leader of the Seattle branch of the International Association of Near Death Experiences (IANDS) and has researched many NDE's since that first 'eureka' moment.

While 'the shoe on the ledge' account has been reported in numerous books, it has a lesser known parallel with one that occurred forty-six years earlier, in 1930, which was carefully investigated in 1961 and later included in the Journal of Scientific Exploration (vol.12, no.3, 1998) with the catchy title: 'Do Any Near-Death Experiences Provide Evidence for the survival of Human Personality After Death?' by Emily Williams Cook, Dr. Bruce Greyson and Dr. Ian Stevenson.

Mrs. Linda McKnight, in agony due to a gall bladder attack, entered hospital in the early hours of a February morning in 1930. She was immediately put into bed against an inner wall and heavily sedated until she could undergo an operation. She slept soundly until she was wheeled to the operating room.

Although still in considerable pain the following day, Linda, was doing as well as could be expected, but soon became "aware of a sensation of a deep inner cold, and everything began to grow dark." She drifted off into oblivion.

Suddenly, she felt as though: "someone had turned on a flood light and I glowed in its warmth." Her first thought was "no pain, wonderful, I'm free, I can go where I please!" She chose to go to the window of her room, which was not near her bed, and from here she viewed the street four stories down.

She observed the doctor urgently administering heart stimulants by hypodermic, but the Linda at the window was not particularly interested until she was distracted by the arrival of her husband.

"It's too late, sir," the doctor told him. Mr. McKnight leant over her body and said sadly: "Linda, why do you leave us?"

"I turned back." Linda recalled. "I remember thinking it odd he was bowed over a figure on the bed instead of looking at me."

Dr. Wiltse had made the same observation more than forty years earlier when he said "they are watching what they think is I, but they are mistaken."

Linda observed the actions and heard conversations between the doctor, her husband and the nurses, and this helped her come to the realisation that the figure on the bed was her own.

"As if someone snapped a rubber band," she stated, "I was jerked [back]... into cold, into blackness, into oblivion. Then there I was in bed with the pain again and people standing around."

Later, Linda felt a need to prove this experience had really occurred. "I remembered seeing a Christmas tree on the balcony below," she recalled, (and remember, this was February!) "and a whole area of sheets flapping in the wind."

She asked the nurse to look, but quickly added: "Don't tell me. Let me tell you. There's a Christmas tree on the balcony below." She also described the flapping sheets.

The nurse had to open the window and lean out to see these, but was able to confirm both the tree and the drying area of the sheets, just as Linda had described them.

"Then I knew I had died and came back again." Linda said.

Jean Morrow also related a similar experience that had occurred to her in 1956 during the birth of her first child, and her account was also included in the Journal of Scientific Exploration.

With her blood pressure dropping alarmingly as a result of blood loss, she heard the words "Oh my God, we're losing her!"

"I was out of body at once and on the ceiling of the operating room looking down, watching them working on a body." Jean recalled. "I knew I wasn't dead, it took a while to recognise the person I was viewing was me!"

Then she found herself hovering over her mother in the waiting room. Jean was astounded to see that her mother was smoking.

"My Mom doesn't smoke," she insisted later.

Jean then moved through a dark tunnel toward an extremely bright light, met her deceased grandmother, and reviewed her life before being resuscitated.

When Jean mentioned to her mother later that she had seen her smoking, her mother was amazed and admitted that while waiting, she had "tried one or two because she was so nervous."

Another veridical account, that of Mr. W. A. Laufmann, had originally been included in a book with the dubious title, 'The Phenomena of Astral Projection' (1951) by Sylvan Muldoon and Hereward Carrington.

A travelling salesman, Mr. Laufmann was out-of-town when he developed a grave illness and was immediately hospitalised. At this time he became conscious of something like a fleecy ball releasing itself from his physical form.

"I was standing in the middle of the room," he stated, "and distinctly saw my dead body lying upon the bed... I started to leave the room and met one of the physicians and was surprised that he said nothing to me, but since he made no effort to stop me I walked out into the street where I met an acquaintance of mine, Mr. Milton Blose."

What Laufmann later told the interviewers reminded me again of Dr. Ritchie who had described approaching a man in the street who walked right through him.

"I tried to greet Mr. Blose by hitting him on the back," Laufmann explained, "but my arm went through him... it was impossible for me to attract his attention."

Laufmann watched his friend cross the street and look at a miniature ferris wheel on display in a shop window.

Blose was later able to confirm that he was in that town on that day and had, indeed, paused to look at a miniature ferris wheel in a shop window.

Then I read an account that totally un-nerved me! This one appeared in the London Sunday Express on May 26, 1935.

In 1911, sixteen-year-old W. Martin was walking past a wall in a street in Liverpool, England. Due to a sudden gust of wind, the wall fell and he was hit on the head by a huge copingstone.

People in the street rushed to his aid and managed to remove the stone. Someone ran to get a doctor, but all felt there was no hope for the young chap.

"Now all this time," Martin later stated, "it appeared as though I was disembodied from the form lying on the ground and suspended in mid-air in the centre of the group and could hear everything that was said."

Aware that his family would be devastated by his death, he felt a strong urge to be with his mother. "Instantly I was at home and father and mother were just sitting down to their midday meal."

He recalled his mother sitting bolt upright in her chair as he entered the room, saying "Bert, something has happened to our boy!" Shortly afterwards, a telegram arrived advising them of the incident, and they rushed out to catch the next train to be with him.

Martin remained invisibly with his parents on the train until he suddenly found himself in a strange bedroom where a woman he recognised as neighbour Mrs. Wilson had just given birth.

The doctor was holding the infant in his hands when Martin became aware of "... an almost irresistible impulse to press my face through the back of the baby's head."

"It looks as though we have lost them both," the doctor announced, and again Martin "... felt the urge to take the baby's place in order to show him he was wrong, but the thought of my mother crying turned my thoughts in her direction."

He then observed himself in bed. His mother was indeed crying as she sat beside him, and he longed to comfort her.

"...and the realisation came that I ought to do the same thing as I felt impelled to do in the case of the baby," Martin reasoned, "and climb into the body in the bed. At last I succeeded, and the effort caused the real me to sit up in bed fully conscious."

Martin amazed his parents by repeating almost word for word some of their conversations, both at home and while on the train. His mother

165

remarked that when some people came close to death, she supposed they were gifted with second sight.

A few weeks later, Martin pointed out that he had also been close to birth as well, and told them that their neighbour Mrs. Wilson had a baby that day but that "it was dead because I would not get into its body."

The family subsequently learned that Mrs. Wilson died on the same day as the accident, after delivering a stillborn girl.

"I am convinced," young Martin reflected 24 years later, "that if I had willed myself into that baby's body, today I would be a Miss Wilson instead of still being W. Martin."

There was no way of verifying or disproving this old newspaper account, so I filed it away as a strange, interesting but dubious story.

CHAPTER 26

WHEN I VISITED THE HEAVENLY FATHER

Katie's near-death account could certainly be called veridical. "That's the one with the beard," she told her mother.

Katie was seven years old in 1982 when she was pulled from a swimming pool. No-one knew how she got there, or even how long she had been underwater. She was not breathing and was rushed to a nearby hospital where a young paediatrician, Dr. Melvin Morse, attended her. Based on the report by the ambulance personnel, she had been clinically dead for at least fifteen minutes. Probably more.

Fifteen minutes! Clinically dead.

A CAT scan revealed massive swelling to Katie's brain. With no gag reflex and an artificial lung machine employed to breathe for her, no-one expected her to survive, least of all Dr. Morse.

Remarkably, Katie made a full recovery within three days. Even more remarkably, she was able to recall a number of events that had occurred throughout the period of her 'death'.

On meeting Dr. Morse for the first time a few weeks later, she told her mother: "That's the one with the beard. First there was this tall doctor who didn't have a beard, and then he came in."

Morse confirmed that a "man without a beard" had attended Katie initially, and agreed that subsequent statements made by Katie were also uncannily accurate.

"First I was in the big room, then they moved me to a smaller room where they did x-rays on me," Katie said, adding that there was "a tube down my nose".

This statement surprised Dr. Morse. Intubations were normally done orally, but Katie had indeed been given a nasal intubation.

Interested in finding out more about the reason for her drowning in case she had suffered an epileptic seizure or blackout by the pool, Morse asked her an open-ended question. "What do you remember about being in the swimming pool?"

Katie's answer stunned him. "Do you mean when I visited the Heavenly Father?"

"That's a good place to start," Morse replied as calmly as he could manage, as yet unaware that the next hour would change his life dramatically.

In 1989, talk show host Phil Donahue devoted an entire show to near-death experiences, which, he announced, "is a subject that's getting a lot of press lately." Katie, whose real name we then discovered was Kristle Merzlock, was among the group of five experiencers invited to share their stories. Drs. Moody and Morse were also present.

Kristle was now 14, and shyly described her experience for the TV cameras: "I got into this darkness, I didn't know where it was, and I heard six sounds, noises, and they scared me, then I saw this light and this woman came out.

Seven years earlier, during her interview with Dr. Morse, Kristle had also described a tunnel opening up. Although this is not mentioned in the television interview, most experiencers report that the light appears at the end of the tunnel, so this is consistent with her original account.

"She said 'my name is Elizabeth and I will help you.'" Kristle continued. "And she brought me into this light, to heaven."

Donahue asked if she knew it was heaven. "Yeah, I had a feeling it was and I saw my body, they had me in the operating room and I saw them sticking things up my nose so I could breathe, and I didn't like it. But I met some of my relatives and they talked with me."

Donahue had four other experiencers and two doctors to interview on a fifty-minute show, so Kristle's segment was necessarily brief. Unfortunately, she did not have an opportunity to reveal who else she met in 'heaven' but in her initial discussion with Dr. Morse a few days after her near-drowning, Kristle had announced: "I met Jesus and the Heavenly Father."

She had also revealed that she met her grandfather, along with two young boys called Andy and Mark who played with her and introduced her to many more people.

"Andy and Mark were "souls waiting to be born," Katie told Morse.

On hearing her story, Morse had consulted the intensive care nurse who had been on duty when Kristle woke up. The nurse told him that the first words the young patient said after regaining consciousness were: "Where are Mark and Andy?"

During the television show seven years after her accident, Kristle responded to Donahue's question about returning to her body: "Well, they asked me if I wanted to return, I said no. I liked it!" she giggled. "And then they asked me, you know, I was seven, and they asked me if I wanted to be with my mother, and I said yes. And then after that I went and visited some more with these people, and then Elizabeth said it was time to go and so I walked a little way, and then I walked back and said 'I don't know how to go' and then she said goodbye and that's the last I remember of it."

In Dr. Morse's book, 'Closer to the Light: Learning From Near Death Experiences of Children', (which of course I immediately ordered at my local bookshop!) Morse wrote that Kristle (referred to as 'Katie' in the book) had vwandered through her house while she was 'dead', watched her sister combing the hair of her Barbie doll, saw her brother playing with his GI Joe figurine, and observed her mother preparing a meal of roast chicken and rice.

Her shocked parents had been able to confirm that this scenario occurred precisely as she had described.

Morse also quizzed her parents about their religious beliefs, but they insisted no-one in the family would have said anything about death to her that would have created such images in her subconscious. Perplexed, he consulted the medical literature, but found nothing of consequence on the subject.

Melvin L Morse, MD FAAP, had graduated with honours from George Washington University School of Medicine with post-graduate training in Neuroscience and a fellowship in Behavioural Paediatrics.

He became an Associate Professor of Paediatrics at the University of Washington, and was honoured by Best Doctors from 1996 to 2006 as being one of the best Paediatricians in America.

During his career, Dr. Morse obtained a two-year fellowship in Haematology/Oncology to study brain tumours and leukaemia at Seattle Children's Hospital. He helped found the Paediatric Interim Care Centre (a nationally acclaimed centre for the treatment of Cocaine Addicted Infants), and the Autism Spectrum Research Clinic in Renton, Washington.

Even with all that experience behind him, Dr. Morse had never encountered anything like this!

Although Moody's ground-breaking book had been published a few years earlier, most doctors had either ignored it or had not even heard of it.

Dr. Morse fell into the latter category, but information on the subject soon found its way into his hands.

He was fascinated to learn that many others had survived a close call with death and had described travelling through tunnels and meeting deceased relatives. Most had also confessed their reluctance to return.

"At time of death," Morse later explained on the popular internet podcast, Coast2Coast, "the brain should be conserving energy by shutting down and not doing anything, but instead it's having complex thoughts about God, the nature of life, and having a life review!"

This realisation led Dr. Morse to enthusiastically respond to the challenge Moody had issued in 'Life After Life', that if anyone researched the topic with an open mind, they would be convinced of the reality of near-death experiences.

He designed a study, then discussed it with various medical colleagues. Most merely scoffed and insisted the topic should not be dignified by scientific investigation.

Some even suggested it was more suited to supermarket tabloids next to stories about bigfoot and alien abductions. The head of psychiatry told him: "Mel, children don't have near-death experiences."

The nurses, however, told a very different story. Many of them confided to Morse that they had heard similar accounts from patients. This was precisely the catalyst Dr. Morse needed to throw himself into further research.

I doubt that Dr. Morse sat on his back doorstep when he asked the universe: "Does a person need to be near death to have a near-death experience?" If he did, then he didn't wait for the universe to conveniently provide an answer. Instead, he enlisted the expertise of an anaesthetist, neurologist, psychiatrist and psychologist and designed a study to be conducted at the Seattle Children's Hospital.

As their control group, they chose 121 children who were critically ill but had not been close to death. Many of these children had been heavily medicated during their illnesses.

He then combed through ten years of hospital records and found twelve children who had literally looked death squarely in the face.

Dr. Morse thoroughly reviewed medical records of all patients involved, carefully documenting the drugs they were taking, the anaesthesia used, the amount of oxygen in their blood and the results of various laboratory tests.

He also checked that all children in both groups had been intubated or attached to an artificial lung machine to ensure their experiences were not caused by lack of oxygen in the blood.

After hundreds of hours of research and questioning, Dr. Morse had his answers.

As Dr. Moody had found when questioning adults, children who experienced an NDE also had difficulty describing what they experienced, and would begin with statements like "well, I kind of remember a really funny thing that I can't exactly tell you."

Most confessed they had not told anyone, including their parents, doctors or nurses, about this puzzling experience.

One eleven-year-old boy Dr. Morse encountered had a cardiac arrest while waiting in the lobby. Doctors gave him mouth-to-mouth resuscitation and heart massage and he was rushed into intensive care. After more than twenty minutes without a heartbeat, one of the nurses, believing their attempts were useless, lamented "I wish we didn't have to do this."

The cardioversion paddles were employed and sent an electrical current through his lifeless body.

The boy opened his eyes. His first words were: "That was weird. You sucked me back into my body!" He then lost consciousness again.

Seven years later, Morse interviewed him. The boy was now a young man of eighteen.

"Well, if you promise not to laugh," he cautioned, "I'll tell you what I remember. I still remember it as if it were yesterday."

Dr. Morse assured him that he would certainly not laugh.

"I heard a buzzing sound in my ears," he began.

During my research, I had occasionally come across other references to "unusual auditory sensations" that occurred while leaving the body.

Some of Dr. Moody's research participants mentioned they had found this annoying, describing a buzzing, ringing or whistling sound. Others had heard it as a roaring, banging or clicking, while some were fortunate to hear more pleasant sounds.

One man who had been pronounced dead on arrival at the hospital said he heard "what seemed to be bells tinkling, a long way off as if drifting through the wind," adding that "they sounded like Japanese wind bells."

A woman told Moody that at the moment she collapsed, she began to hear "a majestic, really beautiful sort of music."

 How many more times would I disregard one comment, only to find it echoed time and again in later accounts?

But, back to this young man's story:

"The next thing I knew," he told Dr. Morse, "I was in a room, crouched in a corner of the ceiling. I could see my body below me... because it was lit up with a light, like there was a light bulb inside me. I could see the doctors and nurses working on me. My doctor was there and so was Sandy, one of the nurses. I heard Sandy say 'I wish we didn't have to do this.' I wondered what they were doing... I heard the doctor say 'Stand back' and then he pushed a button on one of the paddles. Suddenly, I was back inside my body. One minute I was looking down at my face. I could see the tops of the doctors' heads. After he pushed that button, I was suddenly looking into a doctor's face. Man, that hurt." (Closer to the Light, Melvin Morse, MD, 1990)

When asked by Dr. Morse about his prior knowledge of NDE's, the teenager confessed that he had never heard of them. He preferred reading comics to books, and rarely watched television. He insisted that he had told no-one about this experience because "they would probably think I was crazy."

While he had dismissed his experience as a dream, he accurately described his own resuscitation, was able to describe the positions and colours of the instruments around the room, the gender of the attending physicians, and even what they had said during this frantic procedure.

Dr. Morse also observed that this boy was not typical of most teenagers. "I don't feel like partying and drinking as much as my friends do, or doing a lot of stupid stuff," he revealed. "I know there is a better reason for living."

Another child in Dr. Morse's study who seemed mature beyond his years was Cory, who developed leukaemia at the age of three and was dying by the time he reached seven.

After many close calls with death, Cory was sent home to die. At home, he comforted his mother when he said: "Don't worry about my leukemia. I have been to the crystal castle and have talked with God."

Cory then described regularly travelling up a beam of light to heaven. Once there, he explained, he crossed a moat on a rainbow bridge and visited a crystal castle where he met and spoke to many people.

While this might simply sound like a fantastic dream, Cory provided evidence of his celestial travels. He met one of his mother's old high school boyfriends there!

Although Cory's mother was aware that her high school beau had been crippled in an automobile accident long after they left school, she had not seen him for many years, and her son knew nothing about him.

"Don't worry now, Mom," Cory announced, "he said to tell you he can walk now."

Calls to friends later confirmed that his mother's old boyfriend had died on the day Cory spoke of seeing him in the crystal castle.

During his heavenly visits, Cory also met most of the nine children who started chemotherapy on the same day he did, some even before their death had been known by him.

One surprising NDE emerged when an elderly man accompanied his grandson to Dr. Morse's office prior to the boy's tonsillectomy. While Morse was describing the operation to the boy in terms he could understand (and no doubt promising lots of ice-cream for a few days after the operation) the grandfather was sitting quietly at the back of the room.

"I thought he was dozing," Dr. Morse stated in an interview, "when suddenly he looked up and said: "You didn't tell him about the tunnel.""

Dr. Morse's attention immediately switched from grandson to grandfather. Unfortunately, the elderly gentleman chose not to reveal the particulars of the experience. As most operations to remove tonsils usually occur during childhood, we can only presume that the elderly gent's experience occurred long before the publication of 'Life After Life'.

***

The results of Dr. Morse's Seattle study revealed that none of the 121 patients in the control group (those who survived a serious illness but were not near death) recalled anything even remotely resembling a near-death experience. Three had scary hallucinations of monsters, but none experienced out-of-body states, tunnels, lights, or encountered deceased friends.

Meanwhile, eight of the twelve survivors of cardiac arrest clearly recalled at least one NDE element such as being out of their bodies, travelling up a tunnel, seeing a light, visiting with people who had died, encountering a being of light or having a life review.

Dr. Morse's study was published in the American Journal of

Diseases of Children in 1986 and provided strong evidence that the near death experience is not the result of medication, sleep deprivation, lack of oxygen, fear, bad dreams, or subconscious awareness during surgery.

I was amazed to learn that a doctor other than Moody and Kubler-Ross had taken near-death experiences seriously enough to conduct research on them.

Why hadn't I heard about Dr. Morse's study? Had it only been reported in academic journals?

Why hadn't there been newspaper reports about it?

Why hadn't newsreaders announced the exciting news on TV?

Had any other doctors taken NDE's seriously?

How much I was yet to learn!

CHAPTER 27

THEY WOULD LIKE TO MAKE CONTACT

I knocked on Murielle's door. Bill greeted me politely and led me to his reading room.

I had visited Murielle's mediumistic brother-in-law a few times over the past decade, but there had been no earth-shattering revelations, no verifiable information, nothing I could not dismiss as a generalisation or vague possibility.

Why had I returned? Believe me, I asked myself the same question.

Although Bill's first reading had brought through startling information about a new spirit guide (my flying matron, as I flippantly dubbed her) and my psychic friend Rhonda had backed it up with almost identical wording, I was still in two minds.

If communication was genuinely possible, then surely this would confirm that life continued after death.

Rhonda had made various predictions during our years of friendship, predictions that had been uncannily accurate, but was she communicating with a discarnate entity, or were her predictions simply due to an uncanny psychic knack she had of seeing into the future?

Such a prospect was sufficiently stunning, but I would deal with that, I decided, at some other time.

Bill, on the other hand, was not a psychic. He was a medium. He didn't make predictions, he simply claimed the ability to communicate with the departed. A gentle, sincere man in his late 70's, he had a kindly, teddy bear face and spoke with a broad Scottish brogue.

During my second reading, he told me that my maternal grandmother, Nan, was saying how happy she was on the other side, and that she was speaking of the places she had travelled to since her passing, places she could never have visited when she was alive.

That was nice. I might have been happy for her, if only I could believe it really was her. As far as I knew, Nan had never harboured a desire to travel. I'd have been far more impressed if she had commented on the poem I'd read at her funeral, or joked about how she had dimmed the lights in our lounge room later that day.

During another sitting, my old English teacher came forward and promised to continue helping me with my writing projects.

It was true that Miss Holmes had always been most encouraging about my writing during my schooldays, and I had to admit that without referring to her by name, Bill had described her accurately: very thin, grey hair tied back in a bun, glasses perched on the end of her nose. Then again, didn't everyone have at least one teacher who looked like that in the 1960's?

Besides, I had done little writing since I'd left school over thirty years earlier, so I had to wonder why she was still hanging around.

On one occasion, my father's mother announced that she had become a close friend of author Edith Sitwell. I wondered what Nora could possibly have in common with a famous and eccentric English author, other than the fact that my deceased Irish grandmother had been mildly eccentric herself.

This was Bill's last chance. In an effort to assure myself he wasn't simply reading my mind (which, like Rhonda's ability to successfully predict future events, would be an amazing feat in itself) I needed to hear something I didn't know, something that could subsequently be verified.

For twenty minutes I listened to loving messages and calm encouragement from those who claimed to be deceased relatives. No names were provided, merely relationships explained: your father's mother, a brother of your grandfather who says he served in the great war, and so on.

My eyes began to glaze over and I wondered if I would seem rude if I brought this fiasco to a premature end.

Then, Bill paused for a few moments, listening intently. Suddenly, he broke the silence. "Where your father's concerned, you've been separated for a long time and there's been little contact between you and him."

It wasn't a question. Bill rarely asked questions.

Had I indicated, at any time during my previous visits, that I had not seen my father for over thirty years? No. Other than one obscure reference to my father's mother, he had not been mentioned prior to this announcement.

Aware that accomplished impostors could glean information in a number of ways such as body language, facial expressions, answers to previous questions, I carefully remained poker-faced.

"His mother has popped in again," Bill explained. "She is saying: 'that was one of the things that helped me understand how cruel people can be to each other. I had enough of it during my own life and I can empathise and sympathise with your mother.'"

Was it my imagination, or was Bill's broad Scottish accent becoming a lilting Irish brogue reminiscent of my grandmother's?

"Now," Bill continued, "his father is also here and he's saying that if you're interested, they — your father's parents — would like a contact to be made between you and your father. You need not do anything about it. They'll work on it. If they can bring a meeting about, would this be acceptable to you?"

I nodded politely. "Certainly," I said, aware that no such meeting would ever take place. My father and I spoke on the phone occasionally. Very occasionally, very briefly, and only when I initiated it. The prospect of my paternal grandparents setting up such a meeting was nothing short of ludicrous.

I had no choice but to accept that communication between Bill and the 'other side' was nonsense. Perhaps, I considered again, that was because there was no 'other side'. Or, Bill was a fraud. Had I continued to visit him every few years for this moment, to catch him out, expose him? Well, I had finally achieved it.

Victory to me! Why did I also feel betrayed and disappointed? It didn't matter. Best to know the truth.

"They are definitely trying to get you and him together," he insisted as I stood to leave, "because it would be of tremendous advantage for him. They are putting these ideas in his mind. They feel it would be very helpful for him to have contact with you, because of things that are scheduled to happen to him."

I didn't pause to question what these 'things' were. "Wonderful." I smiled weakly and shook his hand. "Thank you Bill. See you next year."

I knew I would ever see Bill or any other medium again.

***

"G'day kiddo!"

The voice on the other end of the phone line was familiar and strange at the same time. I had spoken to my father twice a year when I called him on his birthday and father's day.

"Well, er... um, hello stranger. What can I do for you?" I asked hesitantly.

It had been less than a month since my reading with Bill. Although I held onto a thin hope that his final prediction would come true, I could not imagine it ever happening.

"Net tells me you do Bowen therapy!"

Lynette, his sister's daughter, was a massage therapist. While we shared a common interest in alternative therapies, Lynette and I rarely communicated, so I was doubly surprised she even knew I had trained in Bowen.

"Um... yes. I do."

"Well..." He cleared his throat and I realised this wasn't easy for him. "She says that's what I need. A Bowen treatment."

Surely not. I had heard through the grapevine that he hadn't been well, but surely he wasn't asking *me* to treat him!

"OK, I have no doubt Bowen would do you the world of good. Do you... want me to recommend someone down your way?"

There was a long, uncomfortable pause.

"I... ah... I thought... when you have time... I could come to you... next week maybe.... or when you're available. I'm going to Melbourne next week, so how about..."

"You want ME to treat you?" I felt a smile welling up but resisted giving voice to it. My father was putting his trust in me! My father wanted MY help!

I had dismissed Bill's knowledge of my parents' estrangement as a lucky guess. I had even considered that Murielle might have fed him information, then felt guilty at having such a mistrustful thought.

Then I realized that Murielle didn't even know about my family dynamics.

Now, I had to acknowledge that Bill, or even Murielle if she'd known, could not have arranged this! It was uncanny.

I made the appointment, replaced the receiver and sat staring at the telephone for a few minutes. I needed to carefully consider all the implications of this apparent miracle.

Was it really possible my grandparents were aware of our estrangement?

Had they planted ideas in his mind?

Or, had my father's phone call been just another one of those strange coincidences?

How many coincidences equal credibility?

***

My father didn't simply enter a room. He filled it up. A no-nonsense man with an imposing frame and a booming voice, he had an opinion on everything.

I often wondered how my parents' marriage had lasted for a decade. Mum was a softly spoken, kind and gentle woman. My father was like a bull in a china shop.

The last time I saw him was in 1969, the day of my 21st birthday.

Prior to that, there had been six years of little or no contact between us, but he knew via the grapevine that I was leaving for Europe two weeks later and promised a "special gift" if I agreed to spend my 21st birthday with his family.

The special gift was hardly worth mentioning.

After that 1969 visit, he and his wife had driven me home, intending to drop me off at the front door and be on their way. He parked the car at the front door and I invited them in for coffee, doubting they'd accept. Val, jumped at the opportunity to meet my mother.

"So where's Bert?" Mum asked after I introduced them.

"He... um.... stayed in the car," Val replied with a sheepish grin.

"How silly! Mum scoffed. I'll go out and tell him to come in."

Mum returned a few minutes later, alone but looking smugly satisfied. She had refused to play his game, and I was proud of her.

I put the kettle on, and Val, Mum and I sat down for a chat.

Fifteen minutes later, my father appeared at the door. "Come on," he barked, "I'm not sitting out there all bloody night!" Then he was gone again.

I suspect he had not been the most pleasant travelling companion during the long drive home.

Now, three decades later, I was no longer 21 and Mum was in her seventies and wheelchair bound. I had no doubt she was feeling self-conscious, vulnerable and more than a little nervous.

"Well, well, well," he boomed as I opened the front door. I was instantly taken back to my early childhood.

"Ho ho ho" he would bellow when he arrived at the Christmas eve family gathering, dressed as Santa.

"That's your dad!" my cousin Robert whispered to me during our sixth Christmas Eve gathering. It was the first Christmas Robert and I were old enough to recognise his voice. "Yes, I know," I whispered back. "But don't tell the little ones!"

On this auspicious day, I led him into the living room where my mother was nervously waiting.

"Hello, old girl." He bent to kiss the top of her head in an uncharacteristically gentle gesture.

"Hello, old friend." She smiled.

The ice was broken.

Once on the massage table, I explained Bowen to him as simply as possible. While it was an extremely effective therapy, the technique made little sense to the uninitiated. It required a very brief and gentle pinching and rolling over of small areas of muscle with finger and thumb, followed by a pause of a few minutes, during which time the therapist was required to leave the room to allow the energy to flow unhindered.

After applying a few tweaks, I tiptoed to the door and waited outside for the moves to take effect. I dreaded returning. My father's attitude had always been "if I can't see it or touch it, then it doesn't exist!" He would be confused. If he was confused, then he would also be angry.

My father did not visit therapists who gently pinched muscles. My father visited physiotherapists and surgeons and other specialists. These people didn't tweak and run. To him, this would all come under the 'woo-woo' category.

I took a deep breath and reached for the doorknob. None of this was *my* idea, I reminded myself before entering. "They" had put the idea in his head. *He* had phoned and asked for this. Whatever his reaction, I would handle it.

I gently turned the doorknob.

"What the bloody hell do you think you're doing to me?" he hollered as I opened the door.

I gulped. I was on the verge of taking two steps backward and slamming the door. I was suddenly five years old again and I had just been caught with my hand in the biscuit barrel after refusing to eat my vegetables.

"What do you mean?" I asked as pleasantly as I could, expecting him to leap off the table and grab his jacket on the way out.

"I've got bloody rivers running through me!" he said in amazement.

My father came for more Bowen treatments over the next few months. His wife confided in me that he followed my instructions to the letter, even stopping the car on the long drives home to get out and walk around for a few minutes, as I had advised him to do, and drinking water regularly, something he rarely did.

His health began to improve, and he confessed he had more energy than he'd had for a long time.

"They are definitely trying to get you and him together," Bill had said, "because it would be of tremendous advantage for him."

***

Throughout the past decade I'd spent endless hours on my doorstep, whispering, thinking, asking, pleading for and demanding answers from "anyone or anything out there".

Sometimes, I wondered why I needed more proof.

At other times, I convinced myself I was merely indulging in fanciful dreams to avoid accepting the inevitable.

I had listened to Nan's accounts of ghostly visitors in the month leading up to her death, been present when she commented on the "sweet little dog" she knew nothing about, and observed our lights dimming three times on the day of her funeral.

I had also felt and seen Muffin jump on my bed three weeks after her death (hadn't I?) and witnessed the impossible scenario of Nikki finding Muffin's ball almost a year after I'd secreted it in the back of a drawer in the garage, there to remain out of sight forever.

While I had always been wary of psychic readings, two had described my "flying matron" spirit guide in almost identical words. Rhonda had also predicted Mum's fall even if she had misinterpreted it.

Now, Bill had verbalized my grandparent's request to allow my

181

father to visit. And my father had done so!

How could I keep dismissing these as mere coincidences or an over-active imagination?

I couldn't fight it any longer. I decided to leave my scepticism on the doorstep for safekeeping and find out what, if anything, had been happening in the world of near-death research while my head had been firmly buried in the archaeological sands of the pre-Moody era.

I was off and running again.

CHAPTER 28
ENTER THE SCIENTISTS

By 1997, I had devoted ten years, on and off, to collecting, reading and recording pre-Moody near-death experiences.

The accounts I found were certainly convincing. At the very least, they had dispelled any doubt that Dr. Moody's book had been the cause of this intriguing phenomenon, whatever that phenomenon really was and whatever it meant.

The time had come to find out what, if anything, had transpired since the publication of 'Life After Life'.

On my next visit to the TS Bookshop, I discovered that instead of a few well-stocked shelves (more than enough to impress me a decade earlier) there was now an entire section devoted to death and dying.

How far we had come from "maybe there's something in the religious section".

Alas, most of the books I flicked through were by authors whose credentials were insufficient to convince me they were not merely "cashing in" on Moody's success.

How cynical of me, but I needed to raise the bar. I was teetering on the threshold of belief, but if I was to take the ultimate leap, I told myself that I needed scientific validation.

After an hour of exhaustive browsing — reading book-blurbs can really wear a person out — only two stood out for me. I was surprised to see that both had been published over six years before I had begun my search for answers.

Why hadn't I known about them?

Perhaps, like Dr. Morse's book, they had not been available in Australia at that time, or maybe they'd been tucked away in bookshop storerooms in case they offended customers.

More likely, I had been too obsessed with pre-Moody dates to notice them.

'Life at Death', (1980) by psychology professor, Kenneth Ring provided the results of his own two-year study.

In the introduction to Ring's book, Dr. Moody confessed surprise that his own book had attracted so much attention worldwide and expressed delight that within a year of its publication, several studies were underway to confirm or disconfirm his own preliminary observations.

He mentioned that cardiologist Michael Sabom and "various other physicians" were currently conducting research at a much higher level of systemization than his own.

Fortunately, Sabom's book, 'Recollections of Death', (1982) was also available and this detailed his personal findings as a result of interviewing more than a hundred patients over a five year period.

For once I left my favourite bookshop with a carry-bag that didn't threaten to buckle my knees, and with my bank balance still relatively intact.

***

"I don't believe it!"

That was all cardiologist Dr. Michael Sabom could say in 1976 about the recently published book, 'Life After Life' when psychiatric social worker Sarah Kreutziger brought it to his attention.

Dr. Sabom was an enigma.

A scientist to the core of his being, he was also a regular churchgoer who accepted the church's doctrines of an afterlife because he believed they helped guide proper behaviour. He recognised that faith was totally subjective and unscientific, and insisted there were "no such things as inexplicable phenomena, but merely scientific facts waiting to be discovered."

When colleague Sarah Kreutziger accepted an invitation to do a presentation of Moody's book at their local Methodist church, she asked Dr. Sabom to participate as medical consultant.

He was extremely reluctant to become involved, but on her insistence, eventually agreed to be available at the presentation to deal with any medical questions the audience might have.

In preparation for the talk, Sarah loaned him her copy of the book as it was not yet available in the local bookstores of Florida. He read it, but remained unconvinced. He later wrote in 'Recollections of Death': "My indoctrinated scientific mind just couldn't relate seriously to these 'far-out' descriptions of afterlife spirits and such."

Sarah appears to have been very persuasive. She suggested that in preparation for the talk, it might be helpful if they both conducted brief surveys of hospitalised patients who had survived a medical crisis.

He was convinced no-one would report such an experience, but at least he would be able to tell the audience with a sense of satisfaction that: "We asked!"

The third patient Dr. Sabom interviewed turned his world upside down!

"To my utter amazement," he wrote, "the details matched the descriptions in 'Life After Life'. I was even more impressed by [the patient's] sincerity and the deep personal significance her experience had had for her."

Of course, before revealing her secret, this woman initially needed to be convinced that this curious doctor was not "an underground psychiatrist posing as a cardiologist."

Sabom thought often about that first NDE he heard, and of the woman whose life had been changed by it. Little did he realise that his own life was also about to change dramatically.

He re-read Moody's book, but was still uncomfortable with the unscientific manner in which the data had been collected and analysed.

He was only too aware that "the scientific method of investigation is the systematic collection of objective observations, and that only data collected and presented in a rigorous, unbiased manner are eligible for admission into the generally accepted body of scientific knowledge."

Searching for answers, he contacted Sarah Kreutziger again and together they designed a scientific study with rigorous guidelines. This study commenced only a few months after the initial publication of 'Life After Life' and continued for five years.

It took time and many more interviews before Sabom was convinced. For years, he insisted that NDEs were "*near*" death experiences, not "*after*" death experiences, and therefore doubted they had anything to do with the afterlife.

In 'The Light Beyond' (Moody and Perry, 1988) Sabom wrote: "I can't tell you at what point I believed that this was really occurring. It took a lot of people with NDEs. But when they all started telling basically the same story... the first thing that went through my mind with these people was: 'You have read Raymond Moody's book, haven't you?'"

I could relate to that!

Then Sabom added: "And the patients hadn't!"

While Sabom and Kreutziger were conducting their studies at various hospitals in the southern state of Florida and attracting accounts by other experiencers through their talks at local churches and civic groups, two thousand kilometres north, in Connecticut, a young psychologist was going through a period of soul searching.

Kenneth Ring was feeling spiritually adrift. While volunteering his services in a convalescent home in 1977 in the hope of absorbing the wisdom of some older, wiser person, he chanced to read 'Life After Life'.

Ring's interest in altered states of consciousness had already brought the work of Dr. Elisabeth Kubler-Ross to his attention. This in turn provided him with an awareness of NDEs before Moody's book was even written.

While Dr. Kubler-Ross had not yet published her findings, she claimed to have interviewed over a thousand near-death experiencers. Her enthusiastic lectures, workshops and interviews were creating considerable public and professional interest.

Ring, therefore, had no argument with the contents of 'Life After Life'. In fact, he was inspired by it. But, like his colleague in Florida, he was also aware that a more scientifically structured study would strengthen these findings.

Accordingly, he designed a series of questions that Dr. Moody had not addressed. These questions were almost identical to those Dr. Sabom was asking in Florida.

How common were NDE's? Did everyone who came close to death go through the process, or did it only apply to a few?

Dr. Moody had no way of ascertaining this ratio when he wrote 'Life After Life', as his findings had been based solely on a selection of fifty out of the one hundred and fifty people who came forward specifically to share their experiences with him. He had not interviewed anyone who, following a close call with death, had *not* experienced an NDE.

Similarly, Dr. Sabom had only interviewed three people and had heard one near-death report prior to commencing his study, While it had been uncannily similar to accounts in 'Life After Life', he now wanted to know if all survivors reported NDE's consistent with Moody's findings, or if each one was unique.

Sabom also had further questions.

Did the method by which a person came close to death make any difference? In other words, were NDE's different for those who died as a result of an accident, suffered serious illness, or attempted suicide?

Unknown to each other at the time, Ring and Sabom both made this one of their priorities in their search for scientific validation.

Religious beliefs were also high on Ring's agenda. Did NDE's only happen to those who believed in an afterlife, and did faith contribute to the imagery in these experiences?

Dr. Sabom asked the same question, but he also sought to understand who these people were. What were their social, educational and professional backgrounds?

Through the co-operation of a number of hospitals and psychiatrists, and also by means of local newspaper advertisements, Ring secured the names of one hundred and two patients aged between eighteen and eighty-four who had survived a close call with death or had been resuscitated from clinical death.

During the thirteen months he spent interviewing these survivors, he heard NDE reports from forty nine of them, which was almost half this sample. The remaining fifty three survivors did not recall experiencing an NDE, but were still interviewed to serve as a 'control' group.

Meanwhile, back in Florida, Sabom and Kreutziger interviewed one hundred and sixteen people, and after dismissing those who had voluntarily come forward to report their NDE's, were left with seventy-eight participants.

Of these, thirty-four (about forty-four percent) reported a near death experience.

I considered the implications of these results.

If the findings within these two groups were even vaguely representative of all who had been resuscitated from the brink of death, this suggested that an enormous number of people had experienced an NDE.

Why hadn't I heard about these before I began my own search? Why hadn't they made the front page of newspapers, been the lead story on television news, or had a full page spread devoted to them in a weekly magazine?

I was still to discover that more than two decades after the publication of 'Life After Life', very few took the subject seriously, least of

187

all the media which, it appeared, knew little or nothing about the research that had been conducted.

In 1977, Drs. Moody, Ring and Sabom met at the University of Virginia, along with medical sociologist John Audette, Bruce Greyson (Professor Emeritus of Psychiatry and Neurobehavioural Sciences of the University of Virginia) and other health professionals.

When the group convened, it was clear that both health care professionals and experiencers alike could benefit greatly from an organization dedicated to the research and education of NDEs. Such an organization could offer informational and networking support.

This core group formed the Association for the Scientific Study of Near-Death Phenomena, which changed its name to the International Association for Near-Death Studies (IANDS) in 1981 and appointed Dr. Greyson as editor in chief of their peer-reviewed journal. Greyson served in that capacity until 2008.

Over forty years after its formation, IANDS continues to provide support for NDEr's and to disseminate information for those interested, while also attempting to educate the public on the far-reaching psychological and philosophical implications of this phenomenon.

***

While my search for pre-Moody accounts had been an attempt to convince myself that any reports made following the phenomenal success of 'Life After Life' were not copycat stories fabricated by people who sought fame and fortune, it had not occurred to me that no-one achieved fame and fortune by having an NDE.

Most NDErs could expect no more from those they confided in than a smile, a nod, and perhaps a giggle behind the hand.

Many were admonished for talking nonsense, and some were even referred to psychiatrists! Experiencers were therefore reluctant to share their accounts.

Prior to 'Life After Life's publication, this reluctance was understandable, but I had naively assumed that twenty years after the incredible success of Dr. Moody's book, the entire world was now comfortably familiar with the concept.

IANDS had it right. That just wasn't so.

It also hadn't occurred to me that if a book became a best-seller — and with the notable exception of 'Life After Life', very few books became best-sellers, especially on this subject in the 1980's and 1990's — that everyone in the world had read it, or even that those who had read it had discussed it with others who had not read it.

My partner Barry reminded me that this wasn't so when he related an incident that occurred when he was working as an editor for a major publishing company in 1984.

A well-known author confided to him that he had once been dead but had been resuscitated, then went on to describe how he had "whizzed through a tunnel towards a bright light, and had met deceased loved ones".

"I quickly changed the subject," Barry confessed. "I didn't know where to look or what to say so I just nodded and changed the subject." He later confided to a colleague that the elderly author had "lost it" and was "seeing fairies".

Barry was not alone. When I questioned friends and acquaintances, I found most had no idea what a near-death experience was, other than "almost getting killed".

The few who had heard the term in its correct context assumed it had already been proven scientifically that NDEs were merely the hallucinations of a dying brain.

I started asking relatives, acquaintances, sometimes even random strangers sitting beside me on trains or buses, what they knew about near-death experiences, and whether they knew who Raymond Moody was.

Yes, I confess! I had involuntarily turned into one of those people who had stalked me years ago when I had tried to read Chariots of the Gods!

Only one young girl reacted positively. "Yes!" she said excitedly, "he's a character in that Harry Potter book!"

Then she added tentatively "Isn't he?"

I couldn't confirm or deny it, because at the time, I didn't even know who Harry Potter was.

Then I read a statement by Dr. Sabom that totally destroyed any remnants of my bias.

CHAPTER 29

FINDINGS

In his 1982 book, *Recollections of Death*, Dr. Sabom stated: "Significantly fewer persons with an NDE claimed to have had knowledge of the phenomenon prior to their near-death crisis," adding that "those with previous knowledge reported the experience less frequently."

Wow! So much for copycat stories by people seeking fame and fortune!

Dr. Sabom reminded me that most of his patients began the re-telling of their near death experience with statements like "you won't believe this, but..." or "I've never told anyone about this, but..." or "I know this sounds crazy, but..."

In his wonderful book, Sabom included an account by an 84 year old woman who 'died' during an operation. Unwilling to share her experience with anyone for fear of being laughed at, she chose to record it as a poem.

Her hauntingly familiar words were penned in the 1930's:

> Hovering beneath the ceiling, I looked down
> Upon a body, untenanted – my own
> Strangely at peace, airy, weightless as light,
> I floated there, freed from pain-filled days and nights,
> Until a voice I heard, an urgent call,
> And again I dwelt within my body's wall.

Yes, I was still a sucker for pre-Moody accounts.

***

Sabom and Ring both independently discovered that age, sex, race, education, occupation or cause of death did not appear to have any influence whatsoever over whether a person would encounter an NDE during a near-death crisis.

Of all survivors interviewed, approximately half faced death as a result of serious illness, one quarter were due to suicide attempts, and another quarter had serious accidents.

According to Ring, almost twice as many women as men in the study had their experience due to illness, while most of the men had theirs as a result of accident or suicide.

Regardless of background or cause of death, the experiences remained consistent.

Personal beliefs were also high on both researchers' agendas. Did NDEs only happen to those who believed in an afterlife, and did strong religious beliefs contribute to the imagery in these experiences?

While seventy-one of those interviewed by Ring had strong religious affiliations, twenty-one claimed no interest in religion, and a further seven were agnostic or described themselves as outright atheists. Religious beliefs did not, therefore, appear to be a factor. The same elements continued to occur.

During interviews, all experiencers were encouraged to describe their near-death experience at their own pace and in their own way. Even so, Sabom and Ring both found that the elements Dr. Moody had initially identified remained consistent.

While my own research could hardly be considered scientific, it had confirmed this fact to my satisfaction. The published pre-Moody accounts of NDEs I had gathered had also been consistent with those described in 'Life After Life'

This aspect of NDE reports was important. To take a natural phenomenon seriously, scientists require *repeated* confirmation through observation and experiment, supported by a vast body of evidence. In other words, *what is real is consistently observed.*

No scientist could hope to observe the afterlife, nor could they experiment with death, but there was indeed a vast body of consistently repeated observations available.

If these were dreams or hallucinations, why would people who were unknown to each other and, according to Dr. Sabom, most of them unaware of this phenomena, experience the same or similar dreams or hallucinations?

Both researchers found that the majority of those interviewed reported a sense of deep peace at the point of death, while most in the control group category (those who died and were resuscitated but did not have an NDE) were unaware of any emotions at all during their 'death'.

Nearly a quarter of Ring's experiencers and almost one in three of those in Dr. Sabom's study entered a darkness, which Ring describes as a "transitional one between this world and whatever may be said to lie beyond". Most used words and phrases like "total nothing" or "wonderful blackness" to describe this initial experience. All agreed it was peaceful, comforting and pleasant.

One woman who suffered a cardiac arrest during an operation stated "the thing I could never, absolutely never forget is that absolute feeling of peace, joy... this absolute beautiful feeling... of peace... and happy... it was just absolutely beautiful."

The next feature commonly reported was an out-of-body experience. Over a third of Ring's participants claimed to have had one, although not all of these recalled actually seeing their physical bodies.

Those who did experience this phenomenon often stated that they found themselves high up in a corner of the room, and found this very natural at the time. They were also aware of having acute hearing and sharp mental processes, and observed that the environment was very brightly illuminated.

While most said they felt as if they had been floating, a few reported a sense of moving rapidly through a tunnel or used words that were synonymous with tunnel.

One woman who died during open-heart surgery described it as "a great big drum and this drum was black". Another called it "a void, a nothing... complete blackness," adding that it was "sort of like a dark tunnel".

Almost the identical number of participants in both studies (sixteen in Ring's, seventeen in Sabom's) saw the proverbial 'light at the end of the tunnel' and described it as peaceful, restful or comforting.

Only ten percent of Ring's participants reached the point of entering this light. According to Ring, it is in the light that respondents usually report seeing unforgettable colours and landscapes. Twenty-eight survivors spoke of seeing a landscape of scenic beauty. Ring explained: "the individual may find himself in a meadow or see unusual physical-like structures."

The words 'physical-like structures' grabbed my attention. I wondered if anyone had encountered Jung's temples!

Five claimed to see beautiful flowers on entering the light, and four were aware of lovely music, but all were given only a mere peek of this 'other world' before they returned.

Alas, there were no temples or cities in these surveys, although one woman did report seeing a building with no walls. I tried, but was totally incapable of visualising such a structure. I was beginning to understand what people meant when they despaired of being able to find words to describe what they saw and experienced.

These were important findings! If people were merely making up stories based on information they had read in 'Life After Life' and subsequent publications, then why wouldn't they all mention tunnels, boundaries, deceased loved ones and life reviews?

Why would seven out of every ten declare they had felt peace and joy at the moment of death, but only two of every ten state they had experienced a life review? And why would this ratio remain consistent within each group researched?

Dr. Ring asked the same question. He constructed a ten-point interview scale (very academically called The Weighted Core Experience Index, or WCEI) in order to determine how common each of the Moody elements were.

Don't you just love academics?

According to an article by Professor of Psychiatry and Neurobehavioural Sciences, Dr. Greyson, in The Journal of Nervous and Mental Diseases in 1983, this scale confirmed the initial findings that the number of people experiencing each element declined depending on the level of NDE they reached, from light through moderate to deep.

This set a new standard for evaluating NDEs and would allow future researchers to rate them according to the depth of experience.

Dr. Greyson also developed a Near-death Experience Scale based on sixteen questions carefully designed to differentiate NDEs from those with "questionable claims".

"This is a personal interest of mine," Greyson later stated during an interview, "because I'm a psychiatrist and I've dealt for the past four decades with people who are delusional and who have trouble telling reality from fantasy."

The article in The Journal of Nervous and Mental Diseases described Greyson's scale as being "highly correlated with Ring's Weighted Core Experience Index," adding that it was reliable, valid and easily administered. It was "clinically useful in differentiating NDE's from organic brain syndromes and non-specific stress responses, therefore it assisted in determining which ones unequivocally claimed to have had NDEs from those with qualified or questionable claims."

In other (non-academic) words: "Don't lie to us, we have ways of knowing whether you had an NDE or you're just making it all up!"

Both the Near Death Experience Scale and the Weighted Core Experience Index are still being used by the scientific community today, and both are considered invaluable for evaluation of near-death experiences.

***

Another important development was the subsequent and long-term change of attitude by experiencers.

Dr. Moody had hinted at this at the end of his first book, saying that many "felt that their lives were broadened and deepened by their experience, that because of it they became more reflective and more concerned with ultimate philosophical issues."

As one woman had reported in 'Life After Life': "It made life much more precious to me."

Well, who wouldn't view their life as precious following a close call with death?

Ring also considered this possibility, but his recent period of soul searching prompted him to learn more about this aspect of NDEs. He determined to look at these attitude changes from both sides. In other words, did those who survived death without having had an NDE also report a major change in their philosophy?

His initial findings confirmed our mutual suspicions.

According to Ring, all people who came close to death, whether or not they experienced an NDE, reported that "their lives were altered in significant and drastic ways by the sheer fact of approaching death".

However, while Ring admitted he could not yet provide data to back it up, he felt strongly that experiencers seemed more spiritually aware than those who survived a close call but had no NDE.

A feeling about being "spiritually aware" without being able to back it up was hardly sufficient to convince anyone.

Especially me!

Fortunately, Ring and Sabom independently took this line of questioning a step further and endeavoured to learn about experiencers' subsequent attitudes towards death, including their belief or disbelief in an afterlife.

These results were far more convincing.

Sabom posted a psychologically-validated Dickstein death anxiety scale to all participants. Over eighty percent of the NDErs who responded said they no longer feared dying. On the other hand, almost ninety percent of those who did not have an NDE reported no change in death anxiety.

"This reduction in death anxiety" Sabom reported, "was readily evident not only at the time of the initial interview, but also months or years later."

Ring's research resulted in almost identical statistics. Eighty percent of NDErs in his study said their experience left them with little or no fear of death, while the results of those who came close to dying without experiencing an NDE was almost precisely the opposite.

My own research revealed that pre-Moody NDErs echoed these findings when it came to fear of death.

For example, following her own NDE, sixteenth century nun and mystic, Saint Theresa of Avila wrote: "I was left with very little fear of death, of which previously I had been very much afraid."

Now, who would have thought a mystical sainted Carmelite nun would have been "very much afraid" of death"?

"I had lost something," Gene Albright reported after returning from the other side in 1960. "Something I had lived with most of my life — fear." (The Waiting World, 1975)

"When one day the time comes for me to really die," James Lorne stated after a near-death experience following a heart attack, "I won't try to resist. I'll be ready to follow the call into the beyond." (Glimpses of the Beyond, 1974)

"Dying is a very simple thing," Ernest Hemingway declared in a letter. "I've looked at death and really I know."

"Death is a very much overrated process," Louis Tucker agreed in his autobiography in 1943, after being snatched from its brink as he died of ptomaine poisoning.

Author Katherine Anne Porter died in 1918 during the influenza epidemic. (Incredibly, she was given strychnine to bring her back!)

While it is not known precisely what Porter experienced as she simply called it her "beatific vision", we find a hint in her 1939 novella, 'Pale Horse, Pale Rider', when her main character Miranda is dying of influenza:

"Moving towards her leisurely as clouds through the shimmering air came a great company of human beings, and Miranda saw in an amazement of joy that they were all the living she had known... she knew them every one without calling their names or remembering what relation she bore to them."

The novella ends with Miranda musing: "Now there would be time for everything."

In 1980, at the age of ninety, Katherine Anne Porter finally found her "time for everything". Henry Allen of the Washington Post wrote of her: "having already seen both heaven and hell... she had no fears whatsoever of either the right or the left-handed terrors of eternity."

***

In another work of fiction, 'The Death of Ivan Ilyich', first published in 1886, Count Leo Tolstoy writes of the passing of a cranky old high-court judge in nineteenth century Russia.

While this is a novel, one might pause to wonder from where Tolstoy drew his inspiration when he penned the final death scene:

> At that very moment Ivan Ilych fell through and caught sight of the light, and it was revealed to him that though his life had not been what it should have been, this could still be rectified. He sought his former accustomed fear of death and did not find it.
>
> "Where is it? What death?" There was no fear because there was no death. In place of death there was light. So that's what it is!" he suddenly exclaimed aloud. "What joy!"
>
> "It is finished!" said someone near him. He heard these words and repeated them in his soul. "Death is finished," he said to himself. "It is no more!"

***

When it came to a belief in the afterlife, Ring's results were among the strongest so far in his investigation. He found that experiencers' beliefs in survival after death increased dramatically following their NDE, moving from a previous average position of 'not sure' to 'strongly convinced', while non-experiencers showed virtually no change.

As Archie Matson wrote: "Once a man experiences a thing himself, there can be no more doubting. He knows!"

"I know it to be true," Herman Stulz echoed, "for I have passed through this transition twice and was declared to be dead. I have nothing to fear or be sad over, nothing to make me sorrowful. I had to bury my father, my darling wife and my two sons who have preceded me, for I know as sure as I live I shall again hold them in my arms."

(Herman Stulz, Autobiography, CLDS circa 1971)

One man in Ring's study said he had "thought it was all a bunch of baloney" before his NDE. When asked if he believed in an afterlife now, he stated emphatically "Sure. Definitely."

A racing car driver who almost died as a result of a crash, told Ring: "My attitude toward death [now] is that death is not dying; death is being reborn."

A woman who had a heart attack said she now believed "beyond any question of a doubt that there is something beyond."

Again, Dr. Sabom's results were similar. He found there was a definite increase in belief in an afterlife by "the vast majority of persons with an NDE, a response significantly different from that of persons surviving similar near-death crisis events without an NDE".

Dr. Sabom stated that the NDE experience "represented a privileged glimpse of what was to occur at the moment of final bodily death."

If that wasn't enough to knock my socks off, I was soon to learn that researchers had discovered an even more interesting repercussion of NDEs!

CHAPTER 30

TRANSFORMATIONS

"What's much more interesting to me," Psychiatrist Bruce Greyson admitted during an interview for IANDS, "is not the 'knock your socks off' part of the experience, but the after-effects, the way it changes people's lives."

This was a dramatic new development. It quickly became apparent that most of those who glimpsed 'the other side' returned with an increased sense of compassion and sensitivity and a reduced interest in money or material possessions.

Ego-driven ambition was invariably replaced by a need to be of service, with many finding their niche in humanitarian or service-oriented work such as hospitals, hospices or charity work.

"Psychiatrists and psychologists spend a lot of hard work trying to get people to make fairly small changes," Dr. Greyson stated, "and here in the flash of a second, people are totally transformed. This is a powerful experience!"

The realisation that we each have a mission or purpose was also a common theme among survivors. While acknowledging that each person's mission may not be earth-shattering or newsworthy, experiencers understood that it was crucial for each of us to complete our allotted tasks.

Some experiencers also returned with gifts they neither asked for, nor knew how to use, such as healing or psychic abilities.

Ring observed a marked increase in "...telepathy, clairvoyance and precognition, spontaneous out-of-body experiences and unusual perceptions such as seeing energy fields (auras)".

Transformations

Dannion Brinkley certainly returned with psychic abilities.

You may recall that he had been zapped by lightning while talking on the telephone. It was nothing short of a miracle that he survived this horrific accident, but it took three years of hospitals and rehabilitation before he could walk again!

Brinkley would be the first to admit that he had been a bad boy who had loved nothing more than a good fist-fight! Since his accident, he has devoted much of his time working for hospice in a voluntary role.

He also uses the amazing psychic gifts he brought back, along with the knowledge he gained on the other side, to help the dying through their transitions.

In his introduction to Brinkley's book, 'Saved by the Light', Dr. Moody expressed amazement at Dannion's psychic abilities. "How is it possible," Moody asks, "that a person who has a near-death experience is suddenly able to read minds... I have seen him [do this]... so many times that it has become almost commonplace in my life."

Dr. George Ritchie, who died of pneumonia during world war 2 and was one of the catalysts for Dr. Moody's 'Life After Life', wrote an updated version of his experience (Ordered to Return, 1991) to include details of the profound changes he also underwent following his NDE.

In 1984, Professor Bruce Greyson developed the Life Changes Inventory to quantify changes in attitudes and life styles following an NDE. Of course he did!

Greyson's work in this area has resulted in more than 75 presentations to national and international scientific conferences and over a hundred publications in academic medical and psychology journals.

"What seems to happen," Dr. Ring wrote in 'Lessons From the Light', "is that the NDE unleashes normally dormant potentials for higher consciousness and extraordinary human functioning."

There also appeared to be an increased sensitivity to light, an involuntary ability to manipulate electrical and mechanical equipment (and there are many amusing stories under this category) and an awareness of subtle body changes.

Dr. Melvin Morse believes he knows why this occurs. In his book 'Transformed by the Light', he wrote: "...after scientifically studying hundreds of these experiences, I am convinced that the NDE itself subtly changes the electromagnetic forces that surround our bodies, and each and every cell in it. This change is so profound that it affects things such as personality, anxiety response, ability to have psychic experiences, and even the ability in some to wear a watch."

"In the realm of beliefs, values, behaviour and outlook on life generally," Dr. Ring pointed out in 'Lessons From the Light' that "NDEr's, however different they may have been before their experience, showed astonishing similarities."

"From a psychological standpoint" Ring added, "it was almost as if they had all undergone much the same initiatory ordeal, triggered by the trauma of nearly dying which then, unexpectedly, gave rise to similar, life-transforming insights, and then emerged to speak in a single voice and act from the secret knowledge of a shared vision."

I read that sentence again, slowly.

They "... emerged to speak in a single voice and act from the secret knowledge of a shared vision."

That was really a head-spinning statement! With modern technology snatching so many people from the brink of death these days, I couldn't help wondering what that could mean for the future of humanity, especially when you consider that these profound changes not only effect the experiencer, they also serve as a catalyst for researchers and others to question the meaning of life.

In a recent IANDS interview, Dr. Greyson said: "Studying NDEs for the past 35 years and spending so much time with experiencers themselves has transformed my own views... and helped me outgrow many of the simplistic assumptions of my religious background and my scientific training.

Greyson added philosophically: "I can't say that it has given me answers to the 'big' questions about spirituality and its relationship to our mundane world, but it's made me very comfortable with not having answers."

Transformations following NDE's, however, were rarely easy, and often took a long time to work through. This often resulted in marriage breakdowns and estrangements from family and friends.

When someone returns from the brink of death with an entirely different perspective on life, it is rarely an easy adjustment for spouses or friends, especially if they no longer share common goals, dreams, attitudes and beliefs.

As Greyson pointed out in an interview: "Sometimes people doubt their own sanity after an NDE. Some people feel angry or depressed at being returned against their will, they feel alienated from people who haven't had NDE's, they can't talk about them for fear of being ridiculed. When they have felt unconditional love in the other world they can't be satisfied with the conditional love they feel here."

It became increasingly obvious there was a need for professional counselling for near-death survivors, but in the mid to late 1980's, few health professionals knew anything about these transformational aspects of the NDE.

Forget the aspects! The real truth is that most of them still didn't even know about NDEs!

If survivors sought professional help to deal with what they thought was a unique experience, they would often find themselves clutching a prescription for anti-depressants or being referred to a psychiatrist for treatment of their apparent mental problem.

To address this, Nina Thorburg, RN, of the Massachusetts College of Pharmacy and Allied Health Services joined with nursing, sociology and psychology professionals in 1988 to create the Near-Death Phenomena Knowledge and Attitudes questionnaire.

Academics do love their scientifically-designed questionnaires!

Aimed at discovering attitudes toward and knowledge about near death experiences by intensive or cardiac care unit nurses, registered psychologists and hospice nurses, this questionnaire was developed to ensure that NDErs received the assistance they needed from medical professionals to process their experiences and gain satisfactory answers to their questions.

This in turn would help survivors work through psychological problems that developed due to an inability to discuss experiences openly, along with a sense of 'homesickness for the other side' that many felt, and the difficulty most had adjusting to life back in what they now perceived to be an imperfect world.

Eminent psychiatrist Carl Jung may have benefited from such assistance after surviving a heart attack in 1944.

"Life and the whole world struck me as a prison," Jung had despaired in his 1963 autobiography. "I had been so glad to shed it all, and now it had come about that I, along with everyone else, would again be hung up in a box by a thread."

Saint Theresa felt the same way.

After her near-death experience, she wrote in her autobiography in 1565: "I wanted to remain in this state always and not return to everyday living, for the contempt that was left in me for everything earthly was great; these things all seemed to me like dung, and I see how basely we are occupied, those of us who are detained by earthly things."

Now there, indeed, was an interesting statement from a sainted Carmelite nun!

Author Katherine Anne Porter would agree with her.

"I had seen my heavenly vision and the world was pretty dull after that," she said in an interview. "My mood for several years thereafter was that it was not a world worth living in. (reproduced in The Light Beyond, by Raymond Moody with Paul Perry)

Porter later stated in an interview: "It simply divided my life, cut across it like that ...everything before that was just getting ready, and after that I was in some strange way altered, really. Now if you have had that, and survived it, and come back from it, you are no longer like other people, and there's no use deceiving yourself that you are."

Such despair knew no boundaries. NDErs from all walks of life faced a painful period of adjustment.

One area in which this presented a major problem was the military.

Of course, battle-scarred soldiers also had NDEs, probably at a higher rate than the general public, but most were afraid to talk about them for fear of jeopardising their careers. If they tried to discuss their experience with military doctors or psychologists, they would usually be diagnosed with post-traumatic stress disorder or mental illness and sent to a psychiatrist.

Some were even institutionalised.

To complicate their lives even more, soldiers who suddenly find they cannot tolerate violence do not make effective fighting men. Most return with an overwhelming compassion for all humanity and would rather discuss love and peace than wars and battles.

Generals are usually not impressed by soldiers who want to love their enemy to death!

Unlike many of today's researchers, Diane Corcoran, R.N., Ph.D, was not introduced to near death experiences through 'Life After Life', but as an army field nurse serving in Vietnam in 1969.

She heard them directly from injured soldiers six years before publication of Dr. Moody's book!

"I believe that soldiers are having NDEs at very high rates," Diane stated in an interview. "Up to forty percent of soldiers who are injured are having them because so many of them are injured as a result of traumatic amputations... [and] they really don't have any place to go with their experience."

Diane retired with the rank of Colonel and has since worked

tirelessly to educate the military about this phenomenon to ensure experiencers receive the support they desperately need.

Recently, Diane gave a lecture on NDEs to all the mental health personnel at an army hospital, and asked the audience to put their hand up if they knew anything about NDE's.

"Out of about sixty people in attendance," she said sadly, "only four raised their hands.

CHAPTER 31

IT'S ALL NONSENSE

"It's all nonsense, you know!"

Andy had been working in Alice Springs for many years, so when we literally bumped into each other in a supermarket, we took the opportunity to catch up over coffee. He had married a few years earlier and proudly shared photos of his wife and two beautiful children.

Then he made the mistake of asking me what I'd been up to lately.

I made the next mistake. I told him.

"But how can you say it's nonsense, Andy?" I asked, slightly frustrated by the ease with which he dismissed the subject. "How much do you actually know about NDE's?"

He smiled knowingly. "You forget that as a paramedic I spend most of my life trying to keep people alive in the back of ambulances!"

"I asked you how much you knew about NDE's, not what you do for work."

He shifted uncomfortably in his chair. "Look, I've resuscitated loads of people, ok? They're dead. Ok? They don't go anywhere. Trust me. They just lay there, dead."

Was it my imagination, or was Andy's voice taking on an aggressive tone? He was obviously irritated by my question.

"Tell me then, what do you believe causes these near death experiences!"

He rolled his eyes. "Where do you want me to start?"

"Well," I sighed, waving to the waitress to alert her that I was in dire need of another coffee, "you could start by telling me how much you've read about them."

"Sure, like I have time to read books about people hallucinating!"

Shades of Doc David, I thought. I was determined not to make the same mistake I had made with him and reminded myself to stay calm.

"OK," I said hesitantly, "then you may not know that lots of people who get resuscitated have a story to tell about what happened when they died, and they all describe the same things!

"Ha, of course they do!" Andy laughed. "They've obviously all read the same books!"

My initial reaction was to thump the table and tell him what an arrogant fool he was. Instead, I replied in as calm a voice as I could muster. "Well actually, no, that's not entirely true."

I briefly wondered if I should be pursuing this line of discussion, but it was too late now.

"Most people who have an NDE don't know anything about them, and because they don't talk about them, they usually think they're the only one who's ever had such an experience!"

Andy glanced at his watch. His coffee cup was still half full. I knew it was time to stop telling and start asking.

"Look, I'm not saying these people actually go to heaven and came back to tell about it... um... I'm just... wondering why they would all say the same things, without knowing what other people said, if you follow. If they didn't read the same books, I mean."

"Cerebral Anoxia!"

"Pardon?"

"Inhibited oxygen flow to the brain." Andy looked smug. When the heart stops pumping, the blood stops circulating. Simple. The brain needs blood, the blood carries oxygen. When it doesn't get what it needs...."

"But..."

"And," he emphasised the word with a glare to keep me quiet, "medications. Drugs, anaesthetics, painkillers. Lots of them give patients hallucinations."

"I know," I agreed in an effort to placate him, "when Mum broke her hip they gave her morphine. She insisted there were spiders running up and down the curtain. But these aren't..."

205

"And wishful thinking." He added. "People want it to be true. Their brain doesn't get enough oxygen, they're given medications, they have hallucinations and they want it to be real, they want to know they don't really die. They just..." he shrugged, "interpret the things they see as some heavenly place where we all go and live happily ever after!"

"Andy!" I almost shouted. "No-one wants heaven to be full of spiders! And near-death experiencers don't see things like that, they see tunnels and lights and deceased loved ones! Besides, how could these people see anything at all if their brain's deprived of oxygen? The brain doesn't function without oxygen. Does it? And..."

"The brain..."

And Elisabeth Kubler Ross, surely you've heard of her, she's a highly-respected expert on death and dying and even she says it's all real."

Andy sat and looked at me in silence for a few moments. "You really want this to be true, don't you?"

"It's not about what I want, Andy! NDE's are happening to people all over the world because more and more are being resuscitated, and scientific people are starting to take it seriously. Can you imagine what this would do for people grieving for someone they love, or if they were diagnosed with a terminal illness and scared half out of their wits?"

He leaned forward and patted my hand. "That's very thoughtful of you, but unfortunately, wanting something doesn't make it a fact."

I snatched my hand away in frustration and kept talking.

"Even if the brain did still function, why would everyone who had oxygen-starved brains all see the same things? And if they hallucinate because of morphine, how would they see the same things as a person hallucinating from anaesthetic, or someone on, say, heroin? Wouldn't they all have different experiences, different hallucinations?"

"Hang on, hang on," Andy raised his hand in the air, "the brain is a very complex organ. We don't know everything about how it works, it could be..."

"Exactly!" I interrupted again, aware that the calm line of questioning I had been determined to maintain wasn't working. "We don't know everything about how the brain works. We just assume the mind and the brain are the same thing, but what if... what IF... the mind and the brain are separate? What IF the mind leaves the body when the brain is dead? What IF we don't think with the brain, we think with the mind, and the brain is simply a transmitter and receiver and, I don't know, just interprets it or... channels it or..."

"Channels it?" Andy asked with a look of mock horror. "Are you suggesting the ghost of some long-dead viking is hovering around telling you what to think? Really? I think you're letting your brain AND your mind get carried away."

"Andy," I sighed, "please don't patronise me. I've been reading about this subject for years now. You can't imagine what scientists are discovering about all this. For one thing, no-one's figured out consciousness. What is it, what does it do, where is it produced? Do you know? And if you do, then you're in the wrong job because none of the top scientific minds in the world can agree on a definition or a source!"

"But..."

"You just dismiss it all because you're not taught these things at medical school so you simply accept what you're told. Do you realise that people who are flat-lining have actually seen what other people are doing, or heard what they're saying? They've reported things they couldn't possibly have known about, because they were dead while those things were happening! Not under anaesthetic. Not comatose. Not just very ill. Clinically dead!

Andy glared at me, took a deep breath, then looked down at the table for a long time.

"Andy?" I asked quietly, once again regretting my overly enthusiastic prattle. I wondered why I was trying to convince Andy when I still wasn't sure I'd totally convinced myself.

Finally, he looked up. "I know that," he almost whispered.

"Know what?"

"That people know things that happened while they're supposed to be dead. There was... um... I had... this bloke told me something." he said quietly.

"Andy? What? Tell me!"

He looked back down at his cup. Seconds ticked by like hours.

"Ok," he eventually sighed, "so he died. In the back of the ambulance. I was working on him like crazy for about five minutes."

He looked back down at the table.

"Yes? And?" I prompted.

He kept his gaze fixed on his cup and spoke quietly. "I was talking to him. You know. Trying to bring him back. I knew him. In a town as small as the Alice you get to know people. I said things, things about his family needing him, stuff like that. I knew he couldn't hear me. I mean,

207

he was gone. Nothing there. It was hopeless. But... you know," he shrugged, "you just try. You just... try."

"And he heard you?"

"Well, so he said. Later. He told me he was on the ambulance ceiling and could hear me talking to him."

"But you didn't believe him?" I asked gently, aware that this may be a major turning point for Andy.

"Oh, I believed him all right!" Andy looked up like he had just awoken from a deep sleep and was keen to dismiss a dream he'd had. "I had to believe him, didn't I? I mean, he knew what I'd said. I saw him in the hospital a few days later and he repeated most of the things back to me that I'd said in the ambulance, even things I'd forgotten I'd said!"

"Then what's the problem?" I asked, no longer sure where this conversation was heading.

"No problem." He suddenly smiled, as though he'd finally solved a long-standing puzzle that had been nagging at him. "He just wasn't dead, was he?"

"Not dead? But wouldn't you of all people know if he was dead?"

He laughed heartily. Perhaps a little too heartily. "You'd think so, wouldn't you? But who knows?" he shrugged. "Just because someone's heart stops beating for a few minutes and they're not breathing, who really knows? What's dead, anyway?"

"Indeed," I smiled. "What's dead?"

***

Why were so many people I spoke to in the medical profession adamant it was "fantasy fiction" as Dr. Simmons had once called it?

I might have been swayed by them. After all, they knew far more than I did when it came to medical matters. But whenever I persisted, I discovered they knew nothing about the subject or the research taking place. They were merely expressing a bias.

Many years later, I read about an incident that occurred to Dr. Greyson in the 1980's when he was presenting information about NDEs at an American Medical Association conference.

During the presentation, a cardiologist in the audience stood up and interrupted the lecture. "This is nonsense!" he said dismissively and more than a touch angrily, "In my twenty years of practice, I have never heard of anything like NDE's described." He then demanded to know how it could be proven that patients in these cases were not just making them up.

Immediately, another man in the audience stood up. He politely explained that he had been that doctor's patient, and that he had experienced an NDE.

"And you, sir," he addressed his cardiologist, "were the last person I would have told about my experience!"

The cardiologist looked slightly flustered and immediately sat down.

CHAPTER 32

THE MURDER OF GEORGE

"What's dead, anyway?" Andy had asked.

George Redonaia was dead. He had his own death certificate to prove it!

Proudly describing himself as a "dissident in Soviet Union", George's decision to immigrate to the United States with his wife and young child in 1976 may have been prompted by the memory of his parents' fate. They had been banished to a gulag in the late 1940's for openly expressing their opposition to the totalitarian government, and were subsequently murdered by the KGB in 1956, when George was still an infant.

Adopted by a loving family in Soviet Georgia, George again found himself orphaned at the age of twelve.

A highly intelligent child, he was invited to attend the University of Moscow at fourteen and applied himself diligently to his studies. He emerged at eighteen as a research scientist and was invited to pursue advanced research at Yale.

The KGB denied him permission.

Two years later, George was married and the father of an infant son. He was working as a research psychiatrist and neuropathologist at the University of Moscow when he received a professional invitation from an American colleague to work in Texas.

He applied through official channels and this time was provided with exit visas. It probably didn't hurt that Henry Kissinger, Secretary of State and Foreign Advisor to President Nixon, sent a letter to the USSR in support of his request.

On the day of departure, a Friday, George collected his passport, then waited for a taxi to take him to the airport where he would meet up with his family and prepare to start a new life in Texas.

Once again, the KGB had other ideas.

George tells the story of his 'accident' in a documentary. His English is not perfect, but I have tried to retain the flavour of his personality by using his exact wording wherever possible. I have also used excerpts from a few other sources in order to provide a complete picture of his experience.

In George Redonaia's own words: "I was standing on sidewalk... waiting for cab, when car ran on the sidewalk and hit me. I flew ten metres and fell, then the car runs over me. I was taken to hospital. Doctors did anything they could to help me but I was declared dead. They put me in the morgue and freezer."

According to George, this was no accident. "It was fabricated by KGB. I worked on neuro-transmitter in our brain and I discovered several things, and KGB did not want me to go."

George woke up to find himself in total darkness. "I have no pain and I'm in darkness," he recalled. "I cannot see anything, then I cannot move hand then I cannot move my body and then I understood that I have nothing. But I am."

Shocked to find that he still existed, George wondered: "How can I be when I'm not?" (The Journey Home, 1996)

"I was afraid that I was somewhere without my body," George related in the documentary. "But I was a scientist. I worked on dialectical materialism, historical materialism, and in my idea it's impossible to be somewhere without your body. Where is my main component, my life, my body?"

While participating in the documentary many years later, George recalled his fear and confusion but could also see humour in his experience. "I was scared to death!" he laughed. "But I was already dead!" Then he became serious and said: "...to understand that you are, but you are not. If you think, you are. If I think, I thought, I am."

Recognising he was in "a very different dimension" he reasoned: "But if I am, and if I think, why cannot I think positively what's happening around me? And I began to think about light. I saw light outside of darkness, and it shocked me."

George then "went through that little hole into light" and saw "all these molecules flying around, atoms, protons, neutrons, just flying everywhere."

Such chaotic symmetry brought him tremendous joy, and any concern he had for his lack of a body slipped away when he realised that a physical body was actually a limitation.

"Past, present, and future were somehow fused together for me in the timeless unity of life. At some point I underwent what has been called the life-review process, for I saw my life from beginning to end all at once."

He described this life review as occurring "in that dimension which cannot be described" and explained it like a "holographical view of being inside of your life and then being as a viewer, participating in the play of theatre which is happening there but it is you and you know that you are this."

He felt no remorse or guilt for anything he had done. "I didn't feel one way or another about my failures, faults or achievements. All I felt was my life for what it is. And I was content with that."

His scientific mind observed and questioned everything. "I came to see that reality is everywhere. That it is not simply the earthly life but the infinite life. Everything is not only connected together, everything is also one. I also came to see that a black hole is only another part of that infinity which is light."

"When you leave your body," George was quoted in 'The Journey Home', "you are not in time, and you feel a sense of lightness... you feel light like a feather. You enter into another dimension."

There was that feather again!

George was also amazed that he could be "anywhere instantly, really there, and be aware of everything that was happening."

"Seeing myself, my body, seeing my birth, my parents, my wife, my child, my friends. I saw their thoughts... how their thought moved from one to another dimension, it was incredible experience. I tried to communicate with people I saw. Some sensed my presence, but no-one did anything about it."

Breaking into a broad smile during this interview, George announced: "I could communicate with the children! The very little children who can't speak and can't walk and who were just coming from that place where I was going, and this was amazing, communicating with them. We never spoke in the words, we spoke in mental communication."

In the documentary, 'Life After Life', he provides a stunning example of this. A friend's newborn daughter had been crying for days and had been admitted to hospital. Medical tests had failed to find any cause of her distress. But George knew!

"She had a broken hip and nobody understood why she was crying so loud, and the doctors and parents were very concerned about this. And I said 'don't cry, anyway nobody will understand why you do cry' and she stopped crying and she smiled and it was incredible experience for the people who were around and they looked at her and said 'what's happened? Why she's not crying at this time?' I want to tell them... but I couldn't communicate with them."

When he recovered (I don't want to spoil the ending, but as incredible as it may seem, he DID recover!) George visited his friends and told them: "You know, your daughter is crying because of this, she has a broken hip and this is the diagnosis which you are seeking, and they found that it was true. They were shocked and they were surprised."

Three days after his accident, on the following Monday, George's body was removed from the freezer, washed, and prepared for an autopsy.

"So there I was," he recalled, "flooded with all these good things and this wonderful experience, when someone begins to cut into my stomach. Can you imagine?"

As they made the first cut, "some great power took me" George recalled, "and with neck I think, that part I can't explain, pushed me down and I saw this movement down and then I felt my head ache and I opened my eyes. And this was coming back to my body."

George's eyes flickered. The doctor immediately shone a light into them, and his pupils responded. He was immediately rushed to hospital and resuscitated. "My lungs were collapsed for long time," he said. "I was on respirator for ninety days, but the life came back."

This amazing experience occurred less than a year after publication of 'Life After Life'. It is highly unlikely that any copies of the book were available in the Soviet Union. Accordingly, people were still unaware of this area of study, and were naturally sceptical.

"When I came back to life," George explained, "a lot of different experiences happened. And I experienced a lot of rejection, a lot of fights with the reality of others. But nothing could change my mind. Sometimes, things are beyond our grasp, but I don't try to explain it all because I knew and I believe that God knows better and I believe that I don't need to explain."

In 1989, thirteen years after his 'accident', George and his family were finally allowed to leave the Soviet Union.

Common to most NDEr's, however, George had been transformed by his amazing experience. Once settled in the U.S., this "materialistic scientist and avowed atheist" gained a Ph.D. in the psychology of religion and became the Reverend Redonaia, an ordained priest in the Eastern Orthodox Church, serving as pastor at a Methodist Church in Texas until his death in 2004 aged 48.

Highly-respected near death experience researcher, P.M.H. Atwater, knew George well and also documented his case in her book, 'Beyond The Light'. She wrote that of all the cases she had investigated, George's was "the most dramatic, the longest, the most evidential, and the most soul-stirring."

As keynote speaker at a United Nations conference in the 1990's, George ended his address as follows:

"Many people turn to those who have had near-death experiences because they sense we have the answers. But I know this is not true, at least not entirely. None of us will fully fathom the great truths of life until we finally unite with eternity at death. But occasionally we get glimpses of the answer here on earth, and that is enough for me. I love to ask questions and seek answers, but I know in the end I must live the questions and the answers."

After George's passing, Atwater wrote: "He never failed to share his story and to help others every way he could. My only regret is, he never wrote his own book about his experience. Yet, perhaps he did, on everyone's heart who ever heard him."

***

"What's dead?" Andy had asked months earlier.

"Wouldn't being frozen for 3 days qualify as dead?" I asked him from the back doorstep.

I wondered how he'd reply if he'd been here. He'd probably demand to see the death certificate. I couldn't satisfy that request, but I knew from books and taped interviews that a number of researchers had sighted it.

All the same, Andy would no doubt argue that the hapless George hadn't really died in the first place. The doctor who declared him so had been wrong, and George had merely been frozen for three days, existing in a state of suspended animation which prevented his organs from deteriorating.

If, for reasons I can't even begin to imagine, I chose to climb into my home freezer and remain there for three days, would I survive the experience? Would anyone? I wasn't about to put it to the test, but I doubted it.

Besides, I was healthy, while George had horrific injuries and had been declared dead by a medical professional. Presumably, he had no discernible pulse, and probably no reflexes. If we decide that this does not constitute death, then what does?

If Andy was right and George was not dead, the implications were unsettling. Could this mean that some people might be declared dead long before they really are?

Can a person stop breathing, have no pulse or reflexes, be locked in a freezer for three days, yet still be alive?

This, and I shuddered at the thought, was the stuff of nightmares. Imagine, if you dare, being buried or cremated while you were still alive.

Imagine, if you dare, wanting to scream "hey, stop, don't do this to me! Wait! I'm not dead yet!" while being aware that no-one could hear you and you couldn't even wiggle a finger to attract their attention.

But wait! George wasn't trying to scream "stop, I'm not dead yet!" He wasn't shivering in the freezer, wishing someone would bring him a blanket and make him a nice cup of coffee to warm him up. George was having a lovely time watching flying molecules and chatting to newborn babies.

Andy would say that if you can be revived, then you can't have been dead in the first place! What, then, was dead?

It occurred to me that the only way anyone could prove someone was really dead while they were having a near-death experience was to monitor brain activity to ensure there was absolutely nothing going on in there.

Of course, that was never going to happen. It was hardly ethical to rig a patient up with monitoring equipment in case they died during surgery, and it was also unthinkable to intentionally kill a patient and then resuscitate them.

Or was it?

CHAPTER 33

KILLING TO CURE

In 1991, 35-year-old singer/songwriter and mother of three young children, Pamela Reynolds, was diagnosed with a complex aneurism at the base of her brain.

The prognosis was not good. The aneurism could burst at any time, but surgically accessing this part of the brain was extremely difficult.

In fact, it was almost impossible. Almost.

When Pamela heard about Dr. Speltzer at the Barrow Neurological Hospital in Phoenix, Arizona, she did not hesitate to contact him.

Dr. Speltzer was famous for his expertise in a technique called Hyperthermic Cardiac Arrest.

(Note: a common misconception is that 'cardiac arrest' means heart attack. While cardiac arrest can certainly occur during a heart attack, the term simply means that the heart has stopped beating.)

This radical surgery is known by some in the medical profession as 'standstill', because to perform it, the patient must first be killed!

Dr. Speltzer described the procedure to Pamela, explaining that her eyes would be lubricated and taped shut to prevent them from drying out before a drug was administered to shut her brain down.

This did not mean simply putting the brain to sleep as occurs during anaesthesia. This drug would render Pamela's brain incapable of generating a single thought or recording a single memory. Her body would then be chilled until her heart stopped beating.

Monitoring plugs would be pushed far into her ears to monitor brain activity to ensure there was absolutely nothing going on in there. These earplugs would emit regular and noisy clicks, as noisy as if your ears were encased in block-out headphones while listening to music turned up at top volume!

When Pamela's temperature was lowered sufficiently, the heart and lung machine would be turned off and her body emptied of blood. At this point, she would no longer be breathing. There would be no heartbeat. Her organs would cease to function. No blood would circulate throughout her body. Her brain would generate no activity, or at least none that could be detected by modern medical equipment.

How much 'deader' can one person be?

George Redonaia had no perceptible heartbeat either, and his body had also been frozen. The difference between the two, however, was that Pamela was not placed in a freezer and left unattended for three days. Her vital signs would be extensively instrumented and closely monitored throughout the one hour procedure.

Before the operation began, every monitor attached to Pamela's body would need to confirm that she was clinically dead. She would remain in 'standstill' for at least an hour, then her heart would be restarted. Hopefully!

(And hopefully, Dr. Speltzer did not add the word 'hopefully'!)

It must have been a terrifying prospect, but Pamela had no choice. If she agreed to go ahead with the operation, she would die on the operating table and could only hope she would return to life without the aneurism. If she chose not to have the operation, however, she would die suddenly and soon, perhaps while shopping or eating breakfast!

Pamela chose to die on the operating table.

In a documentary made a few years after the operation, near-death researcher Dr. Michael Sabom stated: "if you wanted to conduct a laboratory experiment where you had someone and took them as close to death, perhaps even into death, as possible, then bring them back and ask them what they could recall, Pam's case probably comes closer to that than any other so far we know of."

Pamela revealed that the first thing she became conscious of during the operation was hearing a sound. She described it as a Natural 'D, as you might expect from a singer/songwriter.

"I remember the top of my head sort of tingling," she recalled. "I felt it was pulling me out of the top of my head. The further out of my body I got, the more clear the tone became. I had the impression it was like a road, a frequency that you go on."

I found the reference to a road very interesting.

Pamela then became aware of a female voice lamenting: 'her arteries are too small', and a male voice replied: 'try the other side'.

"It seemed to come from further down on the table," Pamela recalled. "I do remember wondering, what are they doing because this is brain surgery!"

After the operation, it was explained to her that her femoral (thigh) arteries had been accessed to drain her blood.

Dr. Spetlzer confirmed that this conversation occurred, adding "at that stage of the operation, nobody can observe, hear, in that state. I find it inconceivable that normal senses such as hearing, let alone the fact that she had clicking modules in each ear, that there was any way for her to hear those through normal auditory pathways."

Pamela recalls even more: "...and I remember in [the surgeon's] hand there was a tool that looked to me like the handle on my electric toothbrush, and it had bits and they were kept in this case that looked very similar to the case that my father kept his sockets in. I had assumed they were going to open the skull with a saw, I had heard the term saw, but what I saw looked a lot more like a drill... it had a dent in it, a groove at the top where the saw appeared to go into the handle, but it didn't."

"I heard the saw crank up, Pamela continued. "I didn't see them use it on my head, but I think I heard it being used on something. It was humming at a relatively high pitch and then all of a sudden it went brrrrrr! Like that. It reminded me of... a dentist's office."

Cardiologist Dr. Sabom later stated: "Pamela described equipment and I didn't even know what it looked like, and I confirmed (later) that her description was accurate."

"I just sort of popped out and I was then looking down at the body." Pamela continued. "I knew it was my body, but I was not at all attached to it. I was not that body. I was whatever was looking down at it. My vantage point was sort of sitting on the doctor's shoulder. It was the most aware that I think I have ever been in my entire life. It was brighter and more focused and clearer than normal vision."

"I saw a very tiny pinpoint of brilliant white light way off in the distance, and it began to pull me. I felt a presence. I sort of turned around to look at it, and that's when I saw the very tiny pinpoint of light, and the light started to pull me and there was a physical sensation to the pulling... rather like going over a hill real fast... and there was a sensation, but it wasn't a bodily, physical sensation. It was like a tunnel but it wasn't a tunnel."

"I went toward the light," she recalled happily. "The closer I got to the light I began to discern different figures, different people, and I distinctly heard my grandmother call me. She had a very distinct voice and I immediately went to her. It felt great!"

Then Pamela recalled something that really hit the mark: "I remember thinking, I wonder if I deserve to be here, I'm not a perfect person. And my grandmother said to me: you were a child sent away to school, and as a child, we expected that you would spill your milk. It's the manner which you clean it up that gives us cause for pride."

"I recognised a lot of people." Pamela continued. "My Uncle Gene was there, he passed away when he was only 39. He taught me a lot, he taught me how to play my first guitar. So was my great-great Aunt Maggie who was really a cousin. On Papa's side of the family my grandfather was there. And I saw many, many people I knew and many I didn't know, but I knew that I was somehow connected to them."

"They would not permit me to go further." Pamela said sadly. "It was communicated to me, that's the best way I know how to say it... that if I went all the way into the light something would happen to me physically. They would be unable to put this me back into the body me, like I had gone too far and they couldn't reconnect."

"Is the light God?" Pamela asked while there.

She received the communication: 'No, the light is not God. The light is what happens when God breathes.' And at that point," Pamela said with a sense of wonderment, "I remember thinking: I'm standing in the breath of God."

When reminded that it was time to return, however, Pamela was not so sure.

"Of course, I had made my decision to go back before I ever laid down on that table," she said, "but you know, the more I was there, the better I liked it."

"My uncle was the one who brought me back down to the body. But then I got to where the body was, I looked at the thing, and I for sure did not want to get in it because it looked pretty much like what it was, as in void of life, and I knew it would hurt so I didn't want to get in. But he kept reasoning with me."

'It's like diving into a swimming pool, just jump in!' her uncle encouraged her.

"No!"

'What about the children?' he asked.

"You know what, I think the children will be fine."

'Honey, you've got to go.' He pleaded.

"No!"

After being in 'standstill' for over an hour, the surgical team began the process of warming Pamela's body, then shocked her heart.

"The tunnel was pushing and the body was pulling," she explained. "He pushed me! He gave me a little help there. It's taken a long time, but I think I'm ready to forgive him.

"I saw the body jump, and then he pushed me and I felt it. The sensation of it was rather like diving into a pool full of ice water. It hurt! And I came back with a jolt."

Pamela even recalls the song playing in the operating theatre as she came back into her body - Hotel California, which included the line: "You can check out anytime you like, but you can never leave."

Cardiologist Dr. Michael Sabom researched Pamela's case extensively and concluded that "this is a classic near-death experience occurring under extremely monitored medical conditions where every known vital sign and basically every clinical sign of life and death was being monitored at the time. And that's what makes her case so remarkable and valuable to us."

Pamela's surgeon, Dr. Speltzer, added: "It struck me that this was incredibly perplexing and not understandable with what we know about the brain. Without any brainwave activity it is inconceivable to me that the brain can receive, internalise and maintain memory, but at the same time I think it is the height of egotism to say something can't happen just because we can't explain it."

On reflection, Pamela later summed up what she had gained from this experience: "I see us all as completely different tones. Everyone has a different tone. Now, we could go out of our way to make ourselves sound as much alike as possible, but that would be monotone, and how boring is that? The beauty's in the harmony. I believe that my reason for being is to learn to make harmony with all the variable tones that present themselves."

In an interview nineteen years later, Pamela was asked if she was afraid to die.

"Are you kidding?" she gasped. "I am more afraid to live! Dying is nothing. It's easy... living is hard."

Pamela passed of heart failure in May 2010 at the age of 53, just a few weeks after this final interview.

***

As could be expected, I spent many hours on my think-step, pondering this account.

If dead people were able to describe events and conversations that occurred around them while they had no brain activity, then surely this constituted evidence. Didn't it?

My paramedic acquaintance, Andy, had maintained that people who reported NDE's weren't really dead, but Pamela's case seemed watertight. She had literally been killed in order to perform the delicate operation inside her brain.

Doc David had insisted they only became aware of their surroundings as consciousness returned, but here was a woman being closely monitored by a team of medical staff to ensure there was no heartbeat or brain activity, yet she had been able to repeat conversations that had occurred not at the end, but during the surgery.

How could she have even heard these conversations?

George Redonaia had been locked in a freezer at the morgue when he communicated with a baby and learnt she had a broken hip. If this had subsequently been proven incorrect, his claim could have been dismissed as fantasy.

But it wasn't fantasy. The baby did have a fractured hip. How could George have known this?

I had set out to find pre-Moody NDE's in an effort to prove, to my own satisfaction, that modern-day accounts were not simply copycats. I confess, I had fully expected to discover that the opposite was true.

Now, a decade later, I was having difficulty maintaining my scepticism.

CHAPTER 34

BROW

I turned the collar of my jacket up as I sat on the top of a narrow fence post in the hospital car park. The wind was biting. After numerous attempts, the end of my cigarette finally glowed amber in the dusky light of daybreak, and I inhaled the comforting smoke.

How I hated these times.

More than a decade had passed since Mum had lost the will to live and I had prepared myself to deal with her death.

Leaving work to care for her meant not only giving up the luxury of a steady income, it also meant forfeiting holidays, evenings out, shopping trips, and every other opportunity to leave the house for more than a quick trip to the supermarket.

Coffee and a chat with friends was almost a distant memory. People I once called friends expected more of my time, and when I couldn't oblige, they quietly and unapologetically disappeared from my life, save the occasional rushed phone call and the polite "I must get around to catching up with you one day, it's just that we've been so busy!"

I could deal with it. My mother was more important. Dr. Wong had brought her through her rapid decline ten years earlier, but he hadn't been able to prevent the regular and sudden bouts of unexplained painful bloating.

Occasionally, these could be dealt with by district nurses who, when I phoned them at 9am, vowed they would be there "very soon".

They invariably arrived late afternoon.

On those days, the chair by the front window replaced the back doorstep as my thinking place so I could watch every car go by and pray to whoever might be listening to "please let this be the nurse."

It was the endless hours in emergency rooms that wore me down. They always began with the arrival of the ambulance, the medic examining her and asking a myriad of questions, then a transfer to a stretcher when every movement caused her to cry out in pain.

Arrival at the hospital meant another transfer, this time onto a cold, hard trolley, followed by a long wait before anyone approached us.

The same questions were asked, the same answers were given. Another long wait. Another doctor. A repeat of the questions. The same answers.

I occasionally joked that perhaps we could simply write out the answers and hand out photocopies to all and sundry. Mum never laughed at my feeble attempt to raise her spirits.

Depending on the day of the week and time of the day, we could spend four, five, even six hours in the emergency room. Weekends were horrific. Sometimes we would be placed in a queue, waiting for our turn just to enter the emergency ward.

After she had seen a doctor and I was content that her presence had been officially acknowledged, I would begin pacing the corridors, checking back regularly to see if the curtain was still around her cubicle. If it was, then a trip to the coffee machine or a cigarette in the car park was in order.

Then I would return to the emergency ward to consult with the doctor, who would invariably explain that she was not eating enough fibre and that she needed to increase it dramatically.

She was eating enough fibre. As I was later to discover, that was part of the problem!

Our emergency room visits ended when I helped her into the car and drove her home in the early hours of the morning.

After a restless few hours in my own bed, I would stagger to the kitchen and make her a cup of tea. As I handed it to her, she would smile, struggle to sit up, and say "oh lovely, thank you. I'm feeling so much better this morning."

Panic over. Life back to normal. At least until next time.

Would that be next week? Next month? Who knew?

Would she come home next time?

My mother was now seventy-five years old, and paper thin. When she had been weighed a year ago at the hospital, she had barely reached

35 kilos (around 77 pounds).

At least, I kept reminding myself, we had come through the worst of it. Eleven years ago, she had slept through an entire year. Eleven years ago, she had been rushed to hospital almost on a monthly basis. These days, ambulances only had to call a few times each year.

We could only take one day at a time and hope for the best.

***

"Brow!" Mum said as I wheeled her back to the car.

"What's brow?" I asked.

"Brow. Bran, rye, oats and wheat. The first letters spell brow. That's how I'll remember them."

I nodded. If Dr. Heidi had advised Mum not to eat those foods, then we would both need to ensure she avoided even a hint of them. I had grown to trust this amazing doctor since an acquaintance alerted me to her "unconventional" practice a few years earlier.

"She's a qualified doctor" he explained, "but she has little or no time for conventional medicine since she cured her son of an illness the medical profession gave up on! She uses pulse diagnosis to tune into the body and find out what *it* wants instead of what doctors want to give it or do to it."

More out of curiosity than need, I visited her in 1999 and discovered that pulse diagnosis was only part of her technique. Dr. Heidi worked on auric fields, intuition, and, I suspect, a pinch of psychic ability thrown in for good measure.

Mum had not been out of the house for five years, but I was so impressed with our new unconventional doctor that much to my mother's dismay and constant protests, I insisted on driving her the twenty kilometres to Dr. Heidi's clinic.

The first thing she perceived when meeting my mother was a little unnerving. "Part of your soul is missing," she said. "You lost it somewhere back in your past. Would you like me to see if I can retrieve it?"

Mum nodded without expression, and I smiled inwardly at the progress I had made over the past ten years. There was a time I'd have scoffed at such a claim.

These days I was starting to recognise that anything was possible and everything was probable.

Trying to explain my ever-expanding philosophy to a neighbour, I had likened it to drawing a line in the sand.

"This is the line I mustn't cross!" I said. "I draw the line, I make the rules. On this side, everything is acceptable, on that side, nothing is. Then I learn something, hear something, experience something, and I edge that line just a little further away, and then a bit further. Eventually I'll see there's no need for a self-imposed line at all."

"Hmmm, ok," Carol nodded, "but doesn't that just make you more than a bit gullible? What if Tinkerbell is riding a pet unicorn beyond where you drew your line?"

I shrugged. "Well, I guess if I see Tinkerbell on a unicorn, they both must be there."

"Or you're about ready for the funny farm!" she quipped.

We laughed, but I knew she had a point. Regardless of how confident I pretended to be, I still needed proof and more proof of each new revelation. I still drew that line in the sand.

The concept of heavenly lights and tunnels were becoming second nature to me, but celestial temples and floating doctors had not yet made it to my side of the line.

While I no longer scoffed at the idea of deceased loved ones greeting the dying or nearly-dying, I still considered spirit guides and celestial angels to be fanciful notions.

Now — and I noticed this with some pride — I was accepting that my mother had carelessly misplaced part of her soul, and that this medically qualified doctor was offering to retrieve it.

I silently hoped my mother also accepted it.

"Let's see if we can find out when you lost it," Heidi said, taking my mother's wrist between her finger and thumb, closing her eyes and quietly counting backwards.

"Yes, there it is!" she said quietly. "1956."

Mum and I exchanged amazed glances.

My parents had met at a local dance during world war 2. An air-force military policeman, Bert returned to his post in Papua New Guinea the day after their meeting.

Although my mother was still grieving over the death of her fiancé the previous year, she found herself strongly attracted to the handsome, dashing officer. They corresponded regularly and he eventually proposed in a letter.

Alas, the next ten years were not exactly domestic bliss, due mainly to my father's roving eye. They parted in 1956. Apparently, he took part of Mum's soul with him.

Heidi sat in silence for a few minutes, her eyes closed.

"OK," she sighed. "It's back. Now, let's see what's going on physically."

As she tested various foods and chemicals — reminiscent of the vega test I had arranged so long ago, but this time without electrical equipment — four foods kept emerging as culprits. Bran, rye, oats and wheat. While not prepared to use the word "coeliac", Heidi strongly advised her to stay away from these foods.

These were the very foods I kept piling on her plate in an attempt to heed the advice of numerous doctors who kept insisting she need more fibre, more fibre, more fibre. I had even sprinkled bran over her evening meals regularly!

I spent days researching everything on my bookshelf and in the library on gluten and Coeliac disease. Symptom matches were uncanny and included the inability to gain weight, digestive disturbances, bloating, nausea, even muscle weakness due to ineffective nutrient absorption and poor peristaltic action.

My mother seemed to grow weaker and thinner every day. Her appetite was still poor, her energy levels low.

"No, I doubt she's coeliac!" her new doctor dismissed my suggestion during his next home visit. "People with coeliac disease usually get diagnosed in childhood. But if you want, I guess I can set up some tests" he shrugged, adding that "they might be a bit invasive at her age and in her poor state of health."

"Don't worry," I shook my head, "just forget I even mentioned it."

Along with Barry, Mum and I had moved to a new area five years earlier, and I wasn't about to argue with the only doctor we'd found who was willing to make house calls.

From his very first visit, this one was as determined as Doc David to prove I was totally ignorant about all matters of a medical nature. I wondered if there was a secret newsletter that circulated amongst GPs to alert them to 'difficult relatives of patients who think they know everything but talk nonsense'.

What I learned during subsequent research, however, was that many coeliacs were not diagnosed until late in life when the damage to the digestive system had already taken its toll. Many were not diagnosed at all, in fact.

Some health professionals insisted that most cases of Irritable Bowel Syndrome were due to undiagnosed coeliac disease, and suggested that gluten intolerance may be caused by an excessive intake of offending grains and genetic modification of such grains in modern times.

I changed my mother's diet radically, purchasing gluten-free foods, finding inventive substitutes for threatening foods, preparing and cooking her meals apart from ours.

Her health improved daily. Her appetite also improved. Her energy and her enthusiasm for life increased. I wondered what might have been had we known about this years earlier instead of when she was almost eighty.

If I needed any proof, it came a year later when I discovered a local pizza shop boasting "gluten-free pizzas." Mum had always loved pizzas but the gluten in pastry prevented her from having one. I asked her to choose her toppings.

"Ham and pineapple!" she beamed. When I phoned to order, I asked for assurance that their pizzas were totally gluten-free.

"Absolutely!" was the immediate response.

I had not seen my mother eat so enthusiastically for years. She devoured the entire, albeit small pizza. The following morning, she was again bloated and in pain, and another rush to the emergency room ensued.

I racked my brain. What else had she eaten? Was this episode proof that gluten was not causing these symptoms? It could not have been the pizza, they had assured me it was gluten free. But, just to be sure, I phoned the pizza shop again later that day.

"You're completely sure your pizzas *are* free of gluten?"

"Absolutely!" was the confident reply. "We only use gluten-free pastry!"

"Pastry?" I gasped. "What about the ham?"

"Ham?" he asked, a little quieter than before. "Ham has gluten?"

"Yes!" I shouted down the phone "Ham has gluten! So you didn't use gluten-free ham?"

"Er... no. I– um– we... didn't know that."

I had my proof. Dr. Heidi had been right. Again.

CHAPTER 35

THE RIVER OF FORGETFULNESS

Another element that emerged within the transformative aspect of NDE's was the glimpse of a place where all knowledge seemed to co-exist in a timeless state. Those who were fortunate enough to gain access to this realm reported that they easily and instantly knew all the answers to all the questions they had ever asked, or ever could ask, or hadn't even thought about asking.

Moody had written about this 'instant absorption of knowledge' in 'Life After Life'. One young man had said that the other side was: "...a place where the place is knowledge... you absorb knowledge... you all of a sudden know the answers."

A middle-aged woman said "it was like I knew all things," adding that she still wanted to seek knowledge on this side, because she felt that seeking answers was "...part of our purpose, but that it wasn't just for one person, but that it was to be used for all mankind."

I had wondered at the time of reading these why, if you suddenly knew all the answers, you would still want to seek knowledge. Then I read that most were unable to bring this knowledge they had gained back with them.

Many commented that they returned with a need to try and recapture some of the understanding they had gained in the light but had lost on their return.

Another woman told Moody: "this all-powerful knowledge opened before me. It seemed that I was being told that I was going to remain sick for quite a while and that I would have other close calls. And I did have several close calls after that. They said some of it would be to erase this all-knowing knowledge that I had picked up, that I had been granted the universal secrets and that I would have to undergo time to forget that knowledge."

Moody drew a comparison with the description of warrior Er's near-death experience in Plato's Republic. While dead, Er was told he must return to physical life so he could tell others what death was like. Among many other wonders, Er described souls camped by the River of Forgetfulness, adding: "they were all required to drink a measure of the water... and each one as he drank forgot all things."

In 'The Journey Home', Phillip L. Berman related an account by Lynn Pielage-Kissel who bled to death in 1976 after an horrific accident on a skating rink. After being revived, she recalled: "Instead of information and stimulus slowly filtering into the brain through the senses, I could now absorb almost everything instantaneously, directly from the source."

Gene Albright died in 1960. In an interview for Fate Magazine, he said: "During the death experience I learned that in exactly seven minutes of normal, conscious time, I would return to my body and consciousness. In this very short time I learned more than in my entire previous 34 years. I learned what love is and how it works. I realized that life energy is itself love."

Author Leslie Grant Scott made a similar observation when she died in Ceylon in 1918. "...my consciousness was growing more and more acute," she wrote. "It seemed to have expanded beyond the limits of my physical brain. I was aware of things that I had never contacted."

Scott added: "I have never lost this sense of the underlying unity of all things, but I was obliged to narrow my vision so that it might fit the brain which I had to use."

Years later, I heard an interview with NDE researcher Dr. Jeffrey Long, who spoke of an experiencer who told him that "the universe of knowledge he had during his NDE was like trying to hold an ocean of unearthly knowledge in a tea-cup of his brain."

A tea-cup of his brain? No doubt German physicist and philosopher Gustav Fechner would agree with that quaint phrase. In 'The Little Book About Life and Death', (1836) he discussed the limitations of man's intellect during earthly life:

"In normal life, consciousness can accommodate just one thought and one memory at the same time. We can never access the entire contents of our mind all at once. Our powers of recall can only be in one place at a time; if we want to bring something to mind we have, so to speak, to search our memory with a feeble lantern that throws light in a narrow beam and leaves the rest in dark. Man thus wanders about like a stranger in his own mind."

At the 1937 bicentenary celebration of the Royal Medical Society in England, Sir Auckland Geddes related the strange (at the time) account of a man he knew who had died and returned to tell a fascinating story about gaining knowledge on the other side.

His account is one that I had difficulty fitting into the teacup of my own brain.

Sir Geddes was a qualified physician, a University Professor of Anatomy, British Ambassador to the US, and a military major during world war 1. He was hardly someone inclined to believe everything he heard. His lecture was reviewed favourably in the 1937 Edinburgh Medical Journal under the title 'A Voice From the Grandstand.'

According to Geddes, this man whose story he was about to relate was highly credible but wished to remain anonymous. "It is not a fake!" Geddes insisted. "Without certainty of this I should not have brought it to your notice."

Some suppose that the man he referred to was also a physician, while others firmly believe that Geddes was actually relating his own experience.

This anonymous man, Geddes explained, had spent an agonizing night suffering what he initially believed to be an attack of acute gastroenteritis. By the following morning his condition had worsened, and he recognised the symptoms as acute poisoning.

At no time did the man's consciousness appear to be in any way dimmed, Geddes related, but he suddenly realised that this consciousness was separating from another consciousness, which was also him.

He became aware that the consciousness that remained within his body was beginning to disintegrate, while the consciousness which had begun the process of separation was now altogether outside that body.

I decided this account needed to be read with a strong coffee, otherwise my own consciousness might also begin disintegrating! I was yet to discover how much more complicated it would become.

The anonymous man observed his physical form in the bed, then became aware that he could also see everything in the house and garden, then realized he was seeing not only things at his home, but also in London, and Scotland, and wherever his attention was directed.

Wow! Two decades earlier, author Leslie Grant Scott said much the same after departing from her physical body: "My vision was also extended, so that I could see what was going on behind my back, in the next room, even distant places."

"I could 'see' in either direction with ease." Aubrey Eggleston also agreed after dying of a heart attack in the 1930's.

Seven hundred years earlier, medieval abbot Caesarius of Heisterbach (circa 1180-1240) wrote of his own experience, in 'The Dialogue of Miracles', declaring that his soul moulded like "a glassy spherical vessel, with eyes before and behind, all-knowing and seeing everything at once.

In 1982, cancer survivor Mellen-Thomas Benedict described an eerily similar experience when he died and later stated he saw "every room in the house, and the roof, and even under the house."

More about Benedict later. For now, we'll let Geddes continue his talk.

Sir Geddes explained to the audience that from outside his body, this dying man searched for an understanding of this strange phenomenon and received an explanation from a source he could not identify but chose to call his 'mentor'.

He was told that he was free in a time dimension of space where 'now' was equivalent to 'here'.

This helped him understand that his vision included not only 'things' in the three-dimensional world, but also 'things' in the four or more dimensional places in which he found himself.

He confessed that he could find no words to describe what he saw, but was "conscious of a psychic stream flowing with life through time" and which provided "the impression of being visible." This visibility seemed to him to have particularly intense iridescence.

I paused to try and get my head around this, then wondered if I would ever be capable of understanding such concepts.

I understood that a three-dimensional world (length, width and height) was the physical one in which we lived, but what were "things in the four or more dimensional places"?

What did "a psychic stream flowing with life through time" actually mean?

How could one have "the impression of being visible"? And how could that visibility have "intense iridescence"?

I was afraid that the more I read, the less I would understand, and I was right.

This dying man, Geddes explained, recognized that around each brain there seemed to be a condensation of the psychic which appeared as a small cloud. He then realized he was a condensation in the psychic stream, a sort of cloud that was not a cloud. The visual impression he had of himself was blue.

My own brain was desperately trying to operate in a cloud of condensation. "So, we just become a blue cloud when we die?" I asked him.

As usual, there was no response, so I reluctantly allowed him to continue.

This dying man, Geddes continued, understood that "our brains are just end organs projecting as it were from the three-dimensional universe into the psychic stream and flowing with it into the fourth and fifth dimensions."

The dying man's 'mentor' explained that the fourth dimension was in everything existing in three-dimensional space, and that at the same time, everything in the three-dimensional space existed in the fourth dimension, and also in the fifth dimension.

According to Geddes, the dying man clearly understood that 'now' in the fourth-dimensional universe was the same as 'here' in a three-dimensional view of things.

Thank goodness someone understood! My frustration increased, but at the same time, something nagged at me, something about everything in three-dimensional space existing in the fourth and fifth dimensions.

Was heaven just another dimension? Even with scant knowledge of science (I failed the subject in spectacular fashion in year 8 and had avoided it ever since) I knew that quantum physicists had suggested such a concept.

Physicist Dr. Michio Kaku used carp swimming on the bottom of a shallow pond to illustrate dimensions. In an article entitled 'Black Holes, Worm Holes and the Tenth Dimension', Kaku states:

"To a carp, the universe only consists of two dimensions, length and width... they are incapable of imagining a third dimension beyond the pond. The word 'up' has no meaning for them."

I doubted that any word would have meaning for a fish, but I took his point.

Kaku explained that carp might become vaguely aware of a world beyond the surface of their pond if it rains, because the surface of their pond becomes rippled, and this ripple could be likened to the carp's third dimension. That is, if they were smart enough to recognise it.

"Likewise," Kaku wrote, "although we earthlings cannot see these higher dimensions, we can see their ripples when they vibrate... light is nothing but vibrations rippling along the fifth dimension."

Forget the carp! Were *we* smart enough to recognise this?

In 'The Philosophical Writings of Niels Bohr', this Nobel prize-winning pioneer in quantum physics stated that "anyone who is not shocked by quantum theory has not understood it."

Bohr was right on both counts. I wasn't shocked. And I didn't understand it.

Was 'heaven' just another dimension of the one we currently occupy? Perhaps we only needed a physical body to exist in this dimension, but discarded it when the time came to enter a dimension where such physical encumbrances were no longer necessary.

This brought to mind a diving suite — necessary for deep-sea diving but totally superfluous once the diver emerges from those depths. We would all look a little silly waddling down Main Street it a cumbersome diving suit. Perhaps, we would all look equally silly lugging a physical body around in heaven!

Somehow, that almost made sense. It also hinted at how temples and mountains could exist beyond the earth plane. (i.e. "everything in the three-dimensional space existed in the fourth dimension, and also in the fifth dimension.")

In her book, 'Unseen Adventures' (1951), Geraldine Cummins suggested much the same concept when she wrote: "It seems that we human beings see each other because we are all travelling on the same wavelength; at the same rate of speed. Death may perhaps be defined as simply a change of speed. Our souls cast off our material bodies and occupy bodies of another more rapidly vibrating substance. There are things to be seen beyond the range of the eye, things to be heard the ear has not heard. If we exchange our present senses for others, attuned to different wave lengths, we enter a world not unlike our own."

A change of speed! Of course!

If you watch a fan operating at top speed, the blades spin so rapidly that it's not possible to see individual blades, but does that mean those blades don't exist? Of course not!

The vibratory rate of a dog whistle is beyond that to which our ears are capable of hearing, but dogs can hear it!

Our eyes don't see all the colours in a rainbow. Some anthropologists have even suggested that ancient people saw fewer colours than we do today!

Dimensions. Vibrations. Wavelengths. This concept was actually starting to make a little sense. All the same, it would require many more hours of deep doorstep-pondering and would lead me into a whole new realm of thought about apparitions and apports and even disembodied voices.

But I mustn't get ahead of myself! Back to Sir Auckland Geddes.

This anonymous man, Geddes revealed, began to see living people on the earth plane and noted different colours and levels of 'psychic condensation' surrounding each one of them. He observed a woman with "purple and dark red condensation" enter his room and hurry away to phone the doctor. He watched as the doctor arrived and examined him.

"He is nearly gone," the doctor announced.

"I was really cross," the man reported to Geddes later, "when he [the doctor] took a syringe and rapidly injected my body with something which I afterwards learned was camphor. As the heart began to beat more strongly, I was drawn back, and I was intensely annoyed because I was so interested, and just beginning to understand where I was and what I was seeing. I came back into the body really angry at being pulled back, and once I was back all the clarity of vision of anything and everything disappeared, and I was just possessed of a glimmer of consciousness which was suffused with pain."

That this man was "just beginning to understand" before being pulled back offered some relief to my befuddled brain, which seemed quite incapable of comprehending a fraction of what he had experienced.

The anonymous man acknowledged that once back in the body, he possessed only a "glimmer of consciousness."

It would seem that a "glimmer of consciousness" was all most of us were capable of possessing while occupying a physical body in this third dimension, due, perhaps, to our "teacup of a brain".

Sir Geddes concluded his talk: "This man felt sure it was not a dream," he explained, pointing out that "...it has shown no tendency to fade like a dream would fade."

"What are we to make of it?" he asked the audience.

There was no response.

Today, many could relate to this account. According to most near-death experiencers, a higher understanding during the 'out-of-body' state is common, as is the ability to travel instantly to wherever one's thoughts flow. Many feel anger at being returned to the body, and also retain a clear recall of events which, they insist, are not at all like dreams yet continue to remain clear throughout the years.

Note: they retain a clear recall of events, not the knowledge they have absorbed during their heavenly visit.

One man, however, did appear to bring much of this knowledge back with him.

CHAPTER 36

SPONTANEOUS HEALING

Artist Mellen-Thomas Benedict's death from terminal brain cancer occurred in 1982. Benedict's claims of the knowledge gained during his 'time out' have been tested by a number of scientists, all of whom are in awe of what he has been able to retain. His story was told in Deepak Chopra's book, 'Afterlife'.

In the final weeks of life, Benedict's organs were shutting down. He admitted himself into a hospice program and was being cared for around the clock by a hospice caretaker. In the early hours of one morning, he suddenly found himself fully aware and standing up, looking at his body in the bed.

Suddenly, a magnificent light appeared. Benedict wanted desperately to go to it, but he was also aware that if he did so, he would be dead.

"Please wait." He said. "I would like to talk to you before I go."

What a cheek! But it worked. The entire experience halted as if the pause button on a dvd remote had been pressed.

"I had conversations with the light," Benedict later reported. "[It] changed into different figures, like Jesus, Buddha, Krishna, archetypal images and signs. The information transmitted was that our beliefs shape the kind of feedback we receive."

Benedict learnt much from his telepathic conversation with the light. Then, he rocketed away from the planet.

"I saw the earth fly away," he later wrote. "The solar system whizzed by and disappeared. I flew through the centre of the galaxy, absorbing more knowledge as I went."

Benedict was in good company. As we know, Burris Jenkins accelerated through intergalactic space in 1957, Mary Grohe hurtled through it like a projectile, and Carl Jung viewed earth from far above in 1944.

Throughout the ninety minutes Benedict was 'away', his earthly body showed no vital signs, yet he returned to his body. "I was never told that I had to come back," he states. "I just knew that I would."

Three months later, scans showed absolutely no trace of cancer.

Why didn't Mellen-Thomas Benedict forget everything he had learnt, as others did? According to Benedict, it was because: "I asked never to forget the revelations and the feelings of what I had learned on the other side."

Ask and ye shall receive?

Since that time, Benedict claims he has maintained direct access to Universal Intelligence and can return to the light at will, enabling him to act as a bridge between science and spirit.

That's easy for him to say, but can he back it up? It would certainly seem so. His claims that he can see microcosmic structure has led to him being closely involved in the mechanics of cellular communication and research dealing with the relationship of light to life. This research has provided dramatic perspectives on how biological systems work and how living cells can respond rapidly to light stimulation for high-speed healing.

According to the senior psychologist to the Canadian Olympic Team, Lee Pulos: "It is clear that he is able to simultaneously span several octaves of consciousness from which he can acquire biological information that is extraordinary." (Miracles and Other Realities, 1990)

Dr. Janice Holden, was astounded when "under hypnosis, Benedict was able to give information about, and draw the genetic make-up of a rare neuromuscular disease," adding that: "it is not the kind of thing where one could cheat."

Benedict's miraculous healing may or may not have been the first to occur under these circumstances, but it would certainly not be the last. During the years the followed, a growing number of people would report entering the light as they died, being greeted by a being of light and given information, then returning to life either totally healed or well on their way towards it.

A brand new phenomenon seemed to be emerging.

In 2002, Anita Moorjani, an Indian woman born in Singapore and living in Hong Kong, was diagnosed with Hodgkin's lymphoma. Despite all efforts to heal her, Moorjani's tumors rapidly spread throughout her lymphatic system. Four years later, her body was no longer able to continue functioning and her organs began shutting down.

In 2006, Moorjani lapsed into coma and was admitted to hospital. "It's too late to save her," the doctor told her husband.

"Who's the doctor talking about?" Moorjani asked. "I've never felt better in my life! And why do Mum and Danny look so frightened and worried? Mum, please don't cry. What's wrong? Are you crying because of me? Don't cry! I'm fine, really, dear Mama, I am!" (Dying To Be Me by Anita Moorjani, 2012)

Moorjani thought she was speaking these words out loud, but no-one heard them.

It is not clear whether she was clinically dead at any time. The oncologist sent her to the radiology lab so he could do a full body scan, but in order to slide her into the MRI capsule, she needed to be disconnected her from the portable oxygen tank. When this took place, she began to choke and gasp for air due to the build-up of fluids in her lungs.

That was just her physical body. Her 'other' body felt wonderful.

"I can move around freely now without any help!" she realized. "And my breathing is no longer labored, how amazing this is!"

Then her father arrived. He had died seven years earlier. "Sweetheart," he said, "I want you to know it's not your time to come home yet."

Now, this was a statement I had heard more than once during my research!

"But," he added, "it's still your choice whether you want to come with me or go back into your body."

Anita Moorjani was given a choice! I had only come across a few cases where this happened, such as Percy Cole who had died during dental surgery. Cole's guide, Dorothy, had said "you can stay here with us if you like."

"This is as far as you can go," Moorjani's father then warned. "If you go any further, you cannot turn back."

Deciding that life was too painful, she made the decision to go towards death. What followed is a very personal story which needs to be told in Anita Moorjani's own words. Her book, 'Dying To Be Me', provides this complete and compelling story.

While not wishing to spoil the ending (her book is really more about what she learnt while on the other side, and why she chose to return) Moorjani's eyes flickered open thirty hours after lapsing into a coma and willingly embracing death.

Her doctors ran tests two days later, and these confirmed that her organs had miraculously started functioning again.

Five weeks after being admitted, further tests revealed that the numerous tumors doctors had scanned and described as "the size of lemons" had miraculously vanished.

She was completely free of cancer.

She was also a totally changed person. What she learnt served as the catalyst for her rapid healing.

Today, Anita Moorjani tours the world giving inspirational talks to packed audiences.

Two years after Moorjani's amazing experience, Dr. Eben Alexander — a scientifically-minded, dyed-in-the-wool sceptic about all things 'paranormal' — also journeyed beyond the veil.

Dr. Alexander was a highly trained neurosurgeon. For over two decades he had operated on countless brains. He understood brains. He knew that consciousness was merely a by-product of the brain. He knew that once the brain was no longer able to function, it meant 'lights out'.

Well, that is until he awoke in tremendous pain on a November morning in 2008. When his wife came to check on him, he was having a grand mal seizure! He was rushed to hospital and diagnosed with e-coli Meningitis. Less than one in ten million people per year contract this disease, and only a fraction survive.

By the time the diagnosis was made, the likelihood of Alexander's survival was down to just two per cent. His chance of neurological recovery, however, was zero.

In other words, if a miracle occurred and he lived, his level of intelligence would probably be comparable to that of a relatively smart carrot!

Alexander spent seven days in deep coma. Doctors considered ceasing all treatment to allow him the dignity of dying peacefully. Meanwhile, Dr. Eben Alexander was having the experience of a lifetime.

A week after being admitted to hospital, his eyes flickered and opened.

A slow and painful recovery lay ahead. It took about two months for Alexander's neurosurgical knowledge to return, but that it returned at all was indeed a miracle beyond anyone's most optimistic expectations.

Bearing in mind that his brain had been subjected to long-term bacterial attack and had been literally drowning in pus, the medical staff had no doubt that he would spend the rest of his life in a zombie state.

Alexander was intrigued not only by his own miraculous recovery, but also by what happened during the time he was comatose. He described "a real experience in a very real place, more real than this earthly realm."

"Based on my previous view of neuroscience," he explained in an interview a few years later, "there should have been no way to have any kind of rich, ultra-real, interactive experience."

But he did have such an experience. The belief he shared with most members of the medical profession that consciousness could not exist independently of the brain had proven to be false.

"Given the fact that we don't even know how general anaesthesia works," he confessed during this interview, "and we use this every day, we've done it for a hundred and fifty years and we don't have a clue how it takes away consciousness, that should give you an idea how little we really know about consciousness."

As a neurosurgeon, he was in a unique position to share this revelation with his medical colleagues, so he set out to write an academic paper. He came up with nine hypotheses that might have explained his journey.

Eventually, he realised that none of these hypotheses worked to explain what had happened. He discarded the academic paper and poured his experiences into a book. 'Proof of Heaven: A Neurosurgeon's Journey Into the Afterlife' quickly rocketed to best-seller status.

Dr. Alexander had never bothered to read any of the near-death experience material. He had known they were all nonsense. It was only when he finished writing his story that he read his first book on the subject, and then he was blown away by the similarities to his own "very real" journey.

"It was a very real experience because it really happened," Alexander stated emphatically in a later interview. "I see an underlying reality of an afterlife realm that's very real. It's more real, and more fundamental, than this earth-like reality we live in. I know from my experience, it proved to me, that ... we are conscious *in spite* of our brain, and that's a very important concept. The brain is more of a reducing valve, a filter or a veil, and it's there for a purpose."

Quite a conclusion for a sceptical neurosurgeon!

***

Like Dr. Elisabeth Kubler-Ross, sceptical neurosurgeon Dr. Eben Alexander had risked his reputation by publicly declaring that he had no doubt of the existence of an afterlife, while I, who was a long way from being a highly esteemed scientist or neurosurgeon and had no public reputation to protect, still allowed myself to be swayed occasionally by those who scoffed and insisted it was all nonsense.

Of course, I would defend the evidence passionately against these nay-sayers. What did they know?

How much had they read on the subject? Were they aware of the work by Dr. Moody or any of the others who had contributed to the body of evidence lining my bookshelves and scribbled in my notebooks? Did they know about Dr. Eben Alexander or Anita Moorjani? Of course not.

Then, alone on my doorstep, I would second-guess myself again. Perhaps the sceptics were right. Maybe everything in the universe was made of physical matter, including us.

Dust to dust.

What more did I need to convince me? Perhaps I was waiting for someone to knock on my front door and say "Yeah, I know I died, but here I am to show you that we really do survive!"

Be careful what you wish for!

CHAPTER 37

BE CAREFUL WHAT YOU WISH FOR

KNOCK! KNOCK! KNOCK!

"Who on earth could that be at this hour?" Mum called from her bedroom. I was already out of bed and striding down the hall in total darkness.

"Don't open the door!" she warned.

There were glass panels on either side of the front door, and the veranda was well lit by a streetlight. I glanced at the panels as I rushed past the door on my way to the front window, but saw no shadow there.

Reaching the window, I peered into the night and scanned the open expanse of lawn, the driveway and the street. Again, I saw nothing. I returned to the front door and opened it cautiously, safe in the knowledge the security door was locked.

I wondered why Barry had not leapt up to assume the role of protector and bravely search the premises. I knew he always slept soundly, but those knocks were not mere taps!

"Not a soul to be seen!" I reported when I entered Mum's bedroom. "No-one at the door, no-one out the front! It must have just been the creaking of the house."

"Nonsense!" she said, propping herself up in bed and lighting a cigarette to help calm herself. "That was a very aggressive knock! Houses don't make noises like that unless they're about to fall down!"

I shrugged. "I know. But I was there in seconds and I didn't see a thing."

I glanced at the clock. It was just after 1am. Ours was a quiet neighbourhood, far from shops and traffic. As far as I knew, there were no children living nearby who would play such a prank.

Mum looked anxious, and I was also feeling more than a little unnerved. "I think we both need a cuppa!" I smiled.

***

The shrill ring of the telephone woke me around 8am. I was still bleary-eyed through lack of sleep following the fright of our phantom visitor and staggered out of bed as Barry took the call. He spoke quietly, replaced the receiver, then beckoned me to follow as he made his way to Mum's bedroom. Once there, he made the announcement.

"Bert died last night."

My father was dead!

A few seconds passed in silence. Then, Mum looked at me in wide-eyed amazement. "Oh my God."

I knew what she was thinking before she voiced it, and my legs suddenly felt weak. I lowered myself onto the edge of her bed.

"That was him!" she said quietly.

"Three!" I replied. "Just like Nan with the lights!"

Barry looked totally bewildered. "Him? Three? What *are* you two talking about?"

"There were three loud knocks on the front door last night." I explained. "You slept through it! Mum and I both heard them, loud and clear. I was running around peering through windows, trying to see who it was."

"You didn't hear it because it wasn't meant for you." Mum said to Barry. "It was for us. He came to say goodbye."

I thought back and smiled. "And I said there wasn't a *soul* to be seen!" I said. "I guess I was half right!"

I later learned that my father, who had suffered for many years with a number of chronic illnesses, had died in hospital at around 1 o'clock that morning.

CHAPTER 38

THE RESEARCH CONTINUES

Following hot on the heels of the early research conducted by Sabom and Ring, and the subsequent formation of the fore-runner of IANDS in 1977, George Gallup Jnr had directed his staff to conduct a series of national surveys probing attitudes and beliefs Americans held about immortality, with an emphasis on what he termed 'temporary death experiences.'

Gallup's book, 'Adventures in Immortality: A Look Beyond the Threshold of Death' (1983), was based on the findings of these surveys and revealed that nearly two-thirds of the US population believed in an afterlife.

Aware that many Americans were regular churchgoers and as such, may have been inclined to accept their church's teachings about life after death without insisting on evidence, I was inclined to disregard this result.

Far more interesting, however, was the amount of NDEs revealed in this poll. About 35% of those who had come close to death reported having experienced one!

I reminded myself that this poll had been conducted just five years after the initial publication of 'Life After Life' and once again (will I ever learn?) suspected that many of those surveyed had probably wanted to get on the bandwagon and lay claim to an experience they had recently read about.

Was the average person really so desperate for attention?

If I was going to deafen the now-occasional sceptical whispers in my ear, I needed to find more answers. Had the percentages held strong, now that the initial excitement had quietened down?

Were there even any up-to-date statistics available? If so, where would I find them?

Had any other member of the medical or scientific community been inspired to take up Dr. Moody's challenge to "research the topic with an open mind"?

I reviewed my bookshelves. Disregarding my endless collection of pre-Moody NDE accounts, I found only eight post-Moody books on scientific research written by six medical professionals. Two of these books were by Dr. Moody himself!

A recent addition to this pathetically small post-Moody collection was 'The Truth in the Light: Investigation of Over 300 Near Death Experiences' (1995) by Dr. Peter Fenwick, a British Neuropsychologist and consultant at the Institute of Psychiatry.

Fenwick had read 'Life After Life' many years earlier but, like many of his colleagues, he had been sceptical of what he regarded as merely anecdotal evidence without scientific validation. He was later forced to reassess his opinion, though, when one of his own patients described an NDE to him that was very similar to those he had read about in Moody's book.

As a result of this breakthrough, he set about collecting and analysing over three hundred NDE accounts, and in 1987 presented his findings in a television documentary. After its screening, over two thousand letters poured in from people who had also experienced NDE's, many of whom expressed relief that what they thought was a unique experience had also happened to others. Their accounts served as a basis for 'The Truth in the Light'.

Dr. Fenwick later became president of the British branch of IANDS.

Moody, Ring, Sabom, Morse, Currie, Fenwick. Hardly a revolution in medical research!

I was disappointed. The late 70's and early 80's had held so much promise for further understanding of this phenomenon, and it seemed as though it had died with barely a whimper.

How much I still didn't know.

***

As difficult as it is for us to imagine today, in the mid to late 1990's the internet was not a major part of life for most people, myself included. There were very few home computers, and information via the web was still scant.

By the turn of the century, however, a whole new world had opened

245

up, and I discovered there had been far more activity going on behind the scenes than was revealed on bookshop shelves, even those at the Theosophical Society!

To begin with, the internet introduced me to Radiation Oncologist Dr. Jeffrey Long, who had discovered an interesting new way to gather data and make it easy for people to report and share their experiences.

Dr. Long had "stumbled" across the phrase near-death experience in 1984 in a medical journal, but had not taken the concept too seriously. He later wrote in his book, 'Evidence of the Afterlife': "I was born into a scientific family... I developed a great respect for science."

Several years later, however, Long heard a friend's wife tell of her own near-death experience. It sparked his interest and prompted him to embark on a lengthy period of research.

By 1998, Dr. Long was convinced. He formed the Near Death Experience Research Foundation (NDERF) and developed a website to collect accounts from people all over the world in order to study them.

This website also gave experiencers a unique opportunity to describe their NDEs anonymously, but the questionnaire they needed to work through was hardly a walk in the park. It was lengthy and detailed. Those who were not serious about their claims and chose to fill it out for lack of anything better to do would — and probably did — quickly give up, finding more fun watching paint dry.

Provision was even made on this questionnaire for reporting NDEs in a variety of languages to ensure no cultural bias.

In the first ten years, this unique website registered more than 1,300 people who took the time to work through over one hundred questions. Dr. Long examined every aspect of each account and found "remarkable consistency" among accounts across cultures, religions and societies.

Extracts from many of these accounts (which now number in the many thousands) are included in Long's 2009 book, 'Evidence of the Afterlife', in which he lists his "nine lines of evidence" for the validity of the NDE. "I long ago quit believing that death is the cessation of our existence," Dr. Long confessed in his book, adding "it took me a long time to reach this point."

The NDERF website continues to grow daily and provides fascinating reading.

***

I quickly became an internet junkie!

Hundreds of documentaries were available on youtube. Numerous podcasts offered interviews with medical researchers. I no longer needed to regret that I was unable to attend afterlife conferences around the world when the internet allowed me to sit back and watch them for free.

One documentary provided an amusing account by Alan Sullivan, who had been undergoing emergency heart surgery in 1988 when he suddenly found himself rising upward.

"They put stuff over my eyes," he explained, "and still I could see, and I could see through the operating table and I could see what kind of boots he [the surgeon] had on... I'm up looking down at what used to be me. It wasn't me because real me was up here watching."

Alan saw himself on a table covered with light blue sheets. His eyes were taped shut and a framed drape hid his chest from his face, yet he was able to observe that he was cut open to expose his chest cavity.

What he saw next, however, totally confused him. The surgeon, Dr. Takata, began flapping his arms as if he was trying to fly!

Dr. Lasala, a colleague of the surgeon, later confirmed that Dr. Takata would regularly allow other members of the team to prepare the patient before he took over, and that after scrubbing up he would often put his palms flat on his chest to avoid contamination, then point instructions to the team with his elbows.

To Alan, who was floating near the ceiling, this translated as a credible bird imitation!

"I cannot explain how he saw these things," Dr. Takata later confessed.

***

Further searches also brought Nurse Janet Schwaninger to my attention.

In 2002, Schwaninger (co-ordinator of cardiology care at Barnes-Jewish Hospital in Missouri) and her colleagues published the results of a prospective study of cardiac arrest patients they had conducted over the previous three-year period.

They used Dr. Ring's interview schedule, then did a follow-up using Ring's Life Changes questionnaire.

Schwaninger's interest in the subject began when she witnessed the cardiac arrest of a medical colleague in 1989. It had taken seven defibrillations to revive him, and once conscious, he described witnessing the entire event from a vantage point "to the left in the upper corner of the room."

247

He knew how many defibrillations had been required, and also declared that there had been a spiritual entity with him the entire time who had told him that "everything would be ok, no matter how things turned out."

"He'd never heard of NDEs", Schwaninger explained in an interview with Paul Bernstein, adding "I was very moved by how significantly this physician's life changed in the year following his experience."

This prompted Schwaninger to learn more about the subject. Eventually, she drafted a research proposal to be conducted at the hospital. To her surprise, it was approved.

During this study, the results of which were published in the 2002 IANDS Journal of Near-Death Studies, thirty resuscitated patients were interviewed. Of those, seven (about 23%) reported an NDE, and four who did not have an NDE reported having experienced one during a previous life-threatening event.

All eleven survivors said they felt nothing but peace at the point of death, and all but one experienced an out-of-body state. Schwaninger heard reports of meeting deceased loved ones, seeing brilliant lights, and meeting mystical beings. Only one experienced a life review.

Once again, the Schwaninger study revealed that the percentage of elements occurring during NDE's decreased proportionally according to the depth of the experience.

The pattern continued to hold fast.

One intriguing account in this study was related by an experiencer who reported that since their nde, they feel a tingling sensation in their spine whenever they think or say something negative. Perhaps this provides a lesson for all of us, even if we haven't been sensitized by an NDE to be aware of it!

Once the public heard about Schwaninger's research through the media, many contacted her to relate their own experiences.

"Some of them dated back to the 1930's," Schwaninger remarked, "[and]... they all said there was some kind of survival of their soul or consciousness beyond the physical."

She added: "I even had physicians come up to me and say: you know, I had one of those experiences myself."

Another aspect of separate consciousness also emerged during Schwaninger's research.

"There's this whole new awareness of how we treat patients when we think they're unconscious," Schwaninger pointed out. "Medical colleagues have commented: I never thought about it when I said things while the patients were supposedly unconscious, that maybe they could hear what I was saying."

The interview ended with Schwaninger asking those who are researching this area to never give up, because "it's so significant, and there's something so important that's being said by the patients, significant information that's being given to humanity."

"And not just the message is important," Schwaninger continued, "but how we see that such a brief experience can so profoundly change a person's life. How important it is to recognise and address these experiences in the management and care of patients."

***

In 2001, yet another name had burst onto the scene while I wasn't looking.

As with many science professionals, Dutch cardiologist Dr. Pim van Lommel had not taken NDE's seriously. He knew, without doubt, that all brain function ceased during cardiac arrest, and he accepted that it was impossible to have memories or dreams while clinically dead or comatose. That's why it took him almost thirty years to process an experience he had as a young doctor.

In 1969, six years before Dr. Moody coined the phrase near-death experience, cardiologist Dr. van Lommel attended a patient who died on the operating table. The medical team leapt into action and spent four desperate minutes trying to resuscitate him.

The patient's heart eventually responded and he regained consciousness. Everyone was delighted. Everyone, that is, except the patient, who was furious and demanded to know why he'd been brought back!

He later confided to Dr. van Lommel that he had visited "the other side" and he described what he had experienced. It had been so wonderful, he explained, that he had not wanted to return.

Of course, Dr. van Lommel knew this was impossible. He filed it away as an intriguing but inexplicable story, but never really forgot it.

Then, in 1986, he chanced to read 'Return From Tomorrow', Dr. George Ritchie's book about his death during world war 2 and his flight through the night sky and subsequent return to life.

Van Lommel recalled the patient who had also reluctantly returned to life and told him about travelling through a tunnel toward a bright light, seeing colours and beautiful landscapes and hearing divine music.

249

This nudge prompted him to start asking resuscitated patients if they had "any recollection of the period of their cardiac arrest."

He considered it highly unlikely he would find any. After all, apart from Ritchie's experience which occurred in the 1940's, he had only ever heard of one case, and that had been back in 1969.

Over the next two years, van Lommel questioned over fifty survivors. Imagine his shock when twelve of them told him about their NDE's!

Initially, he wondered why he had only heard about one in all his years as a cardiologist. He later admitted it was because "I had not inquired after these experiences, because I had not been open to them."

Throughout the ensuing years, Dr. van Lommel began to suspect it was possible consciousness existed independently from the brain, and that the brain merely served as a kind of receiver, functioning like a television, radio or mobile phone, merely receiving information but not actually generating it.

He was not alone with this suspicion. More and more researchers have reached the same conclusion, including British Dr. Sam Parnia.

In a recent lecture available on the internet, Dr. Parnia asked the audience the following questions: "Why is it that if you put two brain cells together with a little bit of electricity, you suddenly have a thought? Where do thoughts come from? How is it possible that a brain cell can generate thought?"

No-one raised a hand to offer any explanation.

"It doesn't make sense, he pointed out. "It's a brain cell. It makes protein!"

Almost a century earlier, Nikola Tesla — physicist, inventor and a man ahead of his time — was quoted as saying "my brain is only a receiver. In the Universe there is a core from which we obtain knowledge, strength and inspiration. I have not penetrated into the secrets of this core, but I know that it exists."

Science freely admits it still knows little or nothing about consciousness. What is it, and where does it come from? It has been assumed that it is produced by the brain, and that we see, think, believe, feel and understand because of the brain.

NDE's have prompted science to reconsider this belief.

When thousands of people declared clinically dead insist they had remained conscious, then the question must be asked: If this occurs when there is no measurable brain activity, what part does the brain actually play in generating consciousness?

Unable to dismiss his suspicions that the brain was merely a receiver, in 1988 Dr. van Lommel instigated the first large-scale prospective study into the near-death experience.

Prior to this, research on NDEs had been retrospective, meaning that people were asked to come forward and report NDEs that had occurred to them in the past. Alternatively, they were contacted through old hospital records and asked about the time they had been clinically dead.

Because of the time lapse between the experience and the interview, it was often difficult to make an accurate assessment of all the varying factors.

In many cases, medical records were not easily obtained, attending physicians or witnesses could not be contacted, and determining which medication, or how large a dose a patient had been given at the time or how long they had flat-lined was usually impossible.

A prospective study, on the other hand, means that researchers interview patients as soon as possible following their resuscitation. This ensures that all medical records are readily accessible, and that hospital staff are available to provide details of the incident.

Another advantage of prospective studies is that all patients who experienced a cardiac arrest are interviewed, not just those who report an NDE. This provides a comparison between those who had an experience and those who didn't, and offers far more reliable data.

For example, some scientists still insist that NDE's are caused by lack of oxygen to the brain during the period of clinical death, but a comparison between those who have an NDE with those who don't provides evidence that this cannot be a contributing factor.

After all, everyone who is clinically dead for more than a few seconds begins to lose oxygen flow to the brain, so if this was the cause of NDEs, why wouldn't everyone who survives cardiac arrest also hallucinate heavenly realms or have memories of anything at all while they were flat-lining?

The same logic applies to medications, religious beliefs and a variety of other factors.

If only religious people saw heaven, or only those who were given a certain medication imagined they were out of their bodies, it would all be easy to dismiss.

It is still not understood why some survivors of cardiac arrest experience NDE's while others do not, but at least extensive research over the years has been able to reveal that certain factors do *not* cause them.

It is also possible that everyone who dies and is later resuscitated does experience an NDE, but for some reason not everyone remembers it. There have been cases of people whose memories have been triggered months or years later.

Studies also revealed that fewer survivors who had been given painkilling or sedative drugs reported NDE's, negating the belief still held by some that medications cause these hallucinations.

If that was so, one would expect a higher frequency of reports by such patients, not fewer. However, it does beg the question: do medications block survivor's recall of NDE's, and is this why some do not recall an experience?

Funding for research projects are often difficult to obtain, so van Lommel and his colleagues volunteered their own time and expertise.

They continued to do so for the next thirteen years. Between 1998 and 2001, this team of researchers set about gathering 'on the spot' information from resuscitated patients at ten hospitals throughout the Netherlands.

They interviewed 344 survivors, most of them within 5 days of their resuscitation, then used Dr. Ring's Weighted Core Experience Index to analyse them.

When results were correlated, it transpired that 62 of these 344 patients (or around 18%) had an experience.

Around one third of these reported meeting with deceased persons, moving through a tunnel, and/or observing a celestial landscape. Around a quarter said they left their bodies, communicated with a light, or observed colours. Only a few experienced a life review and/or encountered a border.

Again, these percentages remained faithful to previous studies.

In an interview with Dr. Jeffrey Long, van Lommel said: "... patients were clinically dead, flat EEG, no electrical activity in the cortex, and loss of brain stem function evidenced by fixed dilated pupils and absence of the gag reflex, [yet] the patients report a clear consciousness in which cognitive functioning, emotion, sense of identity, or memory from early childhood occurred, as well as perceptions from a position out and above their 'dead' body." (IANDS website interview of Dr. Pim van Lommel by Dr. Jeffrey Long)

Statistical results of this study, published in the peer-reviewed medical journal, Lancet in 2001, confirmed once again that medical factors did not appear to account for the occurrence of the NDE, nor did age, gender, educational standards, demography, religious beliefs, medication, oxygen deprivation, belief in an afterlife or prior knowledge of near-death experiences.

Subsequent 2-year and 8-year follow-ups were also conducted, and scientists were surprised to find that those who had reported an NDE still recalled it with the same degree of vivid detail as they had when initially interviewed.

Imagine being able to do that for a dream or an hallucination!

These follow-ups also revealed positive changes in lifestyles and attitudes, along with a considerably reduced fear of death, while those who did not report an NDE showed no evidence of such changes.

The following intriguing case was included in van Lommel's Lancet article:

In 1979, a 44-year old man was found unconscious in a rain-soaked field in Holland. He was comatose, hypothermic, and had no pulse.

An ambulance arrived and rushed him to the emergency department of Canisius Hospital where, moments before resuscitation was attempted, a male nurse noticed the patient was wearing dentures. He removed these so a ventilation mask could be safely put over the unconscious man's mouth, then placed them in the crash cart.

The patient was successfully resuscitated and transferred to the Intensive Care Unit.

A week later, the same nurse was distributing medication to the patient's room.

"Oh, that nurse knows where my dentures are," the patient announced, then said to the nurse: "You were there when I was brought into hospital and you took my dentures out of my mouth and put them onto that cart. It had all these bottles on it and there was this sliding drawer underneath and there you put my teeth."

As the patient had been comatose from before the time of his arrival at the hospital until he woke up days later in Intensive Care, the nurse asked how it was possible he knew this.

He explained that he had seen it all from above and described correctly and in detail the small room he had been in, and the appearance of those present. He also confessed that he had been afraid they would stop CPR and had tried unsuccessfully to make it clear that CPR should be continued.

The nurse later admitted that as the medical staff had no idea how long the man had been clinically dead before arriving at the hospital, they had been doubtful CPR would prove successful. They had considered giving up on a number of occasions.

Four weeks later, the patient left the hospital a healthy man, complete with his own dentures. He had been deeply impressed by his experience and stated that he was no longer afraid of death.

In the four weeks following publication of his article in Lancet, Dr van Lommel received 265 emails, including many from physicians who wrote to tell him about their own NDEs!

His prospective study set a new standard in NDE research, and more prospective studies were subsequently initiated in hospitals around the world.

Dr. van Lommel resigned as a practicing cardiologist shortly after publication of his Lancet article to devote his time to further research, lecturing on near-death experiences worldwide, and writing a book.

'Consciousness Beyond Life' was first published in 2007 in the Netherlands and rapidly became a best seller. It has since been translated into English and continues to enjoy international success.

***

Then, just when it seemed that nothing new regarding near-death experiences could be studied, when every question had been asked and every answer had been computerised and analysed, when every ounce of data had been tabulated and every percentage carefully examined, another intriguing aspect of the phenomenon came to light.

Dr. Michael Sabom interviewed an American soldier who had served in Vietnam and had been almost fatally wounded in a mine explosion in 1969. He was amazed by what he heard.

"When I came down and hit the ground," he explained, "I remember sitting up... and I came out of my body and I perceived me laying on the ground with three limbs gone." (The soldier lost both legs and an arm in the explosion.)

Later, while undergoing surgery, the critically injured soldier watched from "the upper left" as the medical staff put a tube down his throat, cut his uniform off and removed what little was remaining of his left leg.

While this account is certainly pre-Moody, what's so astounding about yet another experiencer observing his operation?

Well, according to this hapless soldier: "I had no eyesight for about 3 weeks. I literally could not open my eyes... they had been singed and burned." How, then, had he been able to observe his surgery?

The soldier would not be the last non-sighted person to come forward and relate how he had observed his body from beyond it, but I was surprised to discover he was also not the first.

A similar experience had occurred to Gilbert Nobbs, an English officer of the Rifle Brigade. Nobbs published an article in 1939 describing his experience of being shot in 1916 during the first world war.

He described feeling peace and an indescribable happiness as he looked down at his body lying in the shell-hole and could see that he was bleeding from the temple. He was unaware at the time that the bullet lodged in his head had instantly caused permanent blindness.

I was dead," Nobbs added, "and that was my body; but I was happy!"

These are fascinating accounts, but would they stand up in a law court? Australian researcher Harvey Irwin didn't think so.

Aware that anecdotal evidence didn't constitute proof, Irwin set up his own study in 1987 and interviewed twenty-one people who were vision impaired.

Among them, he found three who reported having visual perception during out-of-body experiences. However, all three had residual or peripheral vision, invalidating the results.

All the same, this intriguing possibility eventually led Kenneth Ring to set up a similar study. He contacted various organizations for the blind and placed notices in their braille or audio newsletters, requesting that anyone who had experienced an NDE or an OBE contact him for inclusion in his study.

Twenty-one NDEr's aged between 22 and 70 were interviewed at length. While two of these were classified as severely visually impaired, the remaining nineteen had either been blind from birth or had lost their sight early in life.

Of the twenty-one participants, fifteen stated they had been able to see during their NDEs. Some had viewed their bodies, observed people around them and/or described their surroundings. A few of these reports had also been validated by outside witnesses.

Others described tunnels, lights and celestial landscapes, leading Ring to conclude that the blind do, indeed, experience visual perceptions while outside their bodies.

Brad Burroughs was one of these. His NDE occurred in 1968 when he died of pneumonia.

Brad Burroughs floated up through the ceiling and viewed the neighbourhood, then felt himself being pulled into a tunnel. As he reached the end of this tunnel, he became aware of a tremendous light that appeared to come from every direction. He emerged onto a field and began to walk along a grassy path.

"It seemed like everything, even the grass I had been stepping on seemed to soak in that light. It seemed like the light could actually penetrate through everything that was there, even the leaves on the trees. There was no shade, there was no need for shade...yet I wondered how I could know that because I had never seen before that point."

While Brad may have wondered about it, he appears to have taken his new-found sight in his stride, while some visually-impaired NDEr's found this aspect of their experience frightening and felt more comfortable in the unsighted world to which they were accustomed.

Vicki Umipeg, who had been blind since birth, had (in her own words) "never been able to understand even the concept of light." Vicki's NDE resulted from an automobile accident in 1973. (Of course, Vicki wasn't driving!)

Like Brad, Vicki was sucked into a tube, then rolled out to find herself lying on grass.

As she later explained: "Everything there was made of light... it was like love came from the grass, love came from the birds, love came from the trees."

"It was very foreign to me to be able to perceive anything like that," she later confessed. "It was very discomforting... not a pleasant thing at first. It was rather scary. I couldn't relate to it."

Vicki's testimony can be viewed on a number of youtube documentaries.

Others found that having sight was initially confusing but they relaxed into it as the experience progressed.

Sight-challenged Marsha had an NDE in 1986 as a result of complications during pregnancy, and later reported: "...I don't think it was my eyes. I don't know how it works because my eyes were back here and since they are not right and I could see everything right, there had to be more special vision somehow."

Another blind experiencer, Debbie, died in 1971. Like most NDErs, she didn't want to return to her body, but she had an additional reason for her reluctance: "...because I knew I wouldn't be able to see in it."

Details of this study, along with participants' individual experiences, are included in Dr. Ring's 1999 book, 'Mindsight'.

CHAPTER 39
NOT THE END

Was scientific interest in the afterlife dead? Not at all. If anything, it had gradually became more accepted by medical and scientific professionals over the years.

Until the internet opened up a whole new world for me, I had no idea (and who would?) that peer-reviewed articles about NDEs had appeared in countless medical journals.

During the first thirty years of NDE research (1975-2005) at least 55 researchers or research teams conducted over 65 retrospective and prospective studies in the US, UK, Australia, Europe and Asia, involving over 3,500 research participants and resulting in the publication of over 700 peer-reviewed journal articles.

Wow! And all continued to validate Moody's initial findings.

Nor did I know how common near death experiences were! While various methods of resuscitation had been used throughout history, it was not so long ago that the patient's chest would need to be surgically opened, the ribs spread and the heart manually massaged.

This was obviously a technique, which could only occur in a hospital, and was one that was rarely used. Oral resuscitation and pressure by hands on the chest worked occasionally, but was nowhere near as successful as modern-day resuscitation procedures.

Prior to this, drowned people have been subjected to a variety of hopeful resuscitation techniques, including being rolled over barrels or flopped over the back of a horse which is then made to gallop in the hope this would rid the deceased person's lungs of water or jump-start the heart.

As Dr. David Casarett points out in his book, 'Shocked: Adventures in Bringing Back the Recently Dead', rescuers in days gone by were sometimes encouraged to "beat the victim with whips or sticks", presumably in an effort to get the heart beating again, or to light a pipe and blow the smoke into the victim's mouth or nostrils.

I wondered what the Cancer Council might say about that technique!

In the past three decades, more people have been snatched back from the brink of death than at any time throughout known history.

In the 1980's, defibrillators became standard equipment at most hospitals, and the more recent development of portable defibrillators meant that not only could these potentially life-saving devices be used in the back of an ambulance on the way to hospital, but in many cases they have been available even before an ambulance arrived.

Is it merely a coincidence, I wonder, that this highly effective technique (defibrillators can provide a first shock success rate of 90% or more!) came into regular use so soon after the publication of 'Life After Life'? Was the 'universe' (or however you wish to interpret that word) working through Dr. Moody to prepare us for the innumerable near-death experiences we would soon start hearing about?

Research in the twenty years between 1988 and 2008 by giants in the field of near-death research such as Drs. van Lommel, Parnia, Waller, Yeates, Fenwick, Holden, Ring, Sabom and Greyson have indicated that between 9% and 18% of those successfully resuscitated report a near-death experience, while paediatrician Dr. Morse insists that around 85% of resuscitated children report an NDE.

Perhaps most children are less concerned what others think and therefore less inclined to keep such experiences to themselves!

Results of the Gallup Pole conducted in the U.S. in 1992 suggested that 5% of Americans (or a whopping 13 million people!) had experienced an NDE.

Results of a German study in 2001 indicated that 4% of that country's population laid claim to having an NDE.

That's not 4% of those who died and were resuscitated. That's 4% of the country's population of around 80 million!

Four years later, a telephone and computer survey of the Australian population conducted by Roy Morgan Research revealed that 8.9% of Australians reported taking a peek across the veil.

When you take into account the number of countries in the world, that adds up to a *lot* of people!

Could all those who share their accounts be lying? Why? And why would those who were sceptics before their experience — and there have been many — make up a story to prove themselves wrong?

Could they all be experiencing hallucinations? If so, why are millions of people around the world having the same hallucination?

Some say anecdotal evidence does not constitute proof, and of course, they're right. A few people seeing fairies in the garden or insisting they patted the Loch Ness Monster can easily be dismissed.

But allow me to pose this scenario: if you were being tried for a crime, and millions of people who didn't know you or know each other came forward to testify that they had seen you commit that crime, and all provided very similar accounts, do you think their testimonies would still be considered anecdotal?

Would you be free to walk out of the courtroom at the trial's end?

All those exhausting hours I had spent browsing the bookshelves at the TS Bookshop had also failed to reveal that there had been numerous presentations at scientific conferences around the world, leading up to the first international medical conference on near-death experience in 2006 at Martiques, France.

To coincide with this occasion, eight participants including Drs. Raymond Moody, Pim van Lommel, Sam Parnia and Marcel Beauregard signed a public statement regarding their convictions.

It began: "We are a group of dedicated physicians and scientific researchers working in different scientific fields and from different countries who share a common interest in the subject of near death experiences."

This group statement pointed out that NDE's cannot be reduced to a mere illusion or hallucination, and that "exciting recent scientific studies of NDE's have raised many intriguing questions we hope will be answered by further research."

The group considered it "of the utmost importance that scientists wishing to understand the nature of human consciousness ... conduct research in scientific fields, notably neurosciences, without prejudice."

At last, it seemed science was starting to listen!

In 2008, the University of Southampton announced their collaboration with 30 hospitals, universities and medical centers in the UK, the U.S. and Europe, launching the biggest research project to date, the Aware Study (AWAreness during REsuscitation).

Under the leadership of Dr. Sam Parnia, the AWARE Study aimed to test the validity of out-of-body experiences and claims of conscious awareness during cardiac arrest, and was funded by the Horizon Research Foundation, the UK Resuscitation Council and the Nour Foundation in the US.

One of the methods devised was to place a hidden visual target (a word, number or picture which staff themselves would know nothing about) face up on a high shelf in selected hospital rooms in order to test the perception of any patient experiencing an out-of-body state.

The initial results of the first four years of this project were published in the medical journal, *Resuscitation* in 2014 and revealed that of 2,060 cardiac arrests that occurred during those four years, 140 patients survived, and of those, 101 could be interviewed. Nine reported an NDE. Once again, we see that the rate of recall is *around* 10%. (In this case, 9%).

Unfortunately, none of the nine patients who reported NDEs had been resuscitated in rooms where targets had been placed.

The real question is that even if there had been a target, would the patient have noticed it? As nurse Penny Sartori pointed out, patients experiencing out-of-body states during resuscitation are usually far more interested in what's going on around their physical body on the bed below, or high-tailing it to the waiting room to try and provide comfort to loved ones than to search for things they don't even know exist!

It would be both unethical and counter-productive — not to mention terrifying — for patients to be advised on entering hospital that "we have targets on top of shelves in some rooms, so if you happen to die while you're here and leave your body and go up to the ceiling, please look around, and if you see one, and if you happen to be fortunate enough to survive, please report back and tell us what you saw."

However, veridical perceptions did take place, regardless of targets.

One patient heard an automated voice saying "Shock the patient, shock the patient" and later described rising to a position near the ceiling and looking down on his body. He described a bald, chunky man by his bed, and was able to recognise him the following day.

Medical records confirmed the automated instructions and the identified man's role in the patient's resuscitation. It also confirmed that the patient's observations had occurred during the three-minute period when there was no heartbeat, yet it is known that the brain typically ceases functioning within 20-30 seconds of the heart stopping.

Dr. Parnia felt that this case and similar ones were significant, bearing in mind that it is often assumed [these] experiences are like hallucinations or illusions occurring before the heart stops or after it has been successfully restarted.

Most patients who reported having out of body experiences were able to accurately describe procedures and equipment used during their resuscitation, while members of the control group (that is, those who had undergone resuscitation but had *not* experienced an OBE) had no idea how they had been resuscitated or made guesses based on what they had seen in TV shows.

"I used to really strongly believe that our mind and consciousness comes from the brain," Dr. Parnia stated in an internet presentation. "I had no doubt about it... until I started doing this research, and I had to question all the basic assumptions I had."

Another example of veridical perception during cardiac arrest that may have led to Dr. Parnia's self-questioning was provided during one of his lectures.

Dr. Tom Aufderheide was in the audience and stood to relate his story, which Dr. Parnia later included in his book 'The Lazarus Effect'.

Dr. Aufderheide stated that at the time of the incident, he had only been a doctor for five days. He had been sent to the CCU to see a heart attack patient, but to the young doctor's horror, the patient had a cardiac arrest just as he was introducing himself.

Completely inexperienced in dealing with such an event, his first thought was: "How could you do this to me?"

In those days, the only option when a patient had a cardiac arrest was to give them an electrical shock, and Dr. Aufderheide did just that, numerous times.

Unfortunately, the patient just kept having more cardiac arrests, so Aufderheide stayed with him, shocking him each time he died.

After eight harrowing hours, the nervous young doctor was tired and hungry, but he could not leave, so when the patient's lunch was brought in, Aufderheide ate it at the bedside.

It took thirty days for the patient to regain his health sufficiently to leave the hospital. Shortly before he did, he asked Dr. Aufderheide to come in, shut the door, and sit down.

He then told the doctor about his near-death experience.

He described a tunnel, a light, and his conversations with deceased loved ones.

If this wasn't shocking enough for an inexperienced young doctor to hear, what the patient said next really floored him:

"You know, I thought it was awfully funny... here I was dying in front of you, and you were thinking to yourself: 'How could you do this to me?' And then you ate my lunch!"

Dr. Aufderheide admits he has been fascinated by near-death experience ever since, and now asks patients who had a cardiac arrest if they have a story to tell.

He confirms that around 10% of his cardiac arrest patients admit to having had an experience. (The Lazarus Effect, Dr. Sam Parnia, Rider, 2013)

***

A further two-year study, Aware II, commenced in 2015.

While the technique of placing targets on high shelves is still being employed, two new aspects were included: the monitoring of brain-oxygen levels to determine whether those who experience out-of-body states retain higher levels of oxygen in their brain than those who don't recall an experience, and audio-recording of interviews for future comparisons.

Nurse Penny Sartori was delighted when the AWARE study was announced. She he had become disillusioned with her 17-year career as a nurse in the Intensive Therapy Unit where so many patients died and there was nothing she could do to help.

"I just wanted to hug them all and make things better for them," she later wrote in her book, *'The Wisdom of Near Death Experiences: How Understanding NDEs Can Help Us to Live More Fully'.*

In an effort to understand what these patients were going through so she could find ways to enhance their care, Penny had begun reading everything she could find on death and dying, yet she continued to sink even deeper into depression.

Eventually her reading brought her to books on near-death experiences and she thought "Wow! These people are telling us that death is nothing to be afraid of!"

She confided to another nurse that the only thing that could keep her working in this field was being able to research NDE's. Her confidante simply laughed.

Two years later, she was granted permission by the Ethics Committee to be included in the UK's first long-term prospective study on NDE's under the supervision of Dr. Peter Fenwick, a British Neuropsychologist and consultant at the Institute of Psychiatry and who we met earlier in this book.

The study began in 1997, and for the next eight years, Penny

Sartori's life was consumed by research into NDE's, which gained her a PhD in 2005 and was followed in 2008 by the publication of her thesis as a book, *'The Near-Death Experiences of Hospitalized Intensive Care Patients: A Five Year Clinical Study'*.

In the first five years of the study, Penny heard fifteen NDE accounts. During interviews with thirty-nine recent survivors of cardiac arrest, seven reported NDE's, while eight other patients who did not experience cardiac arrest this time around voluntarily provided accounts of their NDE's from previous occasions.

One of her more intriguing cases concerned a man who had cerebral palsy. He was recovering from a critical illness when he suddenly began deteriorating rapidly.

Later, when he had been revived and Penny interviewed him, he told her about floating to the top of the room, seeing his body on the bed, visiting his deceased father and being told to go back.

He was also able to correctly identify which doctor had examined him, describe the actions of Penny (who was nursing him) and the physiotherapist, both of whom were at his bedside at the time.

He stated: "that other girl was there too, she was hiding outside the curtains, she was worried about me and kept looking to see how I was."

Penny Sartori was able to confirm all aspects of his observations.

Then, she asked him about any changes that may have occurred as a result of his experience. The patient proudly opened his right hand. Prior to this, his hand had been permanently and tightly contracted for many years as a result of cerebral palsy.

Penny consulted with physiotherapists and doctors and was informed that the tendons in the hand would have shortened so much over so many years that such a sudden recovery was "simply not possible!"

Fourteen years later, Penny Sartori interviewed the patient again.

He could still recall his experience with absolute clarity. His hand was still open, although with advancing years it had developed arthritis and now caused him difficulty picking up coins.

He later stated: "If the doctor said to me I was going to die tomorrow then I would just sit back and enjoy it. I'm not saying I want to die but I'm saying I won't be afraid when I do go. I tell everyone I meet not to be afraid of dying."

***

Yes indeed, there had been a lot more going on beyond the

bookshelves than I knew about or had even suspected, and it all came about because a young medical student had asked himself more than a quarter of a century ago whether he had been fortunate to have heard the only two accounts of near death experiences that ever happened, or if, perhaps, there might have been more.

"Would you have a copy of 'Life After Life'?" I had enquired at my local bookshop almost twenty years earlier.

It seemed like a thousand years ago.

The bookseller had fetched the book, opened it, and read the author's words aloud to me: *"I am not under the delusion that I have proven there is life after death."*

As keynote speaker at a conference thirty years after publication of this book, Dr. Raymond Moody made the following statement:

"I never suspected when I was a younger person that I might reach a point in my life when I seriously entertained the notion that it [the afterlife] was a reality. But through a long process, I've now come to a point where I do accept, to my utter astonishment, this is a reality. We *do* seem to survive death."

Now, thirty years after purchasing his 'innocuous little paperback', and having spent endless hours on the doorstep questioning, arguing, pondering, demanding, reasoning and pleading with the universe, I was inclined to agree!

To my own utter astonishment, it seems I now *DO* believe that we survive death!

CHAPTER40

THIS MUST BE WHAT HEAVEN IS LIKE

Desperate to get my mother out of the house where she had held herself captive for so many years, I suggested we travel in a wheelchair-accessible taxi on her birthday in late August and do some shopping.

Apart from two visits to Dr. Heidi, trips in the back of an ambulance to emergency rooms had been her only outings over the past fourteen years. None had been voluntary trips.

Surprisingly, she was excited about the prospect.

We had a perfect day. She shopped for a soft hairbrush and zipped around the supermarket in her wheelchair, excitedly browsing shelves and choosing items I would never have thought to purchase. It had been many years since she had been in a supermarket, and she was amazed at the never-ending array of new products available.

"Oh look, frozen gluten-free chocolate chip cookie mix!" she beamed. "I can make us some of those! And I need to find some tinned tomatoes and curry powder, I'll show you my recipe for curried sausages! And where's the herb section, I need some ground rosemary for the stew next time we make it!"

I glanced at the shopping trolley and immediately began steering her towards the checkout. I wasn't sure I had enough money for all the items she had already snatched gleefully from the shelves or pointed at for me to retrieve.

We ended the day at a café, sipping coffee in the sunshine.

She came home exhausted, but happy.

***

"Norma died!" Mum announced after hanging up the phone a few weeks after her shopping trip.

Norma was my father's sister. She had also remained my mother's friend for almost seventy years. She was ninety years old, so her death was hardly a surprise. Then again, it was. Like her mother, my feisty Irish grandmother Nora, Norma was a strong, independent woman. She lived alone and "managed very well, thank you very much!"

"Are you ok?" I asked Mum on hearing the news.

"Oh, just a bit shaken," she admitted. "It was so... unexpected."

My mother didn't eat much that night. Not that she ever did, but on this night she merely played with her food.

She didn't say much either. She went to bed early.

She didn't finish her dinner any night thereafter.

***

A few weeks later, the universe presented me with an opportunity to purchase a small second-hand wheelchair-accessible van.

Mum seemed excited and looked forward to visiting friends and relatives she hadn't seen for years.

The van sat waiting in the driveway for two weeks because she didn't feel up to going out.

Eventually, she agreed to a drive, and I quickly bundled her into the back of the van before she could change her mind.

We drove to the beachside resort of Sorrento. It was a mild spring day in early October. Not too hot, not too cold. A slight breeze ruffled the palm trees as I eased her wheelchair gently backwards down the van's ramp and wheeled her across the lawn into the shade of a palm tree beside the beach.

She shivered. "It's too cold here."

I re-positioned her in patch of pale sunlight on the walking path. She sat there silently, looking across the bay towards the mauve outline of the distant hills.

Colourful small boats bobbed about on the sparkling water. A few seagulls swooped above us in the pale blue sky, calling to each other.

"I think this must be what heaven is like," she said very quietly.

***

"Do you have something for anxiety?" I asked the pharmacist a few days later. "My mother's sister-in-law died recently and I think it hit her pretty hard."

"What are her symptoms?"

She's not eating and she doesn't seem interested in much any more. I think she's having anxiety attacks because she's having difficulty getting her breath now and then."

"How old is she?"

"She just turned eighty-eight."

My answer surprised me. Could my mother really be eighty-eight? When did she get so old?

I noticed the pharmacist frowned as she handed me a bottle of herbal anti-anxiety pills. It was as though she knew something that I didn't.

Chapter 41

THE BEGINNING OF THE END

"I don't feel very well."

How many times had I heard those words? Twenty-four years had passed since Mum cooked me an omelette and said she didn't feel well, twenty-four years since she went to bed for a year and I had known, without doubt, that she was dying.

During those years, we had coped with numerous ambulance trips to hospital for pain and bloating, and eighteen years ago, for a broken hip.

A decade ago we had also embraced a diagnosis of gluten intolerance and made radical but successful changes to her diet.

"I don't feel very well" had been uttered by my mother a thousand times in the past twenty four years, but this time, I felt a sudden, sick, sinking feeling in the pit of my stomach.

At the same moment my brain registered words from a voice I had not heard for twenty-four years.

This time it said: "The beginning of the end!"

Alpha, omega. And so it begins... the beginning of the end.

I jumped to my feet and grabbed the mobile hoist, wheelchair and lifting straps, then gently but urgently lifted her from the chair, wheeled her down the hallway, and lowered her into her bed.

"It's just like all the other times," I kept telling myself. "She'll feel better in the morning. She always feels better in the morning. It's just another little hiccup. It's ok. We can deal with it. We always have. It's ok."

But deep down, I knew it wasn't ok.

'The voice' had spoken.

At around 2am, my mother called for me. When I rushed to her room, I found her sitting up in bed, vomiting.

I called an ambulance. It took two hours to arrive.

The queue at the entrance to the emergency room at 5am on Sunday morning was unbelievable. Three men, arms covered with tattoos, sat on the floor like rag dolls, their backs against walls and their heads bowed. One man held a blood-soaked rag to his forehead, another nursed his arm and occasionally groaned.

Frail elderly people sat patiently in wheelchairs and looked bewildered as they waited their turn. Children cried and clutched at the skirts of their weary and worried mothers, tugged at the trouser legs of frustrated fathers.

Accident victims and drug-affected teens were skilfully manoeuvred past the queue and into the brightly lit hustle and bustle, disappearing into curtained cubicles.

Were we at war?

Ambulance crews kept wheeling people in on stretchers and depositing them against corridor walls. My mother was on one of those stretchers. Her face was pale and expressionless. Her eyes were closed. I hoped, I prayed that she was sleeping, then wondered how anyone could sleep in such a bright, busy, noisy, jarring environment.

Two hours dragged by. An orderly came and wheeled her into a cubicle. I sat beside her, holding her hand, waiting, worrying, willing her to live.

She'd be ok. Of course she'd be ok. She was always ok. We'd been here before. We knew the drill. She wasn't dying. She wasn't! She wasn't!

Where was the doctor? We'd be going home soon. Her hand was cold. Of course it was cold. She was on a cold, hard stretcher. She'd be warm soon. She could rest comfortably in her own bed. Soon. Why didn't the doctor come?

This time was no different from other times. Why would I think it was different?

Why didn't someone come? Anyone.

Was she still breathing? I stared intently at her chest.

Oh my God, breathe Mum. Breathe! Yes! I could just make out a slight movement as her chest slowly rose and fell, rose and fell. She was still breathing.

269

Of course she was still breathing. Why wouldn't she be still breathing?

Where was the doctor?

Why didn't someone come?

Please. Someone. Please come!

***

I stepped through the hospital's automatic glass doors and emerged into a pale, insipid dawn. I perched uncomfortably on the edge of a large rock in the garden and lit a cigarette. I needed time alone, time away, time to myself, time outside, time to think. I just needed time. I needed time for Mum, time for us.

This can't be happening.

The doctor had arrived and asked me to describe her symptoms and the events leading up to our arrival. Then he had called for a nurse and asked me to leave. As I backed out of the cubicle, he pulled the curtains closed.

This wasn't how it was supposed to happen.

How had I expected it to happen? Did I really believe she would simply drift away gently in her own bed as I sat beside her reading aloud from one of her favourite books? Did I think she might slip quietly away in her sleep and I would find her in the morning looking joyous and contented?

No. I didn't even try to imagine how it might happen, because it was never going to happen!

I wanted the two of us to keep playing cards on rainy days, laugh together at the silly things we saw in the newspaper, giggle our way through a Wii golf game as she swung the remote-controlled golf club from her wheelchair.

I wanted us to watch our favourite movies all over again. I wanted to read her favourite books to her once more.

I wanted us to look through photos of our driving trips around Victoria decades earlier so we could recall the fun we'd had.

I wanted to spend eternity doing all those ordinary, wonderful things we had always done.

I needed her to remind me to weed the garden or prune the overhanging branches. I needed her to prepare meals before I cooked them.

I needed her to talk about her younger days when she danced the nights away with handsome partners and tell me about the things that happened when I was too young to understand.

I needed her to validate my life.

I just needed her.

***

"Your mother is NOT dying!" The doctor insisted as I sat opposite him in the hospital meeting room.

I had arranged the meeting because I felt Mum was not getting enough attention in her final days.

While she had arrived at the emergency room at 5am, she had not been seen until mid-morning. Then she had been left in the cubicle while they decided what they should do with her.

When the nurse had approached me in the emergency room in the early afternoon and advised me that it might be a few days before she could be admitted to that hospital, I had decided it was time to lay down the law. I insisted she be transferred to another hospital immediately so she could get some rest in a quieter, more comfortable environment.

My demands had been met, but not until that evening.

She was transferred to a hospital closer to home at around 8pm, and two weeks later I sat in the meeting room and tried to hold my temper as I glared at a doctor who was trying to convince me that my mother was not dying.

"I asked," I pointed out coldly, "what you can do to make her final hours more comfortable. I know she's terrified of dying and I don't want her to suffer."

"And by the way," I added emphatically, "I can assure you that my mother IS dying."

The doctor sighed, the nurse beside him rolled her eyes, and Kathy, Mum's case manager and occasional sitter who had joined us for the meeting, shot me an angry look.

As a long-time nurse, Kathy knew better than to argue with doctors. It was clear that to this group — as it had always seemed to be with members of the medical profession — I was simply being difficult.

"Look," the doctor said in his most patronising voice, "she's eating well, she's not complaining about anything, she..."

"She's eating well?" I interrupted, my voice incredulous. "Now, that's interesting! She's been here for two weeks and she's eaten no more than

271

a few mouthfuls a day in all that time."

Three pair of eyes turned in unison to look questioningly at me.

As calmly as I could manage, I said "I come here three times a day to feed her. Or at least, to try and feed her. The meal is dumped on the over-bed table beside her and she can't even reach it. No-one bothers to sit her up or help her eat. I try to spoon-feed her, but after two or three mouthfuls she pushes my hand away. Then," I added, aware that I now had their undivided attention, "someone comes and takes the meal away. And you tell me she's eating well?"

There was some shuffling of feet under the table, and clearing of throats. "I'll... I'll look into that." The doctor frowned. Then everyone stood up to leave.

"Wait!" I shouted, aware that my voice sounded more like the crack of a whip. Everyone turned to look.

"I want to take her home. When can I take her home?"

"I'm not sure that's such a good..."

"I want to take her home!" I said again, this time pronouncing each word slowly and emphatically. I needed them to know that I was not interested further discussion on the matter.

"I'll see what I can do." The doctor nodded, his eyes fixed intently on his shoes as he swung the door open. The others followed closely behind him.

I remained seated and tried to regain my composure. I was furious that no-one seemed to know, or care that not only had my precious mother not eaten anything for two weeks, but that she was dying.

How could they not know? I had left her in their care, confident they would do everything possible to make her last few days more comfortable.

Instead, they had practically ignored her.

***

"I want to come home." Mum said when I eventually regained my composure and made my way to her room. "Can I? Please?"

Here eyes were red and watery.

I took her hand and tried not to let my face reveal my shock when I found it cold and limp.

"You'll be coming home soon." I smiled. "I just had a meeting with the doctor and he's going to arrange it."

She closed her eyes and sighed with relief. "I'm so tired."

"You'll be home soon." I squeezed her hand. "Now look, here's lunch! Let's see if you can eat something today."

"Take it away, I don't want any."

She grimaced, then looked at me pleadingly.

"Just take me home. Please?"

CHAPTER 42

GOING HOME

It took a week before the doctor could make the necessary arrangements for her discharge.

Every day I had to explain that "it will probably be tomorrow, the doctor's ordering an oxygen tank to be delivered and it should arrive tomorrow."

Every day she would close her eyes and sigh deeply. It was as though she was gritting her teeth and hanging on until she got home, and it was becoming more and more difficult for her, but we didn't discuss it.

I had given up trying to encourage her. Now, it was as though we both secretly knew that we were trying to beat the clock to get her home and into her own bed so she could finally let go.

I knew she preferred it that way. On a few occasions in the past I had tried to talk about the research I was doing, but each time she had waved me away.

"I don't want to talk about dying!" she had insisted.

***

I spent my time between hospital visits drinking coffee, smoking cigarettes and crying. Then I dried my eyes, splashed water on my face, travelled to the hospital and smiled brightly as I entered her hospital room.

At last, after three agonizing weeks in a noisy, impersonal hospital, the day of her discharge arrived. The doctor phoned to advise me that the ambulance would collect her at 10am the following morning and bring her straight home.

I arrived at 9.30 and sat at her bedside for most of the day. The ambulance eventually arrived at 3.30pm and she was delivered safely to her bed by 4pm. The oxygen tank had been set up the previous day, so I connected her to it and suggested a nice hot cup of tea.

She showed little enthusiasm but made a valiant effort when I brought it to her. I sat on the edge of her bed, held her hand and smiled as we talked about nothing in particular. I knew she wasn't ready to talk about what was happening. She was home, in her own bed. She could see the garden through her bedroom window. I was with her.

That was enough for now.

When she dozed off, I went to the kitchen and cried some more. And smoked some more. Then cried and smoked again.

***

Sometime that evening, she lost her ability to form words clearly.

Of course. She was home at last. She could finally start letting go.

"Would you like a nice soft boiled egg?" I asked her.

I translated "donn wonn, yuss wuwwa" into "don't want, just water."

I brought her a glass of water and held it to her mouth as she took a few sips, still unsure if my interpretation had been correct. Then I went back to the kitchen and cried some more. Each time I thought I was all cried out, the tears just kept right on coming.

I kept wondering how I was going to cope when the moment arrived. I had no doubt I'd be a basket case.

***

Hospice nurses called twice a day. They did whatever they needed to do, silently and efficiently, then left.

Over the next four days I lived in a dream-like state. I was physically and emotionally unable to do anything but sit beside her bed as she dozed or try to understand her when she spoke. Most of the time, I cried and smoked in the kitchen while she slept.

Day turned into night and back into day. I lost count of days and hours.

On the third or fourth day, the hospice nurse paused at the kitchen door as she was leaving.

"Hello, I'm Pam," she said, interrupting another crying session. "I just wanted to let you know that you're mother's seeing faces."

"Faces?" I gulped.

She nodded. "In the trees."

I looked at her questioningly. "What faces? In what trees? I don't understand."

Pam came into the kitchen and sat beside me. She took my hand and squeezed it. "When people are... dying," she explained, almost apologetically, "they often see... ah... people..."

"Yes, yes, I know that. I understand that." I said impatiently. "But why in trees? And which people? What did she say?"

"She didn't know who they were, she just said they were faces in the trees she could see from her window, but they weren't close enough to recognise."

I wondered how Pam was able to understand my mother's speech when I was having so much difficulty doing so.

"But you need to know what it means." Pam continued, squeezing my hand even harder, "They're nearby, and they'll start coming closer. It won't be too long now."

We sat in silence for a few moments while I tried to find my composure.

"How long is not too long?" I asked. "I want it to be over. I don't want her to suffer. How will I know when it's close? Is there anything I can do to get her through this so she doesn't suffer?"

My mouth began to quiver uncontrollably and I bit my lip in an effort to still it. "I just... I want it to be over!"

Pam reached into her bag and handed me a small bottle of drops. "If she gets stressed, put a few drops of these on her tongue, they'll relax her immediately. She's doing well," she assured me. "She doesn't appear to be in any pain. She just wants to sleep. My guess is she'll go to sleep sometime in the next day or two, and then she just won't wake up."

I felt the tears welling up again. "But how will I know when it's close? I need to be there. I have to be with her. What if I'm on the phone, or if I go to the toilet, or..."

"If she wants you there," Pam interrupted, "then you'll be there. But if she prefers to be alone, then she'll wait until you're not there."

I looked at her incredulously. "How could she do that... I mean... she wouldn't... I..."

"Love," Pam smiled sympathetically, "I've been a hospice nurse for more than thirty years, and I've seen it way too many times to ever doubt it. People choose their time. Some want loved ones with them, some hang on to wait for a special person to arrive, and others prefer to wait until everyone leaves before they let go."

Pam put her arm around my shoulder. "Whatever happens, know that it'll be the way she wants it to be. If you're not there when it happens, it's because for reasons only she can know, she didn't want you to be there. I want you to promise me that if it happens like that, you never need to feel guilty about it. It will be *her* choice."

I gave her a weak smile to thank her. Hospice nurses had come and gone for four days. This was the first time one had spoken to me about anything to do with the process of dying. I was grateful to her.

***

On the fifth night, one of our two cats jumped onto my mother's bed.

Smudge had never jumped on my mother's bed! Although she was a mild-mannered, passive, loving cat, when I reached down to move her she let out a blood-curdling growl and flattened her ears hard against her head. She let it be known she would not tolerate being moved. Then, she fixed her stare on the window and the hair on her back stood up.

I knew the time was close.

I dragged a big heavy lounge chair down the hall and into Mum's bedroom, wrapped myself in a blanket and curled up beside her bed.

Could I do this? Could I sit here and watch her die? Did I have the courage to remain here with my mother until the very last moment?

I owed her at least that much, but was I strong enough?

***

Throughout the long hours that followed, the lounge chair beside her bed became my doorstep while I thought about all I had read, and all that had happened over the past 24 years.

I thought about the hospice nurse's advice.

I tried to prepare myself for the possibility that someone might come to greet my mother and take her away.

Would I know who it was? Would I see them too? Would I be aware they were here?

Would my mother be conscious at the time, or would she be in a coma and unable to share this glorious moment with me?

If she was conscious, and she saw someone and spoke their name, who might it be?

Her mother? Probably.

Heaven Knows

Dr. Karlis Osis had revealed to me through *Deathbed Observations by Physicians and Nurses* that "mothers were the most dedicated greeters."

Nan had died twenty-one years earlier, and Nan's own mother had "moved into room 7" shortly before she died.

Yes. It seemed likely Nan would perform that same duty for her own daughter.

Then there was Patricia, my twin sister who had died at birth. Perhaps she had stayed with us in spirit throughout these years and would come to claim her mother back.

Suddenly, agonisingly faced with the heart-breaking reality of losing my mother, my logical mind – or what I thought was my logical mind – wiped out everything I had come to believe, forgot everything I'd read and heard, dismissed everything, and told me it was all nonsense.

Nan's visits twenty years ago by her mother, her old doctor and her infant nephew had merely been the hallucinations of a dying brain, it said.

The three knocks on the front door at the moment of my father's death? Children playing tricks, it whispered. Or maybe the wind. A nocturnal bird tapping on the door.

Had I really seen my old dog, Muffin, jump on my bed three weeks after she died?

Of course not, it scoffed. My grief had merely invaded my dreams.

As for Muffin's ball miraculously appearing behind a cushion on the couch for Nikki, well that was nothing short of ridiculous! I had never been the world's greatest housekeeper. I was sure I'd secreted it in the garage a year earlier, but obviously I'd been mistaken.

Hadn't I?

It was the way our brains protected us from the heartbreaking agony of grief. Nothing more.

Faces in the trees? How silly.

278

Yes, Dr. David had been right twenty years ago. Fantasy fiction. Wishful thinking.

No-one was coming.

Death was death. Over and out.

My mother wasn't going to a better place.

There wasn't a better place.

My mother was dying.

Dying meant ceasing to exist.

Everyone knew that.

Didn't they?

CHAPTER 43

THE END

In the sixty-three years I had been on this earth, I had never once heard my mother raise her voice. Even when I had misbehaved as a child, she would scold with me such a calm, loving voice, it sounded more like praise!

When she spoke from a distance, I would usually need to move closer to hear her. "Time you got the wax out of your ears," she would joke. "Time you learnt to speak up!" I would chide back.

I would never hear that gentle, sweet voice again.

Now, she could not even form words. Her tongue had difficulty finding the right position to form L, N, D, T or Th. "Did the nurse come yet" became something like "ee ya ursh caar yeah?"

Added to that, everything she now tried to say was almost whispered. Her vocal cords were barely functioning.

As she slept, I sat curled up in my old lounge chair beside the bed. A full moon hung suspended in the night sky, bathing us both in its magical, silver light. Framed perfectly by the large bedroom window, it looked like a timeless beacon leading the way to heaven.

I was surprised to find myself silently reciting an old and long-forgotten Irish nursery rhyme:

I see the moon, and the moon sees me,

and the moon sees the one that I long to see.

So God bless the moon, and God bless me,

and God bless the one that I long to see.

282

I watched my mother sleeping. She had been uncomfortable lying flat so was propped up against a large pillow in a half-sitting position. Now and then I moved closer to assure myself she was still breathing. The rhythmic ticking of the wall clock and her slow, gentle inhalations were the only sounds in an otherwise silent night.

At around 2am, it happened. She opened her eyes, stared straight ahead, then began a lengthy but silent conversation with an unseen visitor. She mouthed the words, waggling her finger in the air as though to emphasise a point. She nodded, occasionally shook her head, sometimes even smiled. She appeared to be debating an instruction or negotiating a deal.

She seemed oblivious to my presence. I almost felt like an intruder in a private conversation. I longed to know who she was communicating with.

A few moments later, she whispered "Mumma. Mumma." Then she slowly raised her thumb, placed it in her mouth, closed her eyes and drifted back to sleep.

Was this it? Would she wake up again? At least I knew her mother had come to take her home. How I wished I could also see my beloved Nan.

***

About an hour later, while the entire world appeared to be deep in slumber and I was fighting an overwhelming desire to drift into oblivion, a strong, loud voice broke the silence.

"Nathan?"

I sat bolt upright. Was that really my mother's voice? It had a strength and clarity I had never heard before. Her tone suggested questioning amazement, as though she knew who was there (where?) but could barely believe her eyes.

How was this possible? She had always spoken so softly. For five days she had not been able to speak above a whisper. An hour ago, she had mouthed words silently.

Now, her voice was almost loud enough to wake the neighbours!

A few seconds later, she called again. "Nathan!"

This time it was said with excitement, as though she had just turned a corner and bumped into a long-lost and greatly cherished friend she never expected to see again.

The third time, she called the name, it was laced with love and gratitude.

I recognised that I was experiencing a sacred moment. I sat in silence and watched in awe.

She had even formed the troublesome 'N' and 'th' perfectly. Nathan should have been a whispered ayy-ang, and I would never have known who it was.

But I did know! It was sweet, handsome Nathan, who had once been the love of her life. He had joined the Royal Australian Air Force during the war and trained as a pilot, but died in a fiery plane crash in 1944.

Why Nathan?

"Spouses came in a close second." Dr. Osis reminded me. That made sense. Although they had not been married, they had announced their intention to marry before he died.

I couldn't believe what I was hearing. For almost seventy years, dear Nathan had been waiting in the wings to collect his beloved fiancé.

A few minutes later, and without warning, my mother raised her head, stared ahead, and called again. This time it was to greet someone else. Her voice was still strong and clear.

"Mabel???" Questioningly.

"Mabel!!!" Surprised and elated.

Then, once again with love and appreciation. "Mabel."

My mother's almost-mother-in-law had been devastated when her only son, Nathan, was killed. When the two heart-broken women comforted each other through their grief, their mutual tragedy forged a strong friendship which continued for more than fifty years until Mabel's death in 1998.

No wonder she had chosen to accompany her beloved son on his earthbound journey to take my mother home.

***

My mother woke the following morning, and once again, she could no longer form words. She attempted to speak occasionally, but try as I did, I could make out very little of what she said.

I longed to know if she remembered what had taken place the previous night.

I would never know.

This day would be spent like the previous four days. I sat by her bed, or drank endless cups of coffee and smoked endless cigarettes in the kitchen while she slept.

There was one major difference, however. I was no longer crying. Perhaps I was simply too exhausted, but I also felt a calm acceptance. I knew now, without doubt, that Nathan, Mabel and Nan were right here, waiting for her.

At midday, while I was sitting beside her bed, the telephone rang. I ran to another room to answer it, and as I did, my mother lapsed into a coma. Perhaps she had not wanted me to leave her side and had tried to follow me. I suspect that she was no longer confined to her physical body from that moment.

***

The doorbell rang at 4pm. I opened the door to Pam, the hospice nurse. "I know I'm not due for an hour," she smiled, "but I thought you might like a few hours to yourself. I can stay until 6."

Pam sat with my comatose mother for two hours, promising to call me if anything changed. I sat at the kitchen table and stared into space, half-hoping to catch a glimpse of her greeters.

I hadn't slept for over thirty hours and my mind and body were starting to protest, but I was determined to stay awake and aware. I needed to be there when the end came, and regardless of Pam's warning that she may choose to go when I was absent, I knew my mother needed me there.

At 6pm, Pam came to the kitchen door and announced her departure. I immediately took her place beside my mother's bed.

"Mum." I whispered softly as I took her hand, "I'm going to miss you so much. I know I rarely said it, but I love you, I love you so much. But I want you to know that I'll be fine. Really I will. I promise. So if you want to go with Nan and Nathan and Mabel, then you go. It's ok. I'll be ok. I promise.

And for the first time, I knew I was telling the truth.

I knew I would be ok.

One small tear formed in the outer corner of her left eye and rolled slowly down her cheek.

She breathed out.

She didn't breathe in again.

She had waited for me.

EPILOGUE

I had expected to be a basket case when death finally took my mother, but I was surprisingly calm. I didn't shed a single tear, although heaven knows, I had shed more than enough in the previous three weeks.

I knew now, without doubt, that she was safe. She was with people who loved her dearly.

I was also relieved.

For more than half my mother's life, she had been restricted by her weakening muscles. She rarely complained, never felt sorry for herself.

For the past eighteen of those years, she had been confined to a wheelchair and had grown weaker with each passing year. She sometimes became frustrated by her inability to do the things she loved to do, and I know she felt guilty because she had to depend on me for so many simple tasks.

Through it all she retained her sweet nature, her active and enquiring mind, her gentleness and her optimism.

Now, she could dance again.

How could I cry about that?

***

Three days later, I nervously dialled a phone number.

"Hello, is this Betty?"

"Yes." The voice on the other end crackled with age.

"Is this the Betty who had a brother called Nathan? And was your mother's name Mabel?"

"Yes. That's right. Who is this, please?"

284

"Um... Betty... my name is Sandy and I found your number in Mum's address book. You don't know me, but..."

I hadn't cried for three days, but now, my voice caught in my throat as I blurted out the words: "My Mum died!"

"Oh, I'm sorry dear," she replied, no doubt wondering who this stranger was.

"Betty, my mother was Phyllis Coghlan."

"Phyllis?" she said in surprise. "Oh my dear! My brother just adored your mother!"

"I know, Betty. I know he did. Um... look, do you have a moment? I'd like to tell you something, and I hope you're sitting down."

REFERENCE SOURCES

Adventures in Immortality, by George Gallup, (McGraw-Hill, 1983

After the Light, by Kimberly Clark Sharp, William Morrow & Co, 1995

Allergy Overload, by Stephen Griffiths, Angus & Robertson, 1987

Alone, by Admiral Richard E. Byrd, G.P.Putnam's Sons, 1938

An Ecclesiastical History of the English Peoples, by St. Bede (8th century)

Anatomy of an Illness, by Norman Cousins, W. W. Norton & Co. 1979

An Autobiographical Memoir of Sir John Barrow, by John Barrow, John Murray (1847)

And When I Die Will I Be Dead? Compiled by Bruce Elder, ABC, 1987

Anecdotes de Medecine (French) by Pierre-Jean du Monchaux, 1740

Appointment in Samarra by John O'Hara, Random House, 1934

Being Pakeha Now, by Michael King, Penguin, Hodder & Stoughton, 1988

Beyond The Light, by P. M. H.Atwater, Birch Lane Press, 1994

Black Elk Speaks, by John G. Neihardt, Bison Books, 1971

Black Holes, Worm Holes and the Tenth Dimension (internet article), by Dr. Michio Kaku

Bring Yourself to Anchor (1941) by Commander Archibald Bruce Campbell, Chapman and Hall, 1941

Casebook of Astral Projection, by Robert Crookall, University Books, 1972

Clerical Errors by Louis Tucker, Harper & Bros. 1943

Closer to the Light, by Dr. Melvin Morse, Villard, 1990

Consciousness Beyond Life by Dr. Pim van Lommel, HarperCollins, 2011

Deathbed Observations by Physicians and Nurses by Dr. Karlis Osis, Parapsychology Foundation, (1961)

Dying as a Liberation of Consciousness by Leslie Grant Scott, Journal of the American Society for Psychical Research, 1931

Dying To Be Me by Anita Moorjani, Hay House, 2012

Evidence of the Afterlife by Dr. Jeffrey Long and Paul Perry, HarperCollins, 2010

Experiences Near Death by Allan Kellehear, Oxford University Press, 1996

Gaze Into Heaven by Marlene Bateman Sullivan, Cedar Fort, 2013

Glimpses of the Beyond, by Jean-Baptiste Delacour, Dell Publishing, 1974

Hawaiian Folk Tales, compiled by Thomas G. Thrum, A. C. McClurg Publishers, 1907

Human Personality and Its Survival of Bodily Death by Frederic W. H. Myers, Longmans Green & Co, 1904

I Died and I Went to Heaven by Arthur E. Yensen, self-published,1955

In Search of the Dead by Jeffrey Iverson, BBC Books, 1992

Intimations of Immortality, by Robert Crookall, James Clarke, 1965

I Was Clinically Dead (in German) by Stefan von Jankovich, Engelberg/Schweiz ,1985

Journal of Resuscitation, (article by Dr. Charlier) 2014

Journal of Scientific Exploration, Vol.12 No.3, 1998 (article: 'Do Any Near-Death Experiences Provide Evidence for the survival of Human Personality After Death?') by Emily Williams Cook, Dr. Bruce Greyson and Dr. Ian Stevenson

Journeys Out of the Body by Robert Monroe, Souvenir Press, 1972

Lancet (van Lommel's article) 2001

Lessons From the Light by Dr. Kenneth Ring and Evelyn *Elsaesser Valarino, Insight Books, 1998*

Life After Life by Dr, Raymond Moody, Bantam Books, 1976

Life at Death, by Dr. Kenneth Ring, Coward McCann & Geoghegan, 1980

Livingstone's Africa, Dr. David Livingstone, Hubbard Bros, 1872

Mediumistic Experiences of John Brown, the Medium of the Rockies, Office of the Philosophical Journal, 1897

Memories, Dreams, Reflections by Dr. Carl Jung, Vintage Books, 1963

Mindsight by Dr. Kenneth Ring, Sharon Cooper & Charles T. Tart, Institute of Transpersonal Psychology, 1999

Miracles and Other Realities, Lee Pulos & Gary Richman, Omega Press, 1990

On Death and Dying, Dr. Elisabeth Kubler Ross, Macmillan, 1969

On Life After Death by Elisabeth Kubler Ross, Celestial Arts, 1991

Ordered to Return by Dr. George Ritchie, Hampton Roads, 1998 (originally published as My Life After Dying, 1991)

Otherworld Journeys by Carol Zaleski, Oxford University Press, 1988

Pale Horse, Pale Rider by Katherine Anne Porter, Harcourt Brace & Co. (1939)

Proof of Heaven by Dr. Eben Alexander, Simon & Schuster, 2012

Psychic Odyssey by Percy Cole, Regency Press, 1959

Recollections of Death by Dr. Michael Sabom, Corgi, 1982

Reflections on Life After Life by Dr. Raymond Moody. Doubleday Dell, 1978

Reminiscences of Three Campaigns by Sir Alexander Ogston, Hodder & Stoughton, 1919)

Return From Tomorrow by Dr. George Spire Books, 1978

Saved by the Light by Dannion Brinkley, Random House, 1994

Science and the Near-Death Experience by Chris Carter, Inner Traditions publishers, 2010

Shocked: Adventures in Bringing Back the Recently Dead by David Cassarett, MD, Penguin Putnam, 2015

Stranger Than Life by DeWitt Miller, Ace Publishing, 1955

Suspiria De Profundis by Thomas De Quincey, 1845

The Biography of Mrs. J. Conant by Allen Putnam, William White & Co., 1873

The Death of Ivan Ilyich by Leo Tolstoy (1886)

The Dialogue of Miracles, by Caesarius of Heisterbach (c.1180-1240)

The History of the Franks (Historia Francorum) by Gregory of Tours,(6th century, translated by Earnest Brehaut, 1916)

The Journal of Nervous and Mental Disease, article by Dr. B. Gresyon, 1983

The Journey Home by Phillip L. Berman, Pocket Books, 1996

The Lazarus Effect by Dr. Sam Parnia, Rider, 2013

The Light Beyond by Dr. Raymond Moody, Bantam, 1988

The Little Book About Life and Death by Gustav Fechner, 1836

The Near-Death Experiences of Hospitalized Intensive Care Patients: A Five Year Clinical Study by Penny Sartori, PhD, Edwin Mellen Press, 2008

The Phenomena of Astral Projection, by Sylvan Muldoon and Hereward

Carrington, Rider, 1951

The Power of Positive Thinking by Norman Vincent Peale, The World's Work, 1953

The Present Truth, series of articles by E. J. Waggoner, 1895

The Psychic Handbook, by Craig Hamilton Parker, Vermilion, 1995

There Is Life After Death by Kenneth L. Woodward, article in McCall's, August 1976

The Supreme Adventure by Robert Crookall, James Clarke & Co., 1961

The Truth in the Light by Dr. Peter Fenwick, Headline, 1995

The Vestibule by Jess Weiss, Ashley Books Inc.,1972

The Waiting World by Archie Matson, Harper & Row, 1975

The Wisdom of Near Death Experiences by Dr. Penny Sartori, Watkins Publishing, 2014

Travels in the Central Portion of the Mississippi Valley by H. R. Schoolcraft, 1825

Unseen Adventures by Geraldine Cummins, Rider & Co. 1951

Voices From the Edge of Eternity compiled by John Myers, Spire Books, 1968

You Cannot Die by Ian Currie, Merthuen, 1978 (later published as Visions of Immortality, Element Books, 1998)

CLDS **(Church of Latter Day Saints)** Extracts from the following historical records were included in **Gaze Into Heaven** by Marlene Bateman Sullivan, published by Cedar Fort, 2013:

    A Curious Experience in Drowning, 1886

    A Narrative of the Experience of Horace Abraham Ackley, 1861

    Biography of William Rufus Rogers Stowell, 1893

    Fragments of Experience (1882)

    Herman Stulz, Autobiography, circa 1971

    "Your Good Name" in The Improvement Era, 1947

ABOUT THE AUTHOR

Sandy Coghlan worked in advertising and television in Australia and London prior to becoming an on-air director at a Melbourne TV station in 1979.

Her first book, *Travel Guide to Tasmania* (Penguin) was commissioned by 'Life. Be In It' in 1984, while her articles on health and metaphysical subjects have been published nationally.

Her third book, *Yesterday: A Baby Boomer's Rite of Passage* (2019) is a light-hearted memoir based on letters and diary entries during her sea voyage to Europe and her travels around the continent in 1969/70.

Sandy also wrote 2 chapters for the best-selling metaphysical book, *With A Little Help From My Friends* by Dawn Hill, contributed to *Great Australian Mysteries 2* by John Pinkney and *Working with Mean Girls* by Meredith Fuller, and is featured in the relationship 'bible', *I'll Have What She's Having* by Valerie Parv.

From 1990 until retirement, Sandy qualified in a variety of alternative therapies, and in 1991, wrote and conducted a nutrition correspondence course for pharmacy assistants around Australia. She also taught creative writing and healing techniques at adult education centres.

Sandy now lives with her partner Barry and their two cats in a bayside area of Victoria, Australia and is working on the second book in the *Heaven Knows* series.

Sandy can be contacted at

pegasus@bookorphanage.com

Made in the USA
San Bernardino, CA
05 July 2020

74836531R00168